INSIGHT CITY GUIDE

RoMe

APA PUBLICATIONS

Part of the Langenscheidt Publishing Group

L

✵ INSIGHT GUIDE
ROME

Editor
Cathy Muscat
Art Director
Klaus Geisler
Picture Editor
Hilary Genin
Cartography Editor
Zoë Goodwin
Editorial Director
Brian Bell

Distribution

UK & Ireland
GeoCenter International Ltd
The Viables Centre, Harrow Way
Basingstoke, Hants RG22 4BJ
Fax: (44) 1256-817988

United States
Langenscheidt Publishers, Inc.
36–36 33rd Street 4th Floor
Long Island City, NY 11106
Fax: (1) 718 784-0640

Canada
Thomas Allen & Son Ltd
390 Steelcase Road East
Markham, Ontario L3R 1G2
Fax: (1) 905 475 6747

Australia
Universal Publishers
1 Waterloo Road
Macquarie Park, NSW 2113
Fax: (61) 2 9888 9074

New Zealand
Hema Maps New Zealand Ltd (HNZ)
Unit D, 24 Ra ORA Drive
East Tamaki, Auckland
Fax: (64) 9 273 6479

Worldwide
**Apa Publications GmbH & Co.
Verlag KG (Singapore branch)**
38 Joo Koon Road, Singapore 628990
Tel: (65) 6865-1600. Fax: (65) 6861-6438

Printing

Insight Print Services (Pte) Ltd
38 Joo Koon Road, Singapore 628990
Tel: (65) 6865-1600. Fax: (65) 6861-6438

©2005 Apa Publications GmbH & Co.
Verlag KG (Singapore branch)
All Rights Reserved

First Edition 1988
Fourth Edition 2004
Updated 2005

ABOUT THIS BOOK

This guidebook combines the interests and enthusiasms of two of the world's best-known information providers: Insight Guides, whose titles have set the standard for visual travel guides since 1970, and Discovery Channel, the world's premier source of non-fiction television programming.

Insight Guides provide both practical advice and general understanding about a destination. Discovery Channel and its website, www.discovery.com, help millions of viewers explore the world from the comfort of their own home.

How to use this book

The book is carefully structured both to convey an understanding of the city and its culture and to guide readers through its sights and activities:

◆ The Best Of Rome section at the front helps you prioritise what you want to see. Top museums, churches and ancient sites, family attractions, festivals and best buys are listed, together with money-saving tips, where to find the best pizzas, and a rundown of the city's eccentricities.

◆ To understand Rome, you need to know something of its past: the city's history and culture are described in authoritative essays by specialists with an intimate knowledge of its evolution and present-day challenges.

◆ The Places section provides a run-down of major attractions with main places of interest coordinated by number with full-colour maps.

◆ A list of recommended restaurants and cafés is included at the end of each chapter in the Places section, and plotted on the pull-out restaurants map provided with the guide.
◆ Photographs are chosen not only to illustrate geography and buildings but also to convey the moods of the city and the life of its people.
◆ The Travel Tips section provides information on transport, accommodation, cultural attractions and shopping. There is also an A–Z directory of practical information, and a useful language guide. Information may be located quickly by using the index printed on the back-cover flap.
◆ A detailed street atlas is included at the back of the book, complete with a full index.

The contributors

City Guide: Rome builds on the work of **Udo Gümpel**, editor of the first edition of *Insight Guide: Rome*. A correspondent for German newspapers, he recruited fellow foreign correspondents **Dr Werner Raith**, **Henning Klüver**, **Peter Kammerer**, **Ulrich Friedhoff**, **Horst Schlitter** and **Maria Morhart**. Two Rome-based writers, **Jane Shaw** and **Sam Cole**, worked extensively on subsequent editions of the guide. **Rowlinson Carter** tackled the history chapters; modern Romans were introduced by **Lisa Gerard-Sharp**, who also contributed to other parts of the book; **Jon Eldan** wrote about Food and Drink; **Mari-Beth Bittan** covered Shopping; and **Marc Zakian** contributed the feature on cinema. Additional material was supplied by **Jason Best**.

The work of earlier editors Martin Rosser, Sue Heady, Jane Ladle and Jane Hutchings was much appreciated by **Cathy Muscat**, Insight Guides' in-house editor, who was assisted by **Pam Barrett**.

This edition was updated and substantially re-written by Insight's chief correspondent in Rome, **Giovanna Dunmall**, an Anglo-Italian writer who specialises in travel, architecture and design.

Among photographers responsible for the stunning images are **Frances Grandsen**, **Anna Mockford**, **Nick Bonetti**, **Bill Wassman** and **Alessandra Santarelli**.

The proofreader was **Sylvia Suddes** and the indexer **Penny Phenix**.

CONTACTING THE EDITORS

We would appreciate it if readers would alert us to errors or outdated information by writing to:

**Insight Guides, P.O. Box 7910, London SE1 1WE, England.
Fax: (44) 20 7403-0290.
insight@apaguide.co.uk**

NO part of this book may be reproduced, stored in a retrieval system or transmitted in any form or means electronic, mechanical, photocopying, recording or otherwise, without prior written permission of *Apa Publications*.
Brief text quotations with use of photographs are exempted for book review purposes only. Information has been obtained from sources believed to be reliable, but its accuracy and completeness, and the opinions based thereon, are not guaranteed.

www.insightguides.com

Maps

Map Legend **239**

Travel Tips

THE BEST OF ROME

Unique attractions, festivals and events, top shops, pizzas and piazzas, family outings... here, at a glance, are our recommendations, plus some money-saving tips.

ROME FOR FAMILIES

- **Villa Borghese Gardens** Laid out over rolling hills, this is the perfect city park for picnicking and relaxing. Attractions include museums, a zoo, a hot-air balloon, a boating lake and bikes for hire. *See page 141.*
- **Castel Sant' Angelo** Drawbridges, trapdoors, cannons, ditches and dungeons ...everything but dragons in this ancient castle, full of surprises *See page 110.*
- **Children's Museum** Explora is a delightful "playtown" where kids can touch, draw and play to their heart's content. *See page 218.*

- **Time Travel** on the Time Elevator – an interactive cinematic journey through Rome's colourful history. *See page 218.*
- **Coins in the fountain** A coin tossed in the Trevi fountain is said to guarantee your return to Rome. *See page 93.*
- **A leisurely ride** on the No. 116 electric bus, which weaves its way from Via Veneto to the Vatican. Lovely for sightseeing and a welcome relief for sore feet. *See page 207.*
- **A fairytale house** A trip to the Casina delle Civette, a romantic folly with beautiful stained-glass windows in the grounds of Villa Torlonia, is a relaxing day out. *See page 179.*
- **Toy shop** The enchanting window displays of Al Sogno on Piazza Navona, have attracted children since 1945. *See page 221.*

ABOVE: There are spectacular views across Rome from Gianicolo Hill. **BELOW:** Trevi fountain, repository of coins and wishes.

BEST VIEWS

- **Gianicolo Hill** Worlds away from the tightly packed streets of Trastevere and the traffic, noise and chaos of the city below. *See page 150.*
- **Piazza Venezia** Fine views from the Vittoriano Monument have the added advantage of excluding the hulking monument itself – the ungainly structure that looms in most Roman views. *See page 76.*
- **Piazza dei Cavalieri di Malta** Look through the keyhole of No. 3 for a classic picture-postcard view of St Peter's dome. *See pages 153 and 107.*

- **Caffè Capitolino** Romantic views of terracotta rooftops, ochre facades and countless cupolas from the Capitoline Museum's pretty café. *See page 77.*
- **The Tabularium** Take in the grandiose spectacle of the Forum and the Palatine from a small terrace in the ancient archive of Roman Law. *See page 76.*
- **Pincio gardens** Views from the Villa Borghese gardens stretch from Monte Mario to the Gianicolo and down to the Piazza del Popolo below. *See page 142.*

ABOVE: Beautiful Byzantine mosaics decorate the floor and apse of Santa Maria in Trastevere

UNMISSABLE SIGHTS

- **Colosseum** The most enduring symbol of Ancient Rome. *See page 88.*
- **Imperial Fora** Built by a succession of emperors from Caesar to Trajan. *See page 80.*
- **Vatican Museums** Vast repository of great artworks and home to Michelangelo's masterpiece in the Sistine Chapel. *See page 112.*
- **Basilica di San Pietro** Michelangelo's dome and *La Pietà* are among the most outstanding features of St Peter's, in the Vatican. *See page 105.*
- **Pantheon** Ancient Rome's best-preserved monument. *See page 117.*
- **The Spanish Steps** The lively hub of the sophisticated shopping district of Tridente. *See page 99.*

BEST CHURCHES FOR ART

- **San Luigi dei Francesi** The dramatic paintings by Caravaggio in the Contarelli chapel were the artist's first great religious works and demonstrate his naturalistic approach and mastery of the chiaroscuro technique. *See page 119.*
- **Santa Maria in Trastevere** A pretty medieval church with spectacular mosaics on the facade and in the apse. It's worth taking a pair of binoculars to enjoy the detail. *See page 149.*
- **Basilica di San Pietro** Michelangelo's tender and moving *Pietà* in St Peter's was completed when the artist was only 25 and remains one of his most famous works. *See page 108.*
- **San Pietro in Vincoli** This church houses another Michelangelo masterpiece, the newly restored statue of Moses, one of 40 statues commissioned for the tomb of Pope Julius II. The four Dying Slaves (now in the Accademia in Florence and the Louvre in Paris) were the only other figures he completed. *See page 163.*
- **Santa Maria della Vittoria** So sensual is Bernini's famous sculpture of St Teresa in Ecstasy that many suggest the rapture on her face is more than an expression of piety. *See page 95.*
- **Santa Prassede** The 9th-century church is filled with magnificent Byzantine mosaics. *See page 162.*

BEST BUYS

- **Ice cream** Head for Gelato San Crispino for colouring- and preservative-free ice-cream. *See page 95.*
- **Valentino** Ready-to-wear lines from Rome's beloved designer are still coveted by fashionistas. *See page 221.*
- **Religious kitsch** or just a nice crucifix or rosary from the shops on Via della Conciliazione and around the Basilica of Santa Maria Maggiore. *See page 221.*
- **Handbags** from Fendi and Furla are the ultimate in classic chic. The less discerning can pick up a cheap designer knock-off from any of the street vendors that congregate around tourist hotspots. *See page 221.*
- **Shoes** from Bruno Magli, a prestigious shoemaker for over 70 years, who is experiencing a major rebirth. *See page 221.*
- **Food** Two legendary delis for Roman and Italian specialities are Volpetti in Testaccio and the charmingly old-fashioned Innocenzi in Trastevere. *See page 222.*
- **Jewellery** In New York there's Tiffany, in Paris there's Cartier, in Rome there's Bulgari where extravagant jewellery reigns supreme. Serious money. *See page 222.*
- **Made by monks** The potions and lotions, teas and preserves on sale at Ai Monasteri are all made by Italian monks. *See page 221.*

BEST PIZZAS

- **Formula Uno** (San Lorenzo). The best and most down-to-earth pizzeria in the university quarter, which is known as pizza central. *See page 181.*
- **Da Baffetto** A legendary pizza venue with fast-moving queues outside all night long. Brash but efficient service adds to the quintessential Roman experience. *See page 124.*
- **Clok** Fun and lively with modern décor *See page 151.*
- **O Pazzariello** A Neapolitan pizzeria

with lots of ambience in quite a small space. *See page 125.*
- **Pizza Ré** Serves a huge range of crusty Neapolitan-style pizzas that are always reliable, appetising and well-made. *See page 103.*
- **Zi Fenizia** A kosher take-away in the Jewish Ghetto which has a permanent queue waiting outside. *See page 137.*
- **Dar Poeta** a special dough (which is supposed to be much easier to digest) is this pizzeria's trademark. *See page 151.*

ONLY IN ROME

- **Cat Colonies** There are an estimated 10,000 cat colonies in Rome, many in archaeological areas, such as the Colosseum, Foro di Traiano and in Largo di Torre Argentina. *See relevant chapters.*
- **Priestly Couture** Papal party gear, nuns' underwear, incense burners and more can be found in shops for religious garments and accessories on Via dei Cestari and Via di Santa

Chiara (near the Pantheon). *See page 117.*
- **Cappuccino** Rome is full of atmospheric cafés serving excellent coffee. Piazza Rotonda and Piazza Farnese are prime spots, but the neighbourhood cafés frequented by locals are more fairly priced. *See page 115.*
- **Catacombs** Three of the largest underground burial sites are to be found in the vicinity of the Appian Way. *See page 170.*

BEST FESTIVALS AND EVENTS

- **RomaEuropa** (www.romaeuropa.net) An experimental arts festival held every autumn: a real breath of cosmopolitan air.
- **Estate Romana** "Roman Summer" is the collective name for all the events held outdoors in parks, villas, monuments and ancient sites, from June to September.
- **Festival of Literature** (www.letterature.festivalroma.org) is held

in and around the remains of the Basilica of Maxentius in late spring.
- **Photography Festival** (www.fotografia festival.it), held all over town from April to June.
- **Il Natale di Roma**. On 21 April Rome celebrates its founding with fireworks, music and other events. *For more about Rome's festivals see pages 219-220.*

ABOVE: a contented member of one of Rome's many cat colonies. **LEFT:** pizzas may have originated in Naples, but there are excellent ones to be found all over Rome.

BEST PIAZZAS

- **Piazza Navona** For its baroque grandeur, spectacular fountains and lively, traffic-free atmosphere. *See page 120.*
- **Piazza Farnese** A welcome relief from the chaos of neighbouring Campo de' Fiori. *See page 133.*
- **Piazza Mattei** A small *piazza* with a playful fountain of bronze boys, water-spouting dolphins, and turtles. *See page 130.*
- **Piazza Santa Maria in Trastevere** This neighbourly square buzzes with activity round the clock but never seems crowded. *See page 149.*
- **Piazza San Pietro** Vast, colonnaded square designed by Bernini to accommodate the crowds making the papal pilgrimage. *See page 105.*
- **Piazza del Campidoglio** For the beautifully elegant staircase designed by Michelangelo. *See page 74.*
- **Piazza di Spagna** A spectacular and welcoming urban space, dominated by a twin-towered church atop the magnificent Spanish Steps. *See page 99.*

ABOVE: the fountain in the elegant Piazza Farnese.
BELOW: St Peter's Square.

BEST SMALL HOTELS

- **Casa Howard** Decorated with real flair; each of the 10 rooms has a different theme. *See page 211.*
- **Hotel Abruzzi** Directly opposite the Pantheon; the view is out of this world. *See page 212.*
- **Fontanella Borghese** Stylish, with beautiful old tiles, hardwood floors and an internal courtyard. *See page 211.*
- **Aleph Hotel** Intriguing boutique hotel. Bedrooms inspired by 1930s design and have hi-tech touches and huge beds. There is also a lovely spa downstairs. *See page 212.*
- **Locarno** Appealing Art Deco touches (the ornate cage lift alone is memorable). Oodles of charm and class. *See page 211.*
- **Due Torri** A delightful, historic hotel in a former cardinal's palace on a small, cobbled street. *See page 212.*

MONEY-SAVING ROME

Free Forum
Free entrance to the Forum – you only pay when you get to the Palatine. *See page 80.*

Free churches
All the basilicas and churches in Rome are free, as is the Pantheon. *See page 117.*

Settimana della Cultura
Cultural Week is held all over Italy in late April or May, when entrance is free to all state-run museums and historical sites. If you are visiting Rome at this time you'll make a good saving, though queues can be lengthy and museums crowded. (www.beniculturali.it). *See page 219.*

Bus tours
Buses in Rome are cheap and efficient. An army of small, electric buses (Nos 116, 117 and 119) wind their way through the most scenic parts of Rome where cars and "real" buses cannot venture.

Cheap eats
Anywhere marked *tavola calda*, where you can choose from well-stocked buffets of grilled vegetables, potatoes, rice and pasta dishes, or *pizza al taglio* where you can buy slices of freshly-baked pizza to enjoy on the steps of a nearby fountain or square.

Free Vatican
Entrance to the Vatican Museums is free on the last Sunday of the month but be prepared for long queues. *See page 108.*

'Roman Summer' events
Anything that is part of the Estate Romana programme is usually very cheap (€8–€15) and you can buy a season ticket that makes it even cheaper. *See page 220.*

Porta Portese Anything and everything can be found at the oldest and best known of Roman flea markets, and there are some good bargains to be found. *See page 144.*

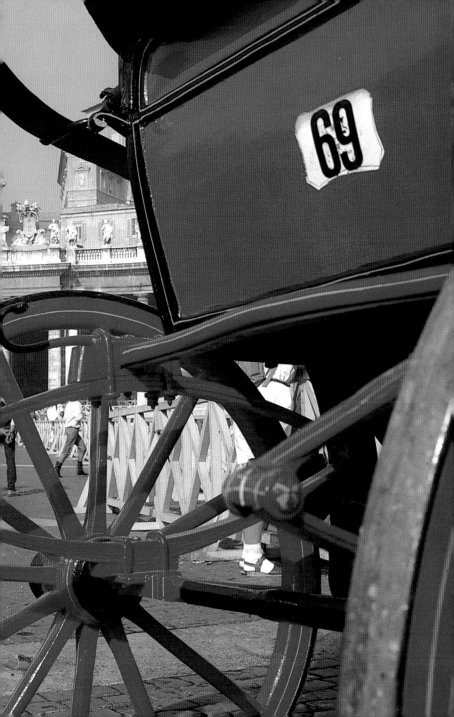

THE ETERNAL CITY

Once the heart of an empire, Rome has attracted poets,
artists, writers and travellers for thousands of years

Dubbed the Eternal City by poets and artists, Rome is one of the most exhilarating and romantic travel destinations in the world. With its soft, ochre-coloured *palazzi*, classical colonnades and dramatic centrepieces such as the Colosseum and the Pantheon, it is a city that inspires the mind, appeals to the senses and captures the heart. As is frequently pointed out on souvenirs and T-shirts, Roma is *amor* spelt backwards.

Home to the Vatican and once hub of a great empire, it has been at the centre of European civilisation for well over 2,000 years. It has attracted travellers for a millennium. Pilgrims came in the Middle Ages – in the "Holy Year" of 1300 alone, some 2 million pilgrims visited the city – and by the 17th century it was seen as a finishing school for European courtiers and gentlemen, the source "of policy, learning, music, architecture and limning [painting], with other perfections which she disperteth to the rest of Europe."

In the 19th century Rome attracted a stream of poets, writers and painters of all nationalities, including Goethe, Stendhal and Henry James. But the English Romantics – notably Byron, Keats and Shelley – were especially drawn to the city, relishing the pathetic charm of greatness brought to its knees. Rome also offered them a retreat from the repressive morality of England, and they saw in Rome's ruins a reflection of themselves: Romantic exiles misunderstood and despised by their own country. At one point there were so many British and North American expatriates living around Piazza di Spagna that it was dubbed "Grosvenor Square".

In Italy itself, Rome is something of a loner, which is both indulged and resented by the rest of the country. It is neither northern nor southern, and, although the capital, it is not considered as sophisticated as fast-paced Milan. It has all the problems of a major metropolis and a few more besides. It has a fantastic archaeological and architectural legacy to maintain, which is both a burden and a source of pride. While traffic pollution erodes the monuments – turning marble into limestone – the civic authorities fight to protect them. As the British journalist George Armstrong remarked: "Rome is the only European capital which each year must spend millions of pounds restoring ruins – restoring them at least to their state of ruin of 100 years ago." ❑

LEFT: view of the Forum, the hub of ancient Rome.

THE MAKING OF ROME

Monarchy, republic, dictatorship, empire: over
a thousand years Rome grew mighty and then
declined into a city of ruins

R omulus and Remus, the twins famously
suckled by a she-wolf, are not the only
candidates for the title of founders of
Rome. One prosaic claim is that an Etruscan
king, a keen equestrian, noted that the dimen-
sions of a valley between two of Rome's 12
hills (not the seven always attributed to it)
would make a wonderful racecourse.

Pliny the Elder (AD 23–79) offered the
more fantastical account of a noblewoman
who was surprised by a male organ soaring
from the ashes in a fireplace. She fell pregnant
and the child of this remarkable union survived to become King Servius Tullius, builder
of the wall around Rome.

Implausible pregnancy is a feature of many
of the legendary accounts, and this is no acci-
dent. Archaeology has unearthed evidence of
scattered settlements in the Roman hills in
1200 BC, but these early Latins were culturally overshadowed by Etruscans, who took
over most of the Italian peninsula from the 9th
century BC, and by Greek colonies established
in the south a century later. Roman historians
acknowledged that one or the other, if not
both, made a significant contribution to the
gene pool of the Roman nation, but in the
interest of chauvinism they preferred a neat
break with the past so that Roman history
could start afresh. Miraculous conception was
just the ticket.

LEFT: the *Augustus of Prima Porta* shows a youthful
emperor looking to Rome's future of *Imperium sine
fine* (rule without end). **RIGHT:** iconic statue of twins
Romulus and Remus, the mythical founders of Rome.

History according to Livy

A large part of Livy's *History of Rome*, written
in the 1st century BC and running to 140 books,
is devoted to weighing up various theories
about the origins of Rome, including one by the
poet Virgil, an exception to the rule in that he
relished the idea of classical Greece as Rome's
cultural and spiritual cradle. Aeneas, the hero
of Virgil's *Aeneid*, is a Greek survivor of the
sack of Troy who drifted to the coast of North
Africa and was sent by the gods to found Rome.
Livy tolerated the idea of Aeneas settling in
Italy and marrying a local princess but he
resorted to miraculous conception to cleanse
Roman blood. King Numitor of Alba Longa,

the ancient Latin capital founded by Aeneas's son Ascanius, was usurped, Livy explains, by his brother Amulius, and Numitor's daughter, Rhea Silvia, was committed to the Vestal Virgins. Paternity of her twins, Romulus and Remus, was pinned on Mars, who consoled her while she was in a cave, hiding from a wolf. Doubting this unlikely story, Amulius had her manacled and thrown into a river, while the twins were placed in a basket and cast adrift to meet their fate. When a drop in the water level left the basket stranded in the mud, the cries of the babies attracted a she-wolf who suckled the boys until they were rescued by a shepherd. Mars later appeared to the twins and pointed them towards their glorious destiny. The twins founded Rome, declares Livy, in 753 BC.

According to popular belief, fraternal relations between the twins later soured over the location and name of Rome. Remus proposed a site on the Aventine Hill and the name Rema; Romulus demanded the Palatine Hill and Roma. The latter was endorsed by the gods when 12 vultures flew over the Palatine compared with only six over the Aventine.

Remus ridiculed the walls his brother was constructing on the Palatine by jumping over them. This was an unbearable affront, which Remus paid for with his life, and the new city walls were ritually annointed with his blood.

GIBBON'S *DECLINE AND FALL*

English historian Edward Gibbon was "musing amid the ruins of the Capitol" in 1764 when he conceived his great work, *The History of the Decline and Fall of the Roman Empire*. This six-volume work covers 13 centuries, starting with the age of Trajan and the Antonines, and shows how Ancient Rome created the forge in which modern Europe was fashioned. The rise of the Teutonic tribes, Charlemagne, the crusades, the Turks taking Constantinople – Gibbon's volumes show that, vast though the Roman Empire was, the shadow it cast down the centuries was greater by far.

Livy's *History of Rome* is not yet over. The population of Rome grew rapidly, he adds, but with a grave imbalance of males over females. Romulus decided to lay on a festival of games so magnificent that all the surrounding tribes were bound to attend. What the visitors did not know was that the women would not be going home. This ruse has been immortalised as the "Rape of the Sabine Women".

Laws of the land

Royal Rome extended over the reign of six kings after Romulus. Codified laws laid down the contractual obligations between patricians and plebeians, the behaviour required of women, and a father's authority over his sons. The patrician class provided priests, magistrates and judges while plebeians were responsible for agriculture, cattle-breeding and trade. Marriage was for life and wives had an equal share of the conjugal property. But the husband was the senior partner. If his wife fell short of "virtue in all things", he could administer appropriate measures, including death. A father exercised absolute authority over his son. He could have him put to work in the fields, imprisoned, flogged, chained, executed, or sold into slavery

The most irksome disparity was between Etruscans and Romans, the former being synonymous with the patrician class, the latter with the plebeians. Differences came to a head over another notorious rape, that of Lucretia, the Roman wife of the Etruscan King Tarquinius Superbus. Although the king was personally blameless, the Roman populace could no longer bear the licentiousness of the Etruscan court. Marcus Junius led the revolt that drove the last of the Etruscan kings into exile. In 509 BC, he was elected one of the two consuls who ruled Rome under a republican constitution.

Republican Rome prospered against the backdrop of an Etruscan attempt to retake the city and restore the monarchy, seen off by Horatius's sterling defence of the bridge leading into the city; the Gallic invasion of 390, when cackling geese sounded the alarm; the Punic Wars with Carthage, with Hannibal leading his elephants across the Alps; the invasions of Gaul and Britain; and the expansion of the Roman Empire to the banks of the Danube. Although the Republic abolished the Etruscan oligarchy, it was still far from democratic. An élite inherited the patrician privileges, and it was only after intense agitation that the plebeians exacted, in 450, the Twelve Tables, a code of laws displayed on bronze tablets in the Forum.

The Romans distanced themselves from the philosophical bent of the Greeks by concentrating on the practical sciences, astrology and Eastern mysticism. The spread of Bacchic rites, however, caused alarm. "This pestilential evil spread from Etruria to Rome like a contagious

disease…" The acceptable form of religion was a mixture of Etruscan traditions and animist spirit worship. Business between humans and gods was governed by a college of pontiffs who pronounced on the significance of birds in flight or bolts of lightning. Flamens (priests) were assisted by Vestal Virgins, recruited as children for a 30-year period of service for which they took a vow of chastity. The penalty for violation of the vow was to be buried alive.

The end of the Republic

Rome made no attempt to develop an industrial or economic base: it simply lived on the proceeds of military booty. The Etruscans

eventually disappeared and the ineffectiveness of Greek campaigns led to the expression "Pyrrhic victory" – their military commander, Pyrrhus of Epirus, was a cunning tactician but, even when he appeared to have won, seemed to lose more men than the Romans. With the final defeat of the great city of Carthage in 146 BC Rome controlled the whole of Italy and most of the Mediterranean basin.

A mighty military machine was needed to run the conquered provinces. Gaius Marius, an officer of humble origins, exploited discontent in the army, and presented himself to the population as a man of integrity willing to engage the corrupt, incompetent ruling clique.

LEFT: Etruscan sarcophagus from the Villa Giulia.
RIGHT: Hannibal's forces cross the Alps

He preached too eloquently, however, and the whole country rose in revolt in the Social Wars of 92–89 BC. An unscrupulous general, Sulla, used the unrest as a pretence for seizing power in 82 BC and installing a military dictatorship. The Roman Republic was dead.

Julius Caesar and Augustus

After Sulla's death, power passed to Pompey. From 59 BC he shared power in the First Triumvirate with Crassus and Julius Caesar, the latter a brilliant commander who conquered Gaul and led his legions across the English Channel. Caesar made sure that a generous share of his booty went back to the capital to

buy political support. The Senate forbade his return to Italy, but in 50 BC he crossed the Rubicon with the intention of seizing power. His pursuit of Pompey led to Egypt, a land of incomparable splendour. Pompey was killed by supposed friends, but Caesar lingered in Rome, besotted by Cleopatra, Egypt's young queen, with whom he had a son. When he returned to Rome, she accompanied him.

Caesar endeared himself to the populace with efficient government and a spectacular building programme, but there were fears that, by marrying Cleopatra, he would, technically, become a king. Jealous senators cut him down, on the Ides of March, 44 BC.

Mark Antony's passion for Cleopatra provides romantic interest through the 13 years of civil war that followed Caesar's murder. Octavian, who took the name Augustus, emerged as victor and first Roman emperor, and Cleopatra's expropriated treasure funded his transformation of Rome from "a city of brick into a city of marble". His conquests abroad vastly enlarged the empire. The Augustan Age was Rome's cultural apex, producing among others Virgil, Ovid and Livy. The civil service Augustus gave Rome kept the empire and its capital going through the malfeasance of some of his successors. Emperors such as Tiberius, Caligula, Nero and Egabalus acted like monsters at the pinnacle of society, while the scholarly Plutarch gave pointers on morality and etiquette.

Honour was restored to the throne by a succession of worthy emperors, notably Trajan, Hadrian and the two Antonines. "In the second century of the Christian era," wrote the author Edward Gibbon, "the empire of Rome comprehended that fairest part of the earth and the most civilised portion of mankind." It was the purpose of the book on which he was embarking, he said, to describe the prosperity and happiness and then, from the death of Mark Antony, to detail the decline and fall.

Constantine and Christianity

By the 4th century, the decline was so far advanced that Emperor Constantine moved the capital to the shores of the Black Sea, to the city he gave his name, Constantinople. Many theories have been advanced to explain this move. Constantinople was certainly nearer the threatened imperial frontiers. Or it could be that Constantine, contemplating legalising Christianity, wished to make a fresh start in a neutral location. Or maybe he hoped to complete the circle begun by Aeneas when he embarked on the *Aeneid*, and to that end he built "The Second Rome" as close as was practical to the ancient site of Troy. Two centuries later, the population of the original Rome had shrunk from over a million to fewer than 20,000 people inhabiting an almost derelict ruin on a dirty river.

Constantine recognised Christianity as a state religion in tandem with paganism in 324, but did not personally convert until he was virtually on his deathbed 13 years later, probably because Christianity alone offered forgiveness for sins as appalling as his. Official recognition was a huge step forward from Nero's days (54–68), when Christians were rolled in wax and used as human candles. But while Christianity made swift inroads in the Eastern Empire, Rome remained pagan for some time after Constantine's death. Eventually, Christianity and paganism fused, the Roman church copying the structure of the pagan priesthood. Images of the goddess Isis metamorphosed smoothly into the Christian Madonna; and the new religion provided leadership to fill the vacuum left by the imperial government's departure for Constantinople.

sure. As a gentleman and a Christian, Alaric spared women and religious buildings. None of this was of much comfort to Honorius. Rome was clearly not safe, so he moved the seat of the Western Empire to Ravenna, "an inaccessible fortress… where he might securely remain, while the open country was covered by a deluge of barbarians".

A quarter of a century later, Rome's worst fears materialised in the person of Attila, the "Scourge of God". Pope Leo I bought him off with a wealthy bride, Honoria of Burgundy. She initially went along with the marriage, but Attila was soon found dead in a pool of blood in the conjugal bed.

Attacks on the city

Although the imperial administration had been transferred to Constantinople, Rome was still the seat of the so-called Western Emperors who increasingly clung to office on the strength of foreign mercenary armies. At the turn of the 5th century, Emperor Honorius engaged the services of Alaric, a Visigoth king, but then found himself in the awkward position of not being able to pay him.

Alaric broke into the city in 410 and helped himself to what was left of the imperial trea-

In 452, Eudoxia, the widow of Emperor Valentinian III (the nephew of Honorius) took the extraordinary step of issuing an invitation to Genseric, whose Vandal hordes had been terrorising the Mediterranean basin for a quarter of a century. Rome was vanquished and Eudoxia married the victor.

German rule

By 467, German tribes were the commanding presence in Italy. The last of the Western Emperors was a German puppet known as Romulus Augustulus; after him, German rulers took direct control. Theodoric the Ostrogoth was an Aryan Christian who spoke

LEFT: marble bust of Julius Caesar. **ABOVE:** the siege of Rome by the Ostrogoth King Vitiges, 6th century AD.

Latin, respected the Roman Senate and restored the city's ancient monuments during his 36 years in power.

German rule over Rome flew in the face of Eastern Emperor Justinian's dream of restoring the empire of old. The Byzantine armies were ultimately successful, but Rome was destroyed in the process. Moreover, it proved impractical to administer Rome from Constantinople, and this opened the way for the local religious authorities to take over the secular reins. To that end, the pope left Ravenna and installed himself in the Castel Sant'Angelo, named in honour of St Michael after he rid Rome of a virulent plague. As kings

of the castle, the popes were poised to become the highest temporal power in the land.

Under Gregory the Great (540–604), papal horizons expanded. Seized by the beauty of Anglo-Saxon youths on sale in the Rome slave-market Gregory was inspired to convert their country to Christianity. The conversion of Ireland and England led in due course to missionary work among the Franks and Germans, and it was the eventual alliance between the papacy and the newly converted Frankish kings, especially against Germanic Lombards who sought to control Italy at Rome's expense, that pushed the papacy yet higher on the ladder of secular authority.

Turbulent times

The partnership between the papacy and the Frankish kings was sealed by Pope Leo III's coronation of Charlemagne as Holy Roman Emperor on Christmas Eve 800. By this act, Leo made it clear that popes preceded emperors. Practically speaking, however, the papacy needed Frankish power, and when that disintegrated after Charlemagne's death, Rome's vulnerability was exposed. The Saracens invaded in 846, looted St Peter's and settled in places like Saracinesco above Rome, where some of their descendants are still to be found.

There was turbulence enough without the Saracens. Romans fought Romans, either as Guelfs, who were more or less loyal to the pope, or as Ghibellines, who preferred the Holy Roman Emperor. A measure of stability was introduced in the 11th century under the influence of the Cluny monastery in Burgundy, which insisted on clerical chastity, piety and discipline. Cardinal Hildebrand, elected Pope Gregory VII in 1073, attempted to claw back papal supremacy over the Holy Roman Empire at the expense of Emperor Henry IV. The contest boiled down to an imperial army versus papal bulls of excommunication. Military might carried Henry to the walls of Rome, whereupon Gregory appealed to Robert Guiscard, the Norman ruler of southern Italy. Guiscard's army included a large number of Saracens indifferent to a squabble between Christians. Their sack of Rome in 1084 surpassed the worst excesses of the Goths and Vandals.

Confusion reigned once again in the 12th century. In Anacletus II, Rome had, of all things, a Jewish pope, who contrived to lose a war with tiny Tivoli. Desperation led to an attempt in 1145 to bring back the republic. The author of this scheme, Arnold of Brescia, was unseated by Pope Adrian IV who, being English, was as unusual in his own way as Anacletus II. Arnold was put to death.

The rot was eventually stopped by Innocent III, who wielded sufficient authority to appoint his own emperor. He disciplined unruly monarchs, launched a crusade against the Moors in Spain and chased the Germans out of central Italy and Sicily. Under Pope Innocent, Rome had a foretaste of Renaissance prosperity and artistic brilliance, and there was probably genuine regret over his undignified death – he was found naked on the floor of Perugia cathedral, apparently poisoned by his enemies.

Boniface VIII replaced him, but he was kidnapped by the French and eventually replaced by a French pope, Clement V. In 1309, France moved the papacy to Avignon, where seven successive French popes lived through the years of the so-called "Babylonian captivity".

Return of the popes

The papacy returned to Rome in 1377 when France was confident that future popes could be made to toe the French line, but it was at once engulfed in the Great Schism, funda-

the arts, it was viewed with some suspicion at the time, with northern Europeans suspecting the popes were merely Italian princes extending their temporal dominions at the expense of their neighbours. These fears were confirmed by Machiavelli with the publication of *The Prince* in 1513, a case study of contemporary political intrigue based on Cesare Borgia, the "nephew" (actually son) of Alexander VI, a Spaniard who had bribed the Sacred College to make him pope then proceeded to develop a form of statecraft "unweakened by pity and uninfluenced by ethics or religious faith". This model was widely emulated, most conscientiously by his son.

mentally a clash between French and Italian ideas about the papacy's role. The row polarised the whole of Europe, setting off early tremors of the Reformation. Two competing popes were joined by a third before the whole lot were swept aside and replaced by Martin V, a Colonna man who "placed the papacy before the Church, Italy before Europe, his Colonna kinsmen before everybody". Predictably, other nobles rose in revolt.

While posterity is indebted to the Renaissance popes for their munificent patronage of

The enormous wealth generated by dubious means made Italy a prize over which the European powers, especially France and Spain, fought for 60 years. Eventually, French, Spaniards, and landless German Lutherans made common cause under the colours of Charles V's imperial army for the infamous Sack of Rome in 1527. The Swiss Guard were killed to a man while priests were beheaded, "old nuns beaten with sticks, and young nuns raped and taken prisoner". St Peter's and the Holy Palace were turned into stables and two-thirds of the city reduced to ruins.

Pope Clement VII, fortunate still to be alive in his Castel Sant'Angelo refuge, decided that

LEFT: Machiavelli, author of *The Prince*.
ABOVE: *Meeting with the Pope*, by Vittorio Carpaccio.

resistance was futile and became the first of a succession of popes who threw in their lot with the Spanish Empire. They borrowed the concept of the Inquisition from Spain and applied it with great rigour. Artists who had fled from Rome drifted back, among them Michelangelo, but the spirit had deserted them. Michelangelo's *Last Judgment* in the Sistine Chapel (1536) is said to reflect the sombre mood of the time.

Reformation and war

The shockwaves of the Reformation in France, Germany and England were felt in Rome. Pius IV (reigned 1559–65) was recep-

tive to Reformation critics, and reconvened the Council of Trent to see what could be done: "The Council shall reform what wants to be reformed, even in our own person and even our own affairs."

Some observers subsequently saw an improvement in the political and religious climate. "Several popes in succession have been men of irreproachable lives," wrote Paolo Tiepolo in 1576, "hence all others are become better, or have at least assumed the appearance of being so.... the whole city has become much more Christian-like in life and manners."

In the meantime, Protestant–Catholic enmity flared, and proceeded to blow itself

out, in the course of the Thirty Years' War (1618–48). The subsequent Peace of Westphalia was a turning point in European diplomatic history. It established the principle of states settling their differences around an international conference table, the genesis of the League of Nations and the United Nations. The papacy was thus deprived of its cherished role as the foremost international mediator.

Napoleon comes to town

In 1796 Napoleon issued a proclamation: "Peoples of Italy, the French army comes to break your chains.... Your property, your religion, and your usages will be respected. We make war as generous enemies, and we have no quarrel save with the tyrants who enslave you." After defeating the papal army at Ancona, Napoleon demanded money and art treasures from the Vatican, and sovereignty over some Papal states. Romans were not sorry to see the French drive the Austrians out of Italy, but they were horrified by the looting of art galleries and punitive French taxes.

Pope Pius VII was bundled across the French border to Valence and Napoleon incorporated the papal territories into the French Empire. He installed his mother in a palace in the Piazza Venezia and gave his sister Pauline to Prince Camillo Borghese. The prince reciprocated by selling his new brother-in-law the Borghese art collection for 13 million francs.

Rise of the Risorgimento

After Napoleon's downfall, papal rule was restored at the Congress of Vienna in 1815, but the same congress also restored Austrian control over large parts of Italy. That kindled the Risorgimento, the rise of modern Italian nationalism, and part of the nationalist conflagration that swept through most of Europe in 1848. Pope Pius IX ("Pio Nono") was perceived as a liberal reformer, but the *sine qua non* of Italian independence was to throw off the Austrian yoke, and the pope could not bring himself to make war on the Catholic Habsburgs. His inhibitions played into the hands of the anti-clerical Giuseppe Mazzini, and it was not difficult to persuade people that an Italian republic was the answer. The pope was deposed from temporal power and a republic proclaimed, with Mazzini as head of a governing triumvirate. In France, however, Louis Napoleon needed Catholic support, and the restoration of the pope seemed a certain way to win it. Giuseppe Garibaldi's 4,000 red-shirted irregulars were no defence against the French army, but rather than surrender he marched his band out of Rome and across Italy to achieve immortality in the history of the Risorgimento.

The reinstated Pio Nono was protected by a cordon of Louis Napoleon's troops while the patchwork of Italian states threw off their princes and united, not behind the republic mooted by Mazzini but, thanks to Count Cavour, a nascent Kingdom of Italy under

beggars. The clerical élite, over the previous century or so, had paid no attention to mundane matters like drainage, at which the ancient Etruscan kings had excelled. Every flood on the Tiber cascaded through the Old City; the surrounding countryside was a malarial wasteland infested with bandits. The spectre of the Paris Commune in 1871 persuaded the city fathers that the new Rome would be better off without a resident working class, so the poor were forced into shanty-towns on the periphery of the city. It was not a prepossessing start for the capital of a newly united nation.

Despite Rome's experiment in social cleansing, Italian politics developed along rel-

Victor Emmanuel II of Sardinia. The pope, meanwhile, had just worked out the doctrine of Papal Infallibility when, in 1870, an explosion rocked the Old Aurelian Wall and the Italian army poured through the breach. The pope barricaded himself in the Vatican and Rome began to adjust to life after 11 centuries of papal rule.

The capital of united Italy

When Rome was proclaimed the capital of the united kingdom of Italy in 1871, a third of the city's population, then about 200,000, were

atively liberal lines into the early 20th century. World War I was, for Italians, virtually a private fight against the pro-German Austrian forces in the north, and Rome itself was not directly implicated. Repercussions came later in the person of Benito Mussolini, the former editor of a Socialist paper who came out of the war "burning with patriotism and bursting with ambition, a *condottiere* of fortune... shrinking from no violence or brutality".

Mussolini and Fascism

Mussolini named his party the Fascisti after the *fasces*, the rods that were the symbol of a magistrate's authority in Ancient Rome. The

LEFT: Giuseppe Garibaldi (1807–82). **ABOVE:** view of Rome in the 18th century by Gaspare Vanvitelli.

party evolved in Milan, dressing its storm-troopers in black shirts and silencing critics by forcing castor oil down their throats. On 30 October 1922, Mussolini marched on Rome, ostensibly to save the country from the peril of Bolshevism. With the king nominally left on his throne, Mussolini pushed through sweeping changes in the appearance and order of Italian society. He bulldozed roads through the historic city centre to speed up traffic. "All merely picturesque things are to be swept away," he declared, "and must make room for the dignity, the hygiene and the beauty of the capital. It is necessary to reconcile the demands of ancient and modern Rome."

RESISTANCE AND REPRISAL

Italian gallantry during the latter part of World War II was conspicuously demonstrated by the shelter given to Jews, anti-Fascists and escaped prisoners-of-war. An escape organisation was set up in Rome by Major S.I. Derry of the British Army, assisted by Monsignor Hugh O'Flaherty, an Irish priest attached to the Vatican, and funded by local people. About 4,000 escapees were shepherded to safety, but these and other resistance activities provoked harsh reprisals. When 10 German soldiers were killed by partisans in an ambush, 335 men were taken from Rome's Regina Coeli prison to the Ardeatine caves outside the city and shot.

Pope Pius XI, a semi-recluse in the Vatican, warmed to the dictator as he restored the crucifix to schools and worked towards a treaty between the Vatican and the Italian state, formalised in the concordat of 1929, when the two sides agreed sovereignty and relations.

Dreaming of a reborn Roman Empire, Mussolini annexed Abyssinia and Albania. He took Italy into World War II on 9 June 1940 when he believed Germany would win. One military disaster followed another, and Mussolini was only deterred from bombing Athens and Cairo when Churchill threatened to retaliate by bombing Rome. By July 1943 the Allies were mopping up in North Africa and preparing to invade Italy via Sicily. Victor Emmanuel III had Mussolini arrested and appointed Marshal Badoglio as head of government. Guessing that Italy would sue for peace with the Allies, Hitler ordered a German occupation of Italy. The armistice was duly declared, Mussolini was made the puppet ruler of a Fascist republic in northern and central Italy, and the German army occupied Rome.

The Allies launched a bombing offensive against Rome, but targets were generally pinpointed, the church of San Lorenzo being one of the rare accidental victims. Rome had no strategic value but for symbolic reasons it was the greatest prize of the Italian campaign. Rome fell on 4 June 1944, yet it was not until 28 April 1945 that Mussolini was captured, shot and hung from a lamppost in Milan.

The onset of corruption

Conditions in Rome immediately after World War II have been grippingly portrayed in contemporary neo-realist films by Vittorio de Sica *(Bicycle Thieves)* and Roberto Rossellini *(Rome, Open City)*. The most familiar backdrop was not the Colosseum, but the high-rise blocks that proliferated under Salvatore Rebecchini, mayor from 1947 to 1956. Property developers bribed bureaucrats and Rome's empty spaces filled with illegal buildings. This system passed effortlessly from the Christian Democrats to the Communists in 1976.

Politically there was nothing edifying about post-war Rome. The 1957 Treaty of Rome spelt out a vision of a Common Market, but life on the ground over the next two decades was blighted by frequent strikes and terrorist attacks. The Italian Communist Party had emerged from the war as the largest European Communist Party outside the USSR, and all the other parties agreed that the Communists must be restrained by any means. No Italian party was large enough to form a government, so the result was a run of short-lived coalitions.

In 1978, political mayhem reached a peak with the kidnapping and murder of Aldo Moro, the Christian Democrat Prime Minister. The same year, Polish Karol Jozef Wojtyla became the first non-Italian pope in 450 years (as John Paul II), and brought international prestige to the Vatican only to see it compromised by disclosures of huge irregularities in the Vatican's finances, including Mafia dealings and the laundering of drug money. The government fought back by taxing the Vatican's business activities and revoking Constantine's AD 324 edict – Roman Catholicism is no longer the state religion of Italy.

Over the next decade the Christian Democrats' dominance faded when coalition partners took important government posts and the judicial system began cracking down on organised crime. The greatest changes came from an anticorruption campaign, begun in 1992 under the name *mani pulite* (clean hands). Out came *pentiti* – mob insiders who gave evidence, breaking the *omerta* (code of silence) which had until then made the Mafia impregnable to mass prosecutions. Hundreds of businessmen and politicians were tried or gave testimony in return for leniency, and the old system of corruption and kickbacks that had ruled post-war Italy began to crumble. The Mafia struck back, and two Sicilian judges were murdered in 1992.

In the wake of the upheaval, multimillionaire industrialist and media-mogul Silvio Berlusconi and his right-wing Forza Italia briefly held power, until the Northern League, a secessionist minority, decided not to participate. In 1996, the centre-left Olive Tree coalition under Romano Prodi brought together a parliament of ex-Communists and hardliners, plus liberal elements. When this fell apart, Prodi moved on to the European Commission. Former Communist Massimo

D'Alema served for two years as Prime Minister, and continued many of the sound fiscal policies of the Prodi government. In 2000, the ruling coalition fragmented yet again, and former Prime Minister Giuliano Amato was called in to lead a technocratic government.

In May 2001, Berlusconi became Prime Minister for the second time, as leader of a right-wing alliance, but Walter Veltroni, a centre-left candidate, won Rome's mayoral elections. Amid protest from the opposition and the trade unions, which led to a series of strikes, the government embarked on a set of reforms of taxes, pensions and the labour market. In Rome, Veltroni has worked hard to make services more

efficient; cultural events have proliferated, and an impressive new lighting system for the Colosseum has been inaugurated. Today's biggest threats to Rome are pollution and traffic congestion. Measures to combat them and to make the city a pleasant environment for the future and to preserve its incomparable past, are being undertaken, but it will be an uphill struggle. The year 2006 will be an important one for Rome and Italy, with general and municipal elections coming up in the same year. After being found not guilty for the fraud charges brought against him in 2004, Berlusconi clings to power; it remains to be seen whether he can charm his way into a third term. ❑

LEFT: Joseph Ratzinger from Germany becomes the 265th pontiff, Benedict XVI. **RIGHT:** strikers demonstrate outside the Colosseum.

Decisive Dates

THE RISE OF THE ROMAN EMPIRE: 27BC–AD211

31 BC–AD 14 Augustus founds the Empire and establishes peace. The arts flourish, especially in Rome. Roads are built to the extremities of the Empire.

AD 64 After setting fire to Rome, Nero builds the Domus Aurea (Golden House).

69–79 Emperor Vespasian has the Flavian Amphitheatre (later renamed the Colosseum) built. The Arch of Titus is erected in the Forum to commemorate the destruction of Jerusalem in AD 70 by Vespasian and his son, Titus.

98–117 The Roman Empire achieves its greatest expansion under Emperor Trajan, extending as far north as the East Friesian islands, east to Mesopotamia, south to North Africa and west to Spain and Britain. The arts flourish across the Empire.

117–38 Hadrian builds walls to secure the Empire's borders.

161–80 Marcus Aurelius reigned as Roman Emperor. His column, with reliefs showing his victories over Danubian tribes, stands in Rome's Piazza Colonna.

193–211 Septimius Severus. A grand arch in the Forum commemorates his victories over the Parthians.

DECLINE AND DEFEAT: 250–1100

250 Christians persecuted under Decius.

284–305 Diocletian. During his reign the Empire begins its decline; he introduces the tetrarchy, whereby four people share power. Renewed persecution of Christians.

312 Constantine defeats Maxentius near Milvian Bridge. Christianity officially recognised. Byzantium, now Constantinople, becomes capital of the Empire in 330.

395 Roman Empire divided. In 404 Ravenna becomes capital of western part.

410 Rome taken by invading Visigoths.

455 Rome plundered by the Vandals.

476 Fall of western Roman Empire. Power assumed by the Germans: first by Odoacer, then by Theodoric, king of the Ostrogoths.

536 Rome captured by Byzantium. East Roman rule in Italy re-established.

590–604 Pope Gregory protects Rome by making peace with the Lombards.

750s Pepin, king of the Franks, aids Pope Stephen III, returns lands taken by Lombards, and lays foundation of temporal sovereignty of the popes by giving the pope the exarchate of Ravenna.

800 Pope Leo III crowns Charlemagne emperor in St Peter's. The Roman Empire is restored in name.

12th century An insurrection takes place during the papacy of Adrian IV (Nicholas Breakspear, the only English pope). Arnold of Brescia, the leader, is executed in 1155.

PAPAL ROME: 1309–1801

1309 Clement V moves the seat of the papacy to Avignon in southern France.

1377 Gregory XI returns to Rome. The resulting "western schism" within the church is finally extinguished only in 1417 with the election of Pope Martin V.

15th century Rome enters a phase of prosperity during the Renaissance. The Popes attract famous artists, including Bellini, Botticelli, Bramante, Donatello, da Vinci, Michelangelo, Palladio, Raphael and Titian.

1527 Charles V's army sacks Rome.

1585–90 Pope Sixtus V commissions Fontana, Bernini, Borromini and Maderno to build and beautify the city. A brief period of prosperity is followed by a steady decline. The Italian peninsula splits into smaller states, among them the

Papal States, with Rome as the capital.

1798–9 Rome becomes a French-style republic. Pope Pius VI dies in French captivity in 1799.

1801 Pope Pius VII concludes a concordat with Napoleon to preserve the independence of Rome and the Papal States. Rome becomes part of the French Empire.

1814 Papal States are restored to Pius VII at the Congress of Vienna.

NEW KINGDOM OF ITALY: 1848–1945

1848 Pope Pius IX gives Papal States a constitution but refuses to intercede for unification. Forced to flee, he does not return until 1850.

1870 Rome and Papal States conquered.

1871 Rome becomes capital of the new kingdom of Italy. The popes live as prisoners in the Vatican.

1922 Mussolini assumes power. Broad streets and monumental new buildings constructed. Suburbs built around the city.

1929 Lateran Treaty between the Italian state and the Vatican makes the latter an independent state with the Pope as head.

1943 Mussolini arrested. The Allies land in southern Italy. The king and government leave Rome.

1944 The Allies liberate Rome on 4 June.

1945 Mussolini is hanged in Milan.

THE REPUBLIC: 1946–PRESENT DAY

1946 After a referendum, Italy becomes a republic. Rome remains the capital; King Umberto II is exiled to Portugal.

1957 The European Economic Community (now European Union) established by the Treaty of Rome, is signed by six nations.

1962 Pope John XXIII opens the Second Vatican Council, which lasts until 1965.

1978 Aldo Moro, prime minister and head of Christian Democrats, is kidnapped and killed by the Red Brigade. Karol Wojtyla becomes the first Polish pope (John Paul II).

1981 Turk Ali Agca makes an assassination attempt on the pontiff in St Peter's Square.

1993 Italy gains government of national unity, headed by President Scalfaro and Premier Ciampi. Giulio Andreotti, seven-times prime minister, is investigated for Mafia association.

LEFT: a reconstruction of the Colosseum.
RIGHT: Prime Minister Silvio Berlusconi.

1994 Elections usher in a new republic. Media magnate Silvio Berlusconi is new prime minister; forced to resign by late 1994.

1995 Andreotti goes on trial.

1996 First left-wing government in Italian postwar history.

1997 Berlusconi receives suspended sentence for fraud. Andreotti trial continues.

1998 Centre-left coalition gives way. Former Communist leader Massimo D'Alema named prime minister.

1999 Projects to prepare Rome for 2000 jubilee culminate in a frenzy of restoration work.

2000 Millions flock to Rome for Holy Year celebrations. Right-wing candidates make major

gains in regional elections; centre-left coalition falls; Giuliano Amato named Prime Minister of a technocratic government.

2001 Berlusconi becomes Prime Minister for the second time as leader of a right-wing alliance. Walter Veltroni, a centre-left candidate, wins Rome's mayoral elections.

2003 Rome hit by a wave of strikes by public-service employees.

2004 Berlusconi acquitted of fraud charges.

2005 Pope John Paul II dies and Joseph Ratzinger from Germany becames Pope Benedict XIV; Berlusconi heads the longest-serving Italian government since World War II.

2006 General and municipal elections.   ❑

THE ROMANS

The citizens of Rome share a glorious history, of which the city reminds them every day, but they often seem quite insouciant about their heritage

Romans are brought up with the demigods of Romulus and Remus and a memory of imperial megalomania. As denizens of the Eternal City, they are exhausted by their ancient wisdom and self-evident superiority. According to Alberto Moravia, the greatest Roman novelist: "The Roman tag of eternal should be understood in the sense of *ennui*, of eternal boredom." Romans have seen it all before – a mood epitomised by the city slogan *"pazienza"*, both a shrug of resignation and a gesture of indifference to their heritage.

Rome is *the* place for contemplating the passage of time and the vanity of human wishes. The world-weary populace has little inclination to relive the glory, decline and fall, but there is a residual melancholy and romantic nostalgia for the grandeur of Imperial Rome. This nostalgia is tinged with a feeling of living in the ruins. Yet the Romans are not inhibited by their heritage; instead, they have domesticated it. Cats command the ruins; housewives hang washing over sacred shrines; and youths scrawl graffiti on noble statues.

Roman society

The Ancient Rome of popular imagination was peopled by emperors and orators, poets and politicians, patricians and plebeians, valiant gladiators and avaricious tax collectors. Repub-

PRECEEDING PAGES: *The Creation of Adam* is the most famous scene from Michelangelo's Sistine Chapel ceiling. **LEFT:** cafés and squares, the public arenas where daily life is played out. **RIGHT:** Roman centurions welcome the tourist invaders – for a fee.

lican Rome had a degree of upward mobility, or at least cultivated popular aspirations, but in practice, society separated into the proletarian masses and a patrician élite. Most of Rome's aristocratic families rose to prominence during the Renaissance. This élite band provided popes and cardinals as well as the noble Corsini, Farnese and Orsini dynasties. The patrician élite survives, often ridiculed as concierges to a decadent heritage.

All roads lead to Rome

In the 19th century, Rome had the smallest middle class of any major European city. But by 1900 a population boom saw the number of inhabitants double; the city was further swollen by the exodus from southern Italy after World War II. In the 1960s, the population reached 2 million, and by the 1990s had topped 3 million. The new arrivals were quickly assimilated by a city that prides itself on its tolerance. Nonetheless, the influx has shaped the composition of Roman society. Yesterday's emblematic types have been replaced by civil servants and clergy, business administrators and boutique owners, not to mention *tifosi*, football fans and the cocky youths Fellini dubbed *vitelloni* (fat calves).

Romans harbour deep attachments to certain quarters in the Centro Storico, from the Ghetto,

still home to several thousand Jews, to Campo de' Fiori, a lively quarter peopled by fruit sellers and furniture restorers. Trastevere, the ancient immigrant quarter north of the Tiber, until recently formed the backbone of the Roman proletariat. Nowadays, its feisty character is submerged under a Bohemian gloss. Testaccio, the hilly 19th-century working-class quarter curled around the former slaughterhouse, is newly fashionable and considered preferable to the *borgate*, the faceless modern suburbs where many Romans have to live. By contrast, Parioli, the leafy suburb north of Villa Borghese, is dotted with chic villas and finds favour with the *nouveaux riches*.

Roman rhythms

According to Moravia, "Foreigners find a certain serenity in Rome," but this is not a sentiment shared by most Romans. The day begins and ends in traffic jams because *Roma intra muros*, based on the "Seven Hills", is periodically closed to cars. To avoid the chaos, many Romans resort to *motorini* (mopeds). En route, they are fortified by strong coffee and *cornetti* (sweet croissants) in a bar.

In the past, mealtimes in Rome were sacred, with offices and shops closing between 1 and 4pm and the majority of workers going home for a cooked meal. Times have changed however, and in what many consider to be a regrettable but necessary drive for greater efficiency, extended mealtimes and siestas have largely become a thing of the past. Office workers now get an hour off for lunch and many shops stay open all day. The exceptions are family-owned shops or small boutiques that still make the most of their three-hour lunch breaks.

Political parasites

As Italy's capital, Rome lives and breathes politics, but it also has a reputation as the flea on the back of long-suffering northern Italy. The anti-Rome prejudice is kept fresh with tales of bloated bureaucracy and crippling inefficiency. In the eyes of other Italians, Romans are seen as greedy parasites and power-brokers bent on keeping the administrative spoils within the family. The city is smothered by a web of political mismanagement and the culture of corruption.

The city is also envied for its monopoly of international institutions such as FAO, the United Nations food organisation. The city hosts two diplomatic corps, with 109 embassies accredited to the Italian government and 59 to the Vatican. According to Moravia, "Rome is an administrative city dominated by two institutions: the State and the Church. That aside, there is no communication, no flow of ideas.".

City of religious sceptics

As a sovereign state and the capital of Catholicism, the Vatican celebrates its triumph over paganism. However, these sentiments are not shared by sceptical Romans. In keeping with their eclectic past, Romans are ritualistic rather than religious, formalistic rather than faithful. In Roman eyes, the Church symbolised temporal power. Today, the Vatican is seen as a political institution, the corporate arm of the papacy, albeit one with a good cashmere gift-shop attached. Anti-clerical attitudes have been confirmed by the financial and political scandals of the early 1980s and the conservatism of Pope John Paul II.

Today, Rome is a secular, sophisticated city, if one coloured by a religious caste of mind. *"Roma venuta, fede perduta"* (Once in Rome, faith is forsaken) runs a cynical local saying. The city may have more than 900 churches,

full-blooded, earthy, exuberant and rebellious, the latter is cerebral and refined, albeit eviscerated. The two traditions meet in a common passion for politics, religion, the family, food and Roman heritage.

The Trastevere poets, commemorated by statues in the riverside quarter, represent the populist strand of Roman society. Gioacchino Belli, the 19th-century dialect poet, was foremost among the satirical poets who railed against the acquisitiveness of Roman rulers. Trilussa, his best-loved modern successor, satirised the ambitions of Mussolini as well as Roman foibles and a fondness for Castelli

but only 3 percent of Romans regularly attend Mass. If the papacy intrudes on daily Roman life, it is only as a source of sexual proscription or a cause of traffic congestion. To the world-weary Romans, the Wednesday papal audience simply serves to clog the city streets with yet more traffic.

Populists and élitists

The stratified society of Ancient Rome has bequeathed two contrasting traditions: the populist and the élitist. While the former is

LEFT: admiring the ancient city from the Gianicolo Hill is a popular Sunday afternoon pastime. **ABOVE:** the market in the working-class quarter of Testaccio.

Romani white wine. *Trasteverini*, the inhabitants "over the Tiber", still pride themselves on their vigour and passion for life.

Pier Paolo Pasolini, the controversial writer and film-maker, followed in the steps of the Trastevere popular poets. Murdered in murky circumstances in 1975, Pasolini was a Marxist, Catholic and homosexual whose disturbing films challenged conventional ideas and sexual mores. As an anti-establishment figure, he immortalised rough Roman youth in his tales of a dying way of life in the city slums.

At the élitist end of the scale lies the intelligentsia, a medley of politicians, professionals, artists and academics. Alberto Moravia, the archetypal Roman intellectual, denied the existence of the species, yet he was the mainstay of sophisticated Roman society for many years, until his death in 1990. His novels reveal a remorseless observer of Roman society. But, like a true Roman, he affected disdain and indifference towards the city of his birth. He only cared for it nostalgically, "like a woman one had once loved". He considered himself a European not a Roman writer, someone who merely used the city as a scenic backdrop to his work.

High-profile Romans by adoption include the virtuoso novelist Italo Calvino (1923–85), who was born in Cuba of Italian parents; the idiosyncratic Dacia Maraini (born in Fiesole in 1936), erstwhile companion of Moravia and a literary lioness of Rome; and Eugenio Scalfari, founder and for 20 years editor-in-chief of *La Repubblica*, Rome's best-selling newspaper, and one of Italy's foremost opinion-leaders until his retirement in 1996.

Giulio Andreotti, seven-times Italian prime minister, was a symbol of longevity in power, and he typified the Roman politician for all seasons. Known as "the eternal Giulio", he was born a stone's throw from Julius Caesar's birthplace and had much in common with his namesake. Also nicknamed *il volpe* (the fox), the Machiavellian Christian Democrat politician was notorious for his patrician disdain as

ROMAN VERNACULAR

Classical Roman writers have enriched the Western world through the language that every educated person once spoke: Latin. The political legacy of Latin is heard in such concepts as "civic", "plebeian" and "pontificate" – terms that define public life to this day. Yet compared with people of other cities, the Romans have not clung to a strong regional dialect. Romanesco, which was once the local parlance, survives only in the Roman clipped speech, rolling accent and certain vernacular expressions: "born in a shirt" means rich. The cadenza romana is a raucous guttural accent in which *questo* (this) is reduced to *'sto; va bene* (fine) becomes a clipped *vabbé* while *andiamo a dormire* (time for bed) is abbreviated to *'namo a dormi*.

Religious and political graffiti represent a Roman art form. Many squares are adorned with plaques containing papal pronouncements or pompous tributes to former emperors. The modern versions are the populist slogans daubed by Roma football fans and the colourful scrawls that appear overnight and are incomprehensible to all but the cognoscenti .

well as his love of power. Andreotti's Roman hauteur and professed piety helped to save him from numerous investigations into alleged Mafia links, until the justice system finally caught up with him in 1995.

Romans at play

Romans might cultivate a philosophical world-weariness but this is rarely reflected in their social life. The 1950s *dolce vita* playground of Hollywood starlets has disappeared, leaving behind a less sophisticated scene. Most of the city's inhabitants feel more comfortable within a populist culture. They enjoy strolling through the gardens of Villa Borghese or admiring the ancient city at sunset from the Gianicolo Hill. On Sunday, football fans flock to Stadio Olimpico to watch Roma or Lazio play at home.

People of all ages feel at home in a packed neighbourhood *trattoria*, tucking into a hearty *saltimbocca all romana* (a dish of rolled veal and ham), *carciofi alla giudea* (artichokes fried in oil) and *misticanza*, a salad of wild leaves, washed down with a robust carafe of wine, often from the local Castelli Romani district.

Bourgeois Romans believe in conspicuous consumption, and Versace-swathed citizens cluster around the *alta moda* shops in Via Condotti while wealthy matrons drape themselves in Fendi furs or Valentino gowns. But Roman enjoyment is generally less evident in glamorous settings such as the opera or a Via Veneto piano bar. Instead, night owls can be found downing a *digestivo* such as Sambuca, Strega or Fernet-Branca near the Pantheon or simply looking cool with a speciality ice-cream on Piazza Navona, while romantic couples may haunt the fish restaurants on the lakes outside Rome. More exotic Roman kicks range from racing around the city centre in customised cars to snorting cocaine or indulging in sexual encounters with Brazilian transvestites. At times, gossip about satanic rites, patrician incest or other deviant sexual practices conjures up the decadence of Pasolini's *Roman Nights*, but it is not a world that most Romans would recognise.

LEFT: the street is a forum for exchanging news and views. **RIGHT:** hanging out at the Campo de' Fiori, a hive of activity day and night.

A tolerant capital

Other Italians regard Romans as both pragmatic and philosophical, shrewd and sentimental, vulgar yet vibrant. The Romans enjoy the contradictions, and in any case do not care in the slightest what others think of them: as masters of *nomifregismo*, a couldn't-give-a-damn attitude, they ignore criticism.

Emperor Vespasian personified Roman shrewdness by charging citizens for using public latrines. Contemporary Roman cynics believe that "when the police are on strike, the traffic's all right". And there is a special name for Roman cunning – *dritto* – the ability to fleece the gullible.

Opinionated and resilient, the Romans still know how to live. They have made Rome, in essence a city of illusion and disillusion, into the most human of European capitals. Romans have a welcoming embrace, offering tolerance and a lack of exclusivity that lies at the heart of their great culture. "All contributions welcome", as the signs say in St Peter's. The promise of Roman citizenship is proffered to all newcomers. Anyone can become Roman in time – even if the official papers fail to materialise – because ultimately, being Roman is a state of mind. As Moravia put it: "There are no Romans, only people who adopt Roman characteristics." ❑

Rome on Film

I talian cinema was born in Rome in 1905. The debut of the country's first feature *La Presa di Roma* – a chronicle of Garibaldi's march into the city – marked the beginning of the Eternal City's enduring love affair with celluloid. Rome remains the heartbeat of Italian cinema; the film community live and work here, and its streets and squares provide a permanent film set.

The silent era was dominated by historical spectaculars, culminating with

Giovanni Pastrone's Punic War kidnap drama *Cabiria* (1914). The success of these toga tales had industrialists and aristocrats queuing to finance Rome's burgeoning film industry.

The birth of Cinecittà

Mussolini viewed film as the perfect propaganda machine for his fascist ambitions. In a vainglorious attempt to trump the Americans he built his Hollywood on the Tiber – Cinecittà – and opened Italy's first film school. Under fascism directors with ideological credentials were bankrolled, but these on-message film-

makers created little of artistic merit. Meanwhile Italy's best directors were either severely censured or went into hibernation.

Neo-realism

The fall of fascism marked the emergence of one of the world's great film movements: neo-realism. Stimulated by post-war wretchedness and tired of escapist spectacle, the *neorealismo* auteurs determined to record the life of ordinary people. At their forefront was Roberto Rossellini who shot his masterwork, *Rome Open City* (1945) on the devastated streets around Via Prenestina. This account of the Nazi occupation revolves around an extraordinary performance from Roman actress Anna Magnani as a defiant matriarch.

The signature film of the neo-realism movement was Vitorrio De Sica's *Bicycle Thieves* (1948). The story of an unemployed man in the slums of Rome was a huge international success. De Sica bankrolled the film himself, used non-professional actors and dedicated his story to "the suffering of the humble".

The second generation of neo-realists included Federico Fellini and Pier Paolo Pasolini. Their subject matter was the Roman underworld of small-time thieves, desperate love and the endemic black market. "We discovered our own country," said Fellini, "and its reality was so extraordinary that we couldn't resist photographing it."

Fellini's collaboration with Cinecittà turned him into the uncrowned king of the studios. He placed his adopted city under a microscope. *Roma* (1972) attacked the Catholic Church while *La Dolce Vita* (1960) satirised the idle Roman rich who hung around the then glamorous Via Veneto. The film left us the enduring celluloid image of Anita Ekberg cooling off in the Trevi Fountain.

It's ironic that Mussolini's film city finally found fame with the Americans he was trying to outdo. Cheap labour, good light and the pleasures of working in Italy brought Hollywood to Rome – turning

Cinecittà into a household name for millions around the world.

Epic heroes and comedians

For over a decade Cinecittà was synonymous with the epic: films like *Quo Vadis* (1951) *Ben-Hur* (1959), Taylor and Burton's *Cleopatra* (1963), and the film that launched a thousand tourist trips, *Roman Holiday* (1953). During the glory years the studios produced over 1,000 films, employing millions of actors, extras, technicians and directors. Modern day studio tours include a surviving section from the set of Cleopatra.

When the public appetite for epics died and neo-realism ran out of steam Rome's film industry hit a downward spiral. Though the public were still hungry for film, the skill of Italian dubbing artists meant that slick and fashionable American films filled Italian cinemas.

And though neo-realism was Italian cinema's artistic zenith, the Italians have always loved their comedic stars. Each city has its home-town clown: Naples will be for ever associated with Toto and Troisi while Florence has Roberto Benigni. When Rome's jester-in-chief Alberto Sordi passed away in 2003 over 80,000 crammed the streets for his funeral. During Sordi's fifty year career he appeared in over a hundred films, including Fellini's 1953 classic *I Vitelloni*. A week after his death, the mayor renamed one of Rome's central streets after him.

Cinecittà's comeback

Home-grown comedy continues to play well, but in recent years there have only been fleeting glimpses of the city in films shown outside Italy. The Roman section of *Night on Earth* (1991) saw Roberto Benigni hilariously careering around town as a taxi driver confessing to his passenger priest. Turkish born director Ferzan Ozpetek uses his adopted city Rome as a

backdrop for films like *Haman* (1997) and *La Finestra di Fronte* (The Window Opposite, 2003) which is set in the ghetto. But the city's most consistently acclaimed film-maker is Nanni Moretti, who runs a production company and cinema here. Moretti is Rome's left-wing Woody Allen. The city is often centre stage in his films, notably *Caro Diario* (1994) where he is seen scootering round the concrete suburbs in search of the essence of Rome. Moretti's languid, ironic storytelling style met with success when his 2001 drama *La Stanza Del Figlio* (The Son's Room) was lauded by international critics.

And after years in the wilderness Cinecittà is back. In 2002, Martin Scorsese reconstructed entire blocks of 19th-century New York slums in the Cinecittà studios for *The Gangs of New York* – watch out for the extras who are all Romans. This heralded a slew of international productions including Mel Gibson's *The Passion of Christ* (2004), Steven Soderbergh's *Ocean's Twelve* (2004) and Paul Schrader's Exorcist prequel, *The Beginning* (2005). Local film makers are crossing their fingers that this will pave the way for a new wave of international success for Italian cinema. ❏

LEFT: Federico Fellini, the godfather of Italian cinema. **RIGHT:** Nanni Moretti scootering round Rome in *Caro Diario* (Dear Diary).

RENAISSANCE AND BAROQUE ART AND ARCHITECTURE

A wealthy, secure papacy and an interval of peace
left a rich legacy of Renaissance and baroque art and
architecture. Between its ancient ruins, Rome is awash with
masterpieces by Bramante, Michelangelo and Raphael, and
arch-rivals of the baroque, Bernini and Borromini

Walking through Rome's Centro Storico, one is frequently amazed by the sheer size and grandeur of the buildings crammed into the narrow, winding streets. At other times one might be struck by an exquisite fountain or façade which, although obviously the work of a major artist and worthy of being the pride of any other city, is ignored by the traffic and pedestrians rushing past. There are exceptions, but a high proportion of these architectural gems date from the period between 1454 and 1670, when, thanks mainly to a securely established papacy, Rome was one of the principal cities in Europe and a centre of Renaissance and baroque art and architecture.

A rebirth

The Renaissance – Rebirth – was a rediscovery and development of the ancient art and culture that had been abandoned after the Roman Empire fell in the 5th century. It began in Italy in the late 14th century and, over the following 150 years, swept across Europe, influencing culture and teaching, and leading to fundamental changes in the way people thought and lived.

Christopher Columbus, Marco Polo and Vasco da Gama discovered new countries and trade routes; Galileo made discoveries about the universe; and philosophers such as Erasmus and Thomas More studied and reapplied

the humanist philosophies of the ancients. While not yet questioning the supremacy of God, they proposed that man was capable of achieving and creating great things without reference to God and the Bible at every turn. This basic change in emphasis led ultimately to a questioning of the dogma of the Catholic Church and to the birth of Protestantism.

It was in art and architecture, however, that the new movement was most visible – in the development of perspective, the more naturalistic presentation of subject matter (especially compared to the Byzantine-inspired style that preceded it) and in the use of classical proportions and styles in building.

LEFT: the Fontana del Moro, Piazza Navona, based on Bernini's designs. **RIGHT:** the fountain opposite the Pantheon, by Giacomo della Porta (1575).

Most of the great artists of the time came to Rome at some point in their careers, either to study the classical proportions of the Forum and other ancient remains, or to complete commissions for the Pope. However, it was really in northern Italy, and particularly in Florence, that the Renaissance developed.

During the middle of the 15th century two factors were responsible for the re-emergence of Rome as a cultural centre. First, the papacy of Nicholas V (1447–55) established a line of popes with time, money and the desire to improve Rome's appearance. Secondly, the Italian League of 1455 ushered in a degree of peace across Italy, leaving the popes free to

Farnesina; and Michelangelo, who designed the Campidoglio as well as painting the Sistine Chapel and sculpting St Peter's *Pietà*.

Artists in residence

Until the 1527 Sack of Rome, artists flocked to the city, working either for the Pope or for the leading families who competed for the papal throne – the Barberini, Borghese, Medici and Pamphili families are among the best known.

Dating from this time are churches such as Santa Maria del Popolo and Santa Maria della Pace (both with Bramante additions), palaces such as those on Via Giulia (for example,

occupy themselves more peacefully with art and architecture.

Many of the changes made over the next 70 years can be seen in Rome today. Nicholas V ordered the demolition of the old St Peter's and the present building was worked on by some of the greatest artists of the 175-year period that it took to complete. Many of the details and interior decorations were executed later, in the baroque period, but Renaissance masters who left their mark include Bramante, whose *Tempietto* on the Gianicolo is regarded as the first truly Renaissance building in Rome; Raphael (as director of works), whose frescoes can be seen in the Vatican and at Villa

Palazzo Clarelli, designed and lived in by Antonio da Sangallo the Younger), and, of course, great works of art, which are to be found in all the main collections but especially in the Vatican, the Palazzo Barberini and the Palazzo Doria Pamphili.

During the latter part of the 16th century, creativity was curbed by a papal decree in response to the threat of Protestantism. The 1563 Council of Trent laid down guidelines for church commissions. Realism was allowed to stay but there was to be no prettification and emphasis had to be put on the worldly suffering of martyrs to remind people of the infernal torments awaiting them if they offended the Church, thus terrifying people into remaining loyal. Niccolò Pomarancio's gruesome frescoes of martyred saints in the churches of Santo Stefano Rotondo and Santi Nereo e Achilleo date from this period. The Accademia di San Luca was founded in 1577 with the purpose of promulgating the Church-approved style of painting.

A major artist of this period was Caravaggio, although his life-like figures and details, such as saints with dirty fingernails, did not meet with undiluted approval from a public used to the daintier figures of Raphael and Michelangelo, or from factions of the Church who found such naturalism blasphemous.

Baroque begins in Rome

While the Renaissance was imported from Florence, the baroque style started in Rome. Although it may seem strange that the purism of the late 16th century should lead to the ornate, baroque style of the 17th, both were provoked by the fear that Protestantism would weaken the power of the Catholic Church. Both styles were intended to promote Catholicism, but while one used shock tactics the other tried gentle persuasion.

By the 1620s, extravagantly decorated churches with *trompe l'oeil* ceiling paintings and gold-encrusted altars were thought more likely to entice people back into the Catholic fold than portrayals of suffering. The basic shapes of these buildings still owed much to classical models but now everything was highly decorated with statuary and reliefs. Size and impact were the main themes explored in baroque architecture.

This was the age of Bernini and Borromini, whose façades grace most main streets and piazzas in central Rome. Bernini's fountains decorate Piazza Barberini and Piazza Navona, and his sculptures are on Ponte Sant'Angelo, in the Villa Borghese and in churches across Rome. The church of Sant'Andrea al Quirinale was one of his masterpieces. It creates an awesome impression in spite of its small size.

Other highlights of the era include the church of Sant'Ignazio Loyola, which belonged to the Jesuits, and the less ornate

Chiesa Nuova. The latter was built for Filippo Neri, who is said to have set his richer followers to work as labourers on the building.

With Rome established as a political and social centre, leading families were keen to demonstrate their wealth and prestige by building massive palaces in the city centre and villas in pleasure grounds outside. Most of them can still be seen today. The Villa Borghese dates from this period, as do parts of the Palazzo Doria Pamphili, the Villa Doria Pamphili and the Palazzi di Montecitorio and Barberini. Once again artists flocked to Rome from other parts of Europe to cash in on the patronage of its great families. Velázquez,

Rubens and Poussin all have major works exhibited in Rome.

During the second half of the 17th century, however, the funding dried up. The turmoil of the Reformation was replaced by political squabbles in which art and architecture had little part to play. There have been plenty of smaller improvement projects and building programmes since the baroque period, but none that has marked the city quite so deeply.

The buildings and monuments of Bernini, Borromini and their contemporaries remain, stunning pieces of work that evoke an era and create a cityscape that is as Roman as the Colosseum and the Forum. ❑

LEFT: beautiful painted ceiling of the Villa Farnesina.
RIGHT: *Bacchus*, by Caravaggio, in the Villa Borghese.

BERNINI AND THE BAROQUE

The Roman baroque style, perfected by Bernini, was the model for European baroque

Gianlorenzo Bernini (1598–1680) was at the forefront of Roman baroque, pioneering sublime and spectacular effects. Although more restrained than elsewhere in Europe, Roman baroque is theatrical, bold, at times bombastic. Bernini's Rome is an open-air gallery of fountains and facades. Palaces and churches boast sweeping curves, majestic facades and theatrical vistas flanked by flights of steps. As a virtuoso architect and sculptor, Bernini worked in broad brushstrokes, with illusionistic verve. At ease with interiors and exteriors, he was a showman renowned for his theatricality and technical brilliance.

Bernini's style found favour with a succession of popes. Even St Peter's is, in part, a Bernini creation, graced by enfolding, keyhole-shaped colonnades. Other masterpieces include the witty design for an elephant to bear the obelisk of Santa Maria sopra Minerva and the graceful angels on Ponte Sant'Angelo. As for palaces, Palazzo Barberini (1629–33) heralded the baroque style and was completed by Bernini, assisted by Borromini, who became his arch-rival *(see opposite)*.

LEFT: Apollo and Daphne displayed with other Bernini masterpieces in the Galleria Borghese. This is Bernini's most famous sculpture. The magnificent, youthful work shows the nymph fleeing from the sun god.

FRANCESCO BORROMINI

Borromini (1599–1667) made use of revolutionary, gravity-defying architectural forms. While Borromini lacked the confidence and all-round virtuosity of Bernini, his churches abound in visual trickery. His work is characterised by a sculptural quality, the alternation of convex and concave forms, and a conspicuous fondness for geometric designs as well as for subtle plays of light and shade.

San Carlo alle Quattro Fontane *(see page 94)* was Borromini's first solo commission. Based on an oval design, the ingenious church is notable for its illusionistic dome. The sinuous, seemingly swaying, walls inspired countless baroque artists.

The great rivalry between Bernini and Borromini has enriched the cityscape and is enshrined in popular legend: on Bernini's Four Rivers fountain in Piazza Navona, the allegorical statue of the River Nile supposedly shields its face, recoiling in horror from the Borromini facade beyond. In fact, Bernini's fountain was unveiled in 1651, a year before Borromini's Sant' Agnese was even started.

BELOW Bernini's Sant'Andrea al Quirinale (1658–70) is a subtle tour de force inspired by Michelangelo's architectural feats.

TOP: Piazza Navona. Rome's loveliest baroque square is home to three fountains and other works by rival architects Bernini and Borromini. In the foreground is Bernini's Fontana del Moro. His sumptuous fountains vie for attention with Borromini's church of Sant'Agnese, with its striking interplay of towers, domes and facade. **ABOVE:** Graceful statues in the Palazzo Barberini, on which both Bernini and Borromini worked.

FAR LEFT: Fountain of the Four Rivers (1651). The four allegorical figures of Bernini's most famous fountain represent the Danube, Ganges, Nile and Plate and allude to the four corners of the world and the pervasive power of the papacy.
LEFT: Bernini's obelisk-carrying elephant outside Santa Maria sopra Minerva church.

THE CITY'S CHANGING FACE

Every city needs to stay modern, but when you have an architectural legacy like Rome's, how can you improve without destroying vital parts of the past?

Rome has been a centre of political power throughout its 2,700-year history. It was home to ancient emperors, then popes; became capital of the new Italian nation in 1870; was the heart of the stillborn empire Mussolini imagined. Each of these periods has left its mark on the city. Rightly or wrongly, the Romans have been blamed for mistreating their archaeological and architectural legacy since ancient times. Emperor Maxentius (AD 306–12) accused contemporaries of tearing down "magnificent old buildings" to get material for new houses. Pope Pius II (1458–64) shuddered at people burning marble monuments to obtain lime. Popular slogans derided Urban VIII's impact: "What the barbarians didn't do, the Barberini did," it was claimed.

The German writer Goethe (1749–1832) made a similar complaint, "What the barbarians left standing, modern architects have destroyed", and the German historian Ferdinand Gregorovius (1821–91) thundered against the Piedmontese remodelling of the papal city. In the 20th century Alberto Moravia classified four-fifths of the city as "a disaster area of civic architecture". Yet these critics stayed in Rome. What draws people to this city, and what keeps them here?

First, Rome has the sort of beauty that provokes passionate response. Every corner seems to have something worth stopping to look at; a green shady courtyard with a dribbling fountain; an extravagant baroque façade;

a colourful street market; or an ancient obelisk that blocks the traffic in a way no modern city planner would allow.

A visible past

Rome is a city standing on the shoulders of its predecessors where layers of history run into each other. Not only were materials taken from older buildings to make new ones, but buildings themselves were adapted to suit changing needs. Medieval church towers rise above the remains of ancient houses; a Renaissance palace balances on top of the Theatre of Marcellus next to a 20th-century restoration of the theatre as luxury apartments; ancient

LEFT: Renzo Piano's state-of-the-art auditorium.
RIGHT: Via del Babuino fountain and message board.

aqueducts run along railway lines leading into Stazione Termini. Even when the buildings have disappeared their shapes remain. One of the key features of Italian city life – the piazza – is a direct descendant of the ancient Forum.

Caesar's improvements

Julius Caesar (101–44 BC) was the first to introduce a programme for improving the city. It was a necessary one, for Rome was nowhere near as splendid as its imperial role demanded. But soon Rome was flaunting its wealth; under Caesar, 640 gladiators wore silver armour at the city's games. The Theatre of Pompey, Rome's first permanent theatre, dates

from this time. It was intended to offer more sophisticated Greek-style theatre than the bloodthirsty spectacles Ancient Romans usually enjoyed, although this civilising gesture met with only limited success. The shape of the round building can still be seen behind Campo de' Fiori; Via di Grotta Pinta follows its curve. The Julian Basilica was also built at this time. The piazza, surrounded by a double row of buildings, had little shops along one side, divided into mezzanine floors with embossed rounded arches (which later became models for Renaissance architecture). It was both a fitting tribute to Caesar and a useful addition for the city's one million inhabitants.

The Emperor Augustus (27 BC–AD 14) liked to boast that he had found Rome made of brick and left it made of marble. The marble remnants we find in today's buildings mostly date from this period. Under Augustus, the urbanisation of the Campus Martius began in the area now covered by the Centro Storico, and was divided into *rioni* – the zones of central Rome that still exist today. The first of the Imperial Fora also date from these years.

Ancient Rome was heavily built up. The *insulae* or apartment blocks rose so high that after the fire of AD 64 destroyed the city centre, a decree of Nero's limited their height to 20 metres (60 ft). In the wake of the fire, disagreement raged between those who wanted the historic, picturesque alleys retained, and Nero, innovator and self-glorifier, who wanted broad avenues and low buildings against which to display monuments dedicated to himself. More practically, Nero forbade the use of wooden ceilings and insisted on the provision of water buckets in houses.

Little of this remains because it was destroyed by Nero's successors (Vespasian 69–79, Titus 79–81 and Domitian 81–96). in order to win popularity and dissociate themselves from Nero, they erected more democratic centres of enjoyment, including the Colosseum, on land originally covered by Nero's lake. Domitian's legacy was the stadium over which Piazza Navona was built.

One of Rome's greatest architects was Apollodorus of Damascus, master builder of Emperor Trajan (98–117), responsible for Trajan's Forum and the covered market behind it – a revolutionary idea, regarded as one of the wonders of the world. Trajan also built a massive bath complex on land previously covered by Nero's Golden House.

Few major buildings have survived from the period between the fall of the Roman Empire and the Renaissance. However, most of the churches that exist today were founded during the Middle Ages, and, although some of them have been completely rebuilt since then, many incorporate medieval fragments – towers in particular. Indeed, towers of a military nature were also erected during this troubled period. Surviving towers include the Torre delle Milizie (1309), which rises above Trajan's Market.

Reconstruction of Rome

In 1447, Pope Nicholas V embarked on a programme that included remodelling many
architectural masterpieces, such as St Peter's.
He also became the patron of artists, crafts-
men, humanists and literary scholars, trigger-
ing a boom in the arts that lasted for well over
200 years. He transferred the seat of papal
power from the Lateran Palace to the Vatican.

Sixtus IV (1471–84) commissioned the Sistine Bridge, the first to be built across the
Tiber for more than 1,000 years. Alexander VI
(1492–1503) fortified the Castel Sant'Angelo
and started work on the Palazzo della Cancelleria. A few years later came Julius II, whose

Sixtus V's (1585–90) main contribution
was to improve communications for pilgrim
traffic. His network of streets built to link all
the city gates is still mostly intact. Via Felice
connected the Porta del Popolo in the north
with S. Maria Maggiore and S. Croce in Gerusalemme. With the existing streets it formed a
system with four nodal points, where obelisks
were erected: Piazza del Popolo, S. Maria
Maggiore, S. Giovanni and S. Pietro. Sixtus
died before he could implement his plan to
demolish the Colosseum, which blocked his
route from the Lateran Palace to St Peter's.

Many of the main sights in Rome's Centro
Storico date from the 17th century, when

architect, Bramante, started work on the new
St Peter's, although he died long before work
was completed, leaving others, including
Raphael and Michelangelo, to take over.

Leo X (1513–21) commissioned Via di
Ripetta, to link the family palace of the Medici
and Porto di Ripetta. Another Medici,
Clement VII (1523–34), had Via del Babuino
built and thus created the "trident" of streets
flowing away from Piazza del Popolo. In 1536
Michelangelo drew up the first plans for the
rebuilt Campidoglio for Pope Paul III.

architects such as Bernini and Borromini
designed buildings and monuments for a
string of popes and papal families. Most of
Piazza Navona belongs to this period, as do
many of the churches, particularly the ornate
ones, such as Sant'Andrea al Quirinale, the
Gesù and Chiesa Nuova.

In the 18th century, works and improvements were on a smaller scale, although two
of the city's most famous sights date from this
time. The Spanish Steps, built to link the
French church of the Trinità dei Monti with
Piazza di Spagna, were completed in 1726,
while the Trevi Fountain, designed by Nicola
Salvi for Clement XII, was finished in 1762.

LEFT: old meets new in the Museo Nazionale Romano.
ABOVE: the Piazza del Popolo.

Utilitarian developments

During the 19th century, most of the changes were utilitarian rather than aesthetic. In 1856 the railway line from Rome to Frascati was opened and the first station was built at Termini in 1862 (although the present building is a 20th-century one). After Unification in 1870 the popes ceased to control Rome and Garibaldi and Vittorio Emmanuel became the figures most often celebrated in statues, street names and monuments (notably the Vittorio Emmanuel monument on Piazza Venezia).

More practical developments included the major roads crossing the city, such as Via Nazionale and Via Cavour; new residential began on the EUR quarter and the Foro Italico, while massive new buildings were erected all over Rome to house institutions such as the university and post office.

The city expands

The idea of building self-enclosed estates on the edge of Rome, the Agro Romano, was first mooted in development plans in 1907. Since 1870 Rome had been the goal of a steady stream of immigrants from the south and the Abruzzi. In 1922 there were about 800,000 inhabitants; by the end of World War II there were 1.8 million. Mussolini decided Rome needed "living space and greatness", and

zones in old neighbourhoods such as Testaccio; and developments on the city's periphery. Further improvements included the embankment, the Lungotevere, started in 1870, which put a stop to the regular, disastrous floods.

The 1920s saw the creation of the Art Nouveau Coppedè Quarter around Piazza Mincio and the Garbatella residential quarter on the city's outskirts. Then Mussolini ushered in a programme of dramatic changes to build a city fit to be the seat of his intended empire. Vast roads were cut through the medieval quarter and parts of the Fori Romani were covered over to create a suitable avenue for Fascist processions. On the outskirts of the city work began building the *borgate* (estates) of Prenestina, Pietralata and San Basilio. These were so depressing both in form and material that Pietralata, Tiburtina and Quarticciolo soon became symbols of wretchedness, inhabited by poor immigrants. Between 1950 and 1976 slums engirdled Rome, while at the other end of the social scale, the wealthy got planning permission to build on the Via Appia. In 1976, after the election of the Communist mayor Carlo Giulio Argan, Rome's great slum clearance began. The *borgate* were given lighting, power, mains water and bus routes. Then came supposedly exemplary new areas such as Tor Bella Monaca and Tor de' Cenci, but in spite of their architectural style and sensible planning they developed the problems typical of such districts worldwide: poverty, poor services and bad communications. Better living standards became a key political issue, including improvements to public transport, especially the grossly inadequate metro.

Rome's rejuvenation

Modern architecture was a rarely seen phenomenon in Rome until a few years ago, when the state-of-the-art auditorium by Genoese architect Renzo Piano, which opened in 2002, spawned a wave of major architectural projects by big-name architects. Its three shell-like concert halls, built around an outdoor amphitheatre and set in parkland, filled a much needed cultural gap and transformed the city's sleepy architectural reputation almost overnight. Currently under construction (with completion scheduled for mid-2006) is the contemporary art centre by Anglo-Iraqi architect, Zaha Hadid. The centre, officially known as the Museo delle Arti del XXI Secolo, or MAXXI, in the northern Flaminio district just across from the auditorium, will contain a complex network of interior and exterior spaces that will house two museums for the state collections of contemporary art and architecture, as well as offering temporary exhibition spaces.

Further out of town, in the unremarkable eastern suburb of Tor Tre Teste, Richard Meier's uplifting Jubilee church *(see page 180, and photo right)*, features three striking white shells, or sails; and in the southern EUR suburb a futuristic congress centre, a suspended, amorphous structure, is being built to a design by Massimiliano Fuksas. Back in the centre, a huge designer hotel opened near the station (on Via Filippo Turati) in 2002, one of the first completely new buildings in the centre in recent years.

The list does not end here: disused industrial buildings have been transformed, one notable example being the Centrale Montemartini museum in Ostiense *(see page 181)*. In the Marconi area, the vast Città del Gusto (City of Taste) complex in a remodelled gra-

nary is a beacon of culture and activity in an industrial wasteland overlooking the Tiber. Not far from Piazza Fiume, Rome's Municipal Museum of Contemporary Art, MACRO, puts an old Peroni brewery to good use. This project follows on the heels of the conversion of the stables of the hilltop Quirinal Palace into a clean, crisp exhibition space.

One of the most long-term and troubled projects has been the construction of a new museum pavilion to house the Ara Pacis, an altar dating from 9 BC, located at the Tiber end of the Piazza Augusto Imperatore. The old structure, built by Fascist architect Vittorio Morpurgo, was considered ugly and no

longer capable of protecting the monument, so in 1996 US architect Richard Meier started work on a new complex that will ultimately contain a bookshop, a small museum and exhibition space, a store-room and a small auditorium.

The project, made of glass, plaster and travertine, has been delayed both for practical reasons (archeological remains were found below it and the foundations had to be modified) and political motives (local architects and politicians did not like the fact that the commision was awarded without a competition), but it looks as if it may finally be ready by the autumn of 2005. ❏

LEFT: Stazione Termini's elegant facade.
RIGHT: Richard Meier's Jubilee Church.

FOOD AND DRINK

For Romans, the very act of eating is celebrated
almost as much as the food itself. Simple yet
delicious dishes are the city's mainstay

Culinary traditions run deep in Rome, reaching back to the ancient peoples who first populated the region. For centuries the Romans have held firm against the influence of many new ingredients, dishes and cooking techniques that have come as a result of Rome's contact with the rest of the world, as well as the fads and fancies of the upper classes, emperors and popes.

Though exotically spiced sauces, fancy game dishes and "delicacies" like fried parrots' tongues dressed with honey, have faded into history, something does remain from the high cuisine of the past: the decided pleasure with which Romans go to table. It is probably not the place to hunt down the top restaurants – few consider *la cucina romana* to be the best of Italy's regional cuisines – but Rome may well be one of Italy's most pleasurable cities in which to eat. Often, what might seem to be slow service is merely the Roman way of stretching the meal out far into the night. In general, restaurants plan on one seating per evening, so you will not be rushed, or pressured to leave. When in Rome, make a point of having a long, lingering meal – and have it in the open air, if the weather is good.

La cucina romana

Quite a lot of the local cuisine involves offal, the so-called *quinto-quarto* (fifth quarter) of the animal. While dishes like *rigatoni con pajata* (pasta with veal intestines) and *trippa*

alla romana (tripe with tomato sauce, Roman mint and *pecorino*) are long-time local favourites, you will find that most restaurants in the centre of town tend to avoid such specialities in favour of dishes from other parts of the country which are more familiar to their clientele, such as pasta with pesto sauce, risotto and polenta.

But you needn't eat innards to eat Roman, and every restaurant will have at least a few home-grown dishes, all of them sharing the frugality that marks the region's food, perhaps better called cooking than cuisine. Expensive restaurants offer adventurous dishes with long names, but the menu of a typical Roman

LEFT: patriotic pasta. **RIGHT:** a leisurely lunch al fresco
is one of the best pleasures Rome has to offer.

establishment tells a different, less complicated story: *spaghetti alla carbonara* (with rendered bacon, egg and *pecorino* cheese), *bucatini alla gricia* (with *guanciale* – cured pork jowl), *cacio e pepe* (with *pecorino* cheese and black pepper) and *all'amatriciana* (with *guanciale* or rendered bacon and tomato sauce) all share an undeniable simplicity. Pasta even makes its way into Roman soups: *pasta e ceci* (chick pea soup flavoured with rosemary) and *broccoli e arzilla* (clear soup of broccoli and skate). *Gnocchi alla romana* (potato dumplings in a meat sauce) are traditionally prepared on Thursday, while *baccalà* (salt cod) is served on Friday.

Nor is fish fussed over: clams tossed with spaghetti and olive oil becomes *spaghetti alle vongole* and *pesce azzurro* (fish from the sea) is baked in the oven *(al forno)* or cooked on the grill *(ai ferri* or *alla griglia).* Two common meat dishes are *saltimbocca alla romana* (veal slices rolled with prosciutto and sage) and *coda alla vaccinara* (braised oxtail in a tomato and celery sauce), but the meat to try is *abbacchio* (milk-fed lamb), which is usually roasted with herbs and garlic or served *alla scottadito* (grilled chops).

Save room for vegetables, which abound in Rome's produce markets all year long and find their way to the table in basic preparations, often steamed or blanched, then briefly sautéed. Romans are the undisputed masters of the artichoke, which are in season from November through to April and traditionally prepared in several ways, among them *carciofi alla giudia* (deep fried), and *carciofi alla romana* (stuffed with garlic and Roman mint and stewed).

A typical winter salad is *puntarelle*, made from shredding the stalks of a locally-grown chicory and serving them with a lemon-anchovy dressing. Summer brings roasted peppers, aubergines and *zucchini* (courgettes) served in a variety of ways, and large tomatoes stuffed with herbs and rice, while in spring you'll see asparagus and *fave con pecorino* (raw broad beans served with *pecorino* cheese).

Many Italians like to have just one main dish and finish off a good meal with a piece of fruit. Accordingly, appetisers and desserts get little attention in most Roman restaurants. A few common starters are melon or figs with *prosciutto* and *fiori di zucca* (deep-fried *zucchini* flowers filled with mozzarella and anchovies). Popular desserts are *torta di ricotta* (ricotta tart), *panna cotta* (eggless firm custard made of cream and served with a fruit sauce) and *tiramisù* (Italian espresso trifle).

The local wines – those from Frascati are the most famous – are probably better than they have ever been, but pale in comparison with wines produced in other parts of the country, which are now much better known and readily available.

Wine bars are very popular in Rome, and offer a great alternative to having a restaurant meal. Choose from usually about a dozen wines available by the glass (or from more than a thousand different labels by the bottle) and a great selection of high-quality cheeses, cured meats, and smoked fish, as well as soups and salads, quiches and gratins, and homemade desserts.

Roman pizza

Although it is the Neapolitans who are credited with inventing pizza, the Romans eat their fair share. There are more *pizzerie* than restaurants in town, and they even have their own version of this staple dish. A Roman pizza is plate-sized, rolled very thin and flat and baked in a wood-burning stove (*forno a legna*), while the Neapolitans usually make a thicker, softer dough with a raised border. A night out at a *pizzeria* (few are open for lunch) is a quintessential Roman experience.

On the go

For Romans, *gelato* (ice cream) is not as much dessert as it is an afternoon or after-dinner snack to accompany a leisurely stroll around town. Accordingly, *gelaterie* are never far away and stay open until late. Other treats that can be picked up from street vendors all over town are roasted chestnuts in the autumn and winter and refreshing *grattachecca* (shaved

tions, *pizza al taglio* is always sold by weight; an *etto* (100 grams) makes a small portion. A good number of these shops also sell *supplì* (fried balls of rice and mozzarella), a classic Roman snack.

The gastronomically curious may like to visit the Museo Nazionale delle Paste Alimentari (daily 9.30am–5.30pm, tel: 06-6991119), on Piazza Scanderbeg near the Trevi Fountain, for fascinating displays of all kinds of pasta. But a visit to a good *alimentaria* is as rewarding as a trip to any museum. You will find regional products from all over the country, but the local cheese to try is *pecorino romano*, made from ewe's milk

ice with syrup) and watermelon wedges in the summer months.

Romans often stop at the local bar a couple of times a day, first for a breakfast of espresso or cappuccino and a *cornetto* (the Italian version of the French *croissant*), then another espresso and perhaps a snack, such as a *panino* or *tramezzino* (small sandwiches) later in the day.

Pizza al taglio (by the slice) is also very easy to find. Thicker than *pizzeria* pizza and topped with dozens of imaginative combina-

into big wheels, which are bathed in brine and aged for 18 months. A by-product of this is *ricotta di pecora*, brought in fresh from the farms and delicious on its own. A memorable sandwich can be made from *porchetta* (whole roasted pig, sliced to order), a speciality of the towns in the hills around Rome.

If you are not travelling any further, take the opportunity to try *mozzarella di bufala* (handmade mozzarella cheese, made from the milk of water buffalos), or several kinds of *prosciutto* from central and northern Italy. Two *alimentari* with particularly good quality and selection are Franchi (200–204 Via Cola di Rienzo), and Volpetti (47 Via Marmorata). ❑

LEFT: for a healthy snack on the hoof. **ABOVE:** a wealth of fresh ingredients go into a good pizza topping.

SHOPPING

Rome is the place for designer goods and specialised
neighbourhood shops, for fine jewellery and fresh
produce. Above all, it's a city where shops are still
as individual as the people who frequent them

Rome is sometimes considered the poor
cousin of the Italian fashion meccas of
Milan and Florence, yet if the truth be
known, not only does it have enough haute
couture, chic clothing and leatherwear stores
to satisfy the hungriest of style-vultures, it has
a lot more besides. The secrets of the Roman
shopping scene are variety, exquisite raw
materials, fine craftsmanship, a range of prices
to suit every wallet, and one of the most beautiful backdrops for shopping in the world, the
Eternal City itself.

Whether you are a backpacker on a budget
or a well-heeled globetrotter with a platinum
Amex card, shopping in Rome is always fun.
The city's window-dressers have a flair for
transforming displays into artistic still-lifes, so
even window-shopping, which costs nothing,
becomes a rewarding experience.

The best buys here are still leather goods of
all kinds – from gloves to bags, jackets and
footwear – haute couture, silk goods and
knitwear. If you have your eye on something
specific, like a Fendi bag, Missoni top or Fer-
ragamo shoes, make a note of prices before you
leave home, so you'll know whether you are
paying less in Rome. In many cases you will
get a bargain. Boutique fashions are also starting to make their mark and offer a wide range
of alternative fashion at interesting prices.

Some attractive old prints and decorative
objects can be found in the city's interesting
antique shops, and fully-fledged collectors can

rely on the prestigious reputations of some of
Italy's top dealers. Genuine Italian handicrafts
are less easy to find in these days of Asian
imports, but some shops stock genuine Ital-
ian-made ceramics and handwoven textiles.
Moreover, many of the more traditional areas
of the city host an ever-increasing number of
talented artisans who sell hand-crafted goods
directly from their workshops.

Exploring the city

Guidebooks to Rome tend to direct readers to
just two shopping areas in the city: the Tridente, the Golden Triangle of shopping
located south of Piazza del Popolo and

LEFT: Tad Conceptstore is one of a new breed of lifestyle stores. **RIGHT:** Beauty Point cosmetic superstore.

between Piazza di Spagna and Via del Corso, and the Centro Storico (Historic Centre), which surrounds Piazza Navona and Campo de' Fiori. And in some ways, they are right to do so. These areas are where you will find the highest concentration of shops, the most aesthetically appealing, well-known or upmarket emporiums, many pedestrianised piazzas and streets, and all the high-fashion names that Italy is known for worldwide, as well as the cream of the international crop.

Yet shopping in Rome is about much more than those two areas. As in any large, international metropolis, other parts of the the city specialise in independent fashion boutiques or

Shopping areas

In ancient times wealthy Roman families would send a slave out into the streets to do the household shopping. These days the shopping is still done by slaves – slaves to fashion. If you're a *fashionista*, then your first port of call should be the streets of the Tridente, particularly Via dei Condotti, Rome's most famous shopping street. Here in the city's haute couture and prêt-à-porter mecca, you'll find all the names that define Italian fashion: Prada, Gucci, Versace, Armani and many, many more. Southwest of the Tridente is the *centro storico*, which includes the main tourist sights of Campo de' Fiori, the Pantheon and Piazza Navona. Here

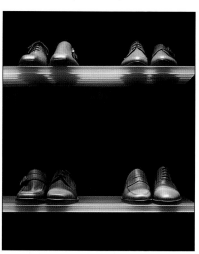

artisans' workshops, and others still host large commercial districts that serve the suburbs. In these latter areas you will find branches of many of the big-name shops located in the city centre, as well as a good number of local speciality stores, such as patisseries, shoe shops or jewellers, that have such good local reputations that even the notoriously lazy Romans are prepared to cross town to see what they have on offer. Often visitors will have a more rewarding, and certainly a more *Roman* experience, if they venture further afield. The shops will be less crowded, the shop assistants less jaded and some of the boutiques quirkier, and cheaper, too.

the fashion pickings are interspersed with quirky boutiques, stylish homeware stores and classy antique shops.

A little further afield but within walking distance are the attractive medieval alleyways of Trastevere, situated across the Tevere (Tiber) River from the southern end of the Centro Storico. Trastevere specialises in artisans' workshops and traditional delicatessens. From here it is a short walk to working-class Testaccio, which is now an up-and-coming area that mixes local, neighbourhood shops with a few trendy boutiques.

To the west of the Tridente (beyond the river) is a bustling area known as Prati, home to offices, apartment blocks and many, many shops. Prati has a good selection of the well-known brands, but not so many of the tourists. Northeast of the Centro Storico and heading towards Termini, the city's main railway station, is a largely 19th-century, boulevard-filled area of Rome containing the congested but also highly commercial thoroughfares of Via Nazionale, Via del Tritone and Via Veneto. Via Veneto is not as chic as it was in its 1960s heyday, while Via Nazionale and Via del Tritone both offer a good range of Italian high-street chain stores. Off Via Nazionale to the southeast is the medieval district of Monti, which is strong on artisans and smaller boutiques.

tive household items, as well as hosting art exhibitions in its airy, warehouse-style space.. The Salario area to the north is an important commercial centre, with upmarket shops catering to the posh Parioli neighbourhood that lies further north; most stay open all day and late into the evening. There are also a branches of a couple of the city's classiest department stores, COIN and La Rinascente.

Many of these areas also support local markets. The best ones to look out for as you explore the city are the Campo de' Fiori produce market, Porta Portese flea market in Trastevere and the multicultural Nuovo Mercato Esquilino *(see pages 145)*.

The streets flanking the western side of the railway station and around Piazza Vittorio Emanuele II make up Rome's principal multi-ethnic area, and this is reflected in its import-export clothing stores and exotic foodstuff havens. To the east of the station is the suburb known as San Lorenzo, a politically radical area which is harsh on the eye but big on local colour, and now home to ethnic and artisan stores, as well as art galleries. Studio Marsi, in Via dei Marsi, has gained a good reputation for customised, vintage clothing and decora-

LEFT: classic bags and shoes at Fratelli Rossetti.
ABOVE: Laura Biagiotti (left) and Tad Conceptstore.

Getting around

Getting from one area to another in Rome is easy. If you are staying in the city centre and are armed with a decent map you will be able to walk almost everywhere, and will definitely find it a more pleasant experience than trying to jam yourself onto one of the packed buses that chug through the car-ridden city's central thoroughfares. Keep an eye out for the small electrical buses that snake quietly through the city, however, as they can provide welcome relief for tired feet. For the more outlying areas there is always a handy bus from the city centre, or a metro stop not too far away, to make it easier to carry your purchases home.

When to hit the shops

Opening hours in Rome are a law unto themselves. What British and American visitors find most surprising is the tendency for many shops to close for at least two hours at lunch time and for the whole of Monday morning. However, shopping hours in Italy are changing. In highly commercial and touristy areas such as the Tridente, Via del Corso, the Trevi Fountain and Via Nazionale, most shops, especially the chain stores, department stores and high-fashion boutiques, now operate a so-called *orario continuato* (continuous opening hours), sometimes also called the not-quite-English *orario no-stop*, both of which mean

they do not close at lunch time. Often these stores will not close on Monday morning either. As soon as you are off the main tourist trail, however, or if the shop is a smaller boutique, traditional opening hours will generally be respected.

Sunday opening is another recent novelty on the Roman shopping scene. Again it's mainly the big names, chain stores and department stores in touristy areas that open on a Sunday. Another thing to remember is that in July and August, as the heat starts to become oppressive, local and independent shops may close on Saturday afternoon, and most close for at least two weeks for their annual holiday.

Roman service

It won't be long before you experience a phenomenon well known to regular visitors to Rome – the unhelpful shop assistant. Although there are many exceptions, most notably the designer boutiques who are dependent on tourist trade, and the small independent stores, the Roman retail trade is not known for polite customer service. Shop assistants may seem either too bored or too busy talking to pay you any attention. Don't take it personally; simply ask firmly for what you want and you'll find the assistants usually snap to attention.

Bargain hunting

Discounts are not generally given in most types of stores, although you may be able to get one if you are making a large purchase. One exception are the many large *profumerie* (perfume and cosmetics stores) where most items are sold at *prezzo scontato* (discount price). Another and rather more pain-free way of getting reliable bargains is the end-of-season sales *(saldi)*. The main sales periods are in January (after January 6) and February, and mid-July to mid-September. At other times of the year, interesting deals can often be had at stores showing a *liquidazione* sign, which indicates a closing-down sale.

For good quality second-hand cashmere, silk and linen garments, try Blue Cachemire in Via di San Fransesco, Trastevere. They are not exactly cheap, but they are extremely good value. And for hand-made shirts and blouses in 100 percent cotton, go to Tessuti Camiceria in Viale Mazzini, in Prati. Again, we're not talking about knock-down bargains, but excellent value for made-to-order garments.

Another way to get your designer goods cheaply is to buy them from the North African street-vendors who populate the city's most touristy thoroughfares and bridges. Of course, they are selling bags that only *look* like real Prada, Gucci, Fendi and Louis Vuitton numbers, often to an unsuspecting international clientèle. Remember, though, that when you are given prices that are a fraction of those of the original labels, the goods are definitely not the real thing, and that trade in counterfeit goods is actually illegal.   ❑

LEFT: old-fashioned specialist shops still thrive.

The Artisan Scene

As you wander through the medieval alleyways of Rome's historic centre, you will often hear the distant whir of a drill or the insistent clipping of a chisel. Chances are a house is being renovated nearby but it could be one of the city's many *artigiani* (artisans) – a carpenter, furniture restorer or plasterer, perhaps – hard at work in his or her workshop. Rome has for centuries attracted men and women skilled at trades requiring simple tools, an artistic sensitivity and, above all, the deft use of their hands. A quick glance at some of the city's historic street names confirms this. In the heart of medieval Rome, around Campo de' Fiori, you will find the hat-makers' street (Via dei Cappellari), the jacket-makers' street (Via dei Giubbonari) and the carpenters' street (Via dei Falegnami), all in close proximity.

Nowadays, however, the emphasis has changed, and the term *artigiano* is used in a more liberal sense – some would say too liberally – and defines anyone involved in the small-scale, hand-made production of anything from candles to clothing. Many foodstuffs (particularly pasta) and cosmetics are also sold with labels stating that they are *di lavorazione artigianale* (of artisanal production). This simply means that the production is not industrial in scale or means.

Old-fashioned skills and *botteghe* (workshops) co-habit with new ones, and in the same street you are likely to find an antiques restorer next to a potter, a frame-maker beside a jeweller, a specialist in *faux* marbles, gilding and lacquer work rubbing shoulders with a Tiffany glass-maker. Although the city centre seems to have an overwhelming devotion to collectors and restorers of antique furniture and objects, interspersed among them are other, more decorative types of artisans and artists. Yet it is in other, less central districts that the artisan scene is particularly evident and constantly expanding. In the characteristic Trastevere area the artisan scene is well-established but in some cases too tourist-oriented to be really interesting. More recently, the leafy and pleasant medieval streets of Monti and the grimy yet vibrant San Lorenzo quarter have become home to an increasingly diverse, cutting-edge and high-quality array of artisans.

Most real artisans will be quick to tell you that the quality most needed to succeed is a passion for what they do. The hours are flexible (they can open just in the evening, or by appointment only) and

if they are centrally located they will see a regular tourist trade, but often the hours are long and days off are spent finishing off something promised to a client. And there are few financial incentives. Although some subsidies are available, their granting is so complex and slow that few artisans are able to benefit effectively.

For the buyer though, the advantages of artisan-produced goods are obvious. In these days of mass production and the runaway success of the Ikea formula (even in Rome), artisans can provide welcome relief and a generous dose of originality and genuine skill. ❑

RIGHT: instrument restorer at Mohsen.

PLACES

A detailed guide to the city with the principal sites
clearly cross-referenced by number to the maps

Rome is crammed with great sights. In no other city are the accumulated layers of history so evident. Every corner and crest seems to lead to a famous monument, church or square.

However, for first-time visitors trying to grapple with the layout of its 12 hills – not the seven usually attributed to it – the city can seem confusing. The best way to orientate oneself is to look upon Via del Corso as a spine, with the leafy Villa Borghese quarter at the top, the archaeological zone at the bottom, the *Centro Storico* to the west, Piazza di Spagna to the east, and the Vatican and Trastevere on the far bank of the River Tiber.

The first three chapters cover the main archaeological sites – namely the Capitol, Forum, Palatine and the Colosseum – reflecting the city's foundation and key episodes in its history. Trevi Fountain and the Spanish Steps are the focal point of the next two chapters, which cover these most iconic of Rome's landmarks and the maze of streets around them.

What is referred to as the *Centro Storico,* or historic centre, is the dense centre of Rome contained in the great bend of the River Tiber; this is covered in the chapters on Piazza Navona and the Pantheon; and Campo de' Fiori and the Ghetto.

The Vatican and Trastevere chapters take you across to the west bank of the Tiber for a tour of St Peter's and the Vatican Museums, and the fashionable Trastevere district and the Gianicolo (Janiculum Hill) for one of the finest views of the city.

After this, the book dips into the quarters verging on these key areas – the Villa Borghese quarter, the Aventine and Testaccio, Monti and Esquilino, and other neighbourhoods beyond the usual tourist routes. Thence to more peripheral areas such as the Appian Way and beyond to Mussolini's Rome – EUR to the south, and Foro Italico to the north – and the university enclave of San Lorenzo. For those who want to escape the noise and heat of the city, there's a selection of day-trips into Rome's environs.

Advice on getting around the city, shopping, nightlife, accommodation and other essential information is contained in the *Travel Tips* section of this guide. And with the attached map of the city's best restaurants, you'll never go hungry.   ❑

PRECEDING PAGES: the Spanish Steps are buzzing with activity day and night; refreshment stands are a familiar sight in the city centre.
LEFT: the Dome of St Peter's offers fine views and is a good place to get your bearings.

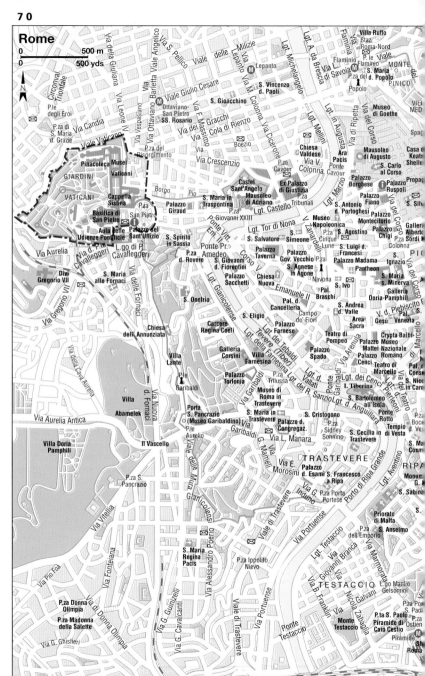

Rome

0 — 500 m

0 — 500 yds

N

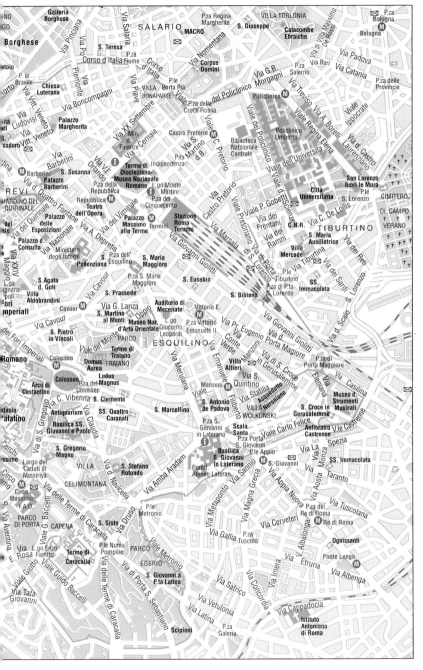

THE CAPITOLINE HILL

The Capitoline Hill was the political power centre of the ancient world, beautified by Michelangelo's designs during the Renaissance and now home to the world's oldest museums. Close by, the stark Vittoriano monument overlooks the hectic Piazza Venezia, linking the ancient world with our own

Map
on page
74

The Capitoline Hill started life as a fortified stronghold and later became the city's religious and political centre. As a 12th-century guidebook, *Mirabilia Romae (The Marvels of Rome)* stated: "The Capitol was the head of the world, where consuls and senators abode to govern the earth." At only 50 metres (150 ft), it may be the lowest of the city's 12 hills, but Rome was founded at its feet. During the Renaissance, it was glorified with the Piazza Campidoglio, a harmonious square designed by Michelangelo, and second only to Piazza San Pietro in its architectural symmetry.

The twin crowns

In ancient times the hill looked quite different, with steep cliffs of porous tufa rock falling steeply on all sides of its twin crowns. On the southern crown, known as Campidoglio (the Capitol), stood the Tempio di Giove (Temple of Jupiter), which was the religious hub of the state. Originally the size of a football pitch, it was begun by the Etruscan kings and dedicated in 509 BC, the first year of the Republic. Behind its six-pillared, south-facing frontage a great anteroom led to the shrines of three great gods – Jupiter, Juno and Minerva. Every New Year's Day, the consuls were inaugurated in a formal cere-mony on the Capitol. The triumphal processions followed Via Sacra, the holy road, coming up the hill from the Forum. Remnants of the basalt paving of this street can be seen quite clearly from Via di Monte Tarpeo. Anyone guilty of treason was thrown from the Rupe Tarpea (Tarpeian Rock), the Capitol's southern precipice.

The other crown of the hill housed the temple to Juno Moneta, the goddess who is supposed to have warned the Romans of an attack by Gauls in

OPPOSITE AND BELOW: Michelangelo's staircase leads to the Campidoglio, watched over by the twin gods, Castor and Pollux.

390 BC by making her sacred geese
honk. The mint also stood here,
hence the word *moneta*, meaning
money. The site is occupied by the
church of **Santa Maria in Aracoeli**
❶ (St Mary of the Altar in the Sky).
The church hides behind a 13th-cen-
tury brick façade, but its origins go
back much further, as its ancient
columns testify. Records from AD
574 mention a church on this site that
was considered old even then. The
interior features an ornate coffered
ceiling dating from 1572–75 and a
striking Cosmatesque floor. This
style of intricate, geometric poly-
chrome patterns is named after
Lorenzo Cosmati (1140–1210), its
inventor. In the first chapel on the
right are Renaissance frescoes by
Pinturicchio from the life of St
Bernard. The recent restoration of the
Chapel of San Pasquale Baylon
brought to light some beautiful 13th-
century frescoes concealed behind
16th-century works.

*The Etruscan statue
of the she-wolf dates
from the 5th century
BC. Romulus and
Remus were added in
the Renaissance.*

BELOW: Santa Maria
in Aracoeli.

Piazza del Campidoglio

In between the hill's two peaks sits
the **Piazza del Campidoglio** ❷
(Capitol Square). In ancient times it
was the site of the Asylum, a sacred
sanctuary that protected the persecuted, said to date back to the time
of the founder of the city, Romulus.

The magnificent square, its buildings and the broad staircase leading
up to it were designed by Michelangelo for Pope Paul III, who wanted a
majestic setting for the reception of
the Holy Roman Emperor Charles
V on his visit to Rome in 1536.

As it turned out, the square
wasn't completed until the 17th century. Standing guard at the top of the
Cordonata, as the staircase is
known, are two imposing statues of
Castor and Pollux. The piazza's centrepiece is a first-rate copy of an
immense equestrian statue of
Emperor Marcus Aurelius. The
original is kept inside the Palazzo
Nuovo *(see next page)*.

Ancient Rome

Straight ahead is the **Palazzo Senatorio**. At the bottom of its double staircase is a fountain of Minerva flanked by two gigantic reclining statues that represent the Nile (left with the Sphinx) and the Tiber (right with the she-wolf). The two grand *palazzi* on either side of the square – Palazzo Nuovo (New Palace) and Palazzo dei Conservatori (Conservators' Palace) – house the oldest public museums in the world, the Musei Capitolini.

The Musei Capitolini

The **Musei Capitolini** ❸ (Capitoline Museums; tel: 06-39967800; Tues–Sun 9am–8pm, last entry one hour before closing; audioguides in English; admission charge) are entered via the Palazzo dei Conservatori, on the right of Michelangelo's Cordonata.

The **Palazzo Nuovo** has a rich collection of ancient sculpture. The most famous piece here is the *Dying Gaul*, a beautifully evocative statue of a fatally wounded warrior, a Roman copy of a 3rd century BC Greek statue. Other highlights among the rows of busts of emperors, statesmen and philosophers include the voluptuous *Capitoline Venus*, the red marble satyr that inspired Nathaniel Hawthorne's novel, *The Marble Faun*, and more earthly subjects, including a drunken woman and children with various animals. Look out also for the Mosaic of the Doves from Hadrian's villa and the 2nd-century mosaic of theatre masks.

One of the most famous exhibits in the **Palazzo dei Conservatori** is the much-copied she-wolf wet-nursing Romulus and Remus. The wolf is Etruscan, dating from the 5th century BC, but the twins were added in the 15th century by Pollaiuolo. Other highlights here include a graceful 1st-century figure of a boy removing a thorn from his foot; an earlier Venus; a splendid collection of late Renaissance and baroque art, including works by Caravaggio, Guercino and Rubens; and fragments of a colossal statue of Constantine in the courtyard.

The two palaces are connected via a passage lined with artefacts

Map on page 74

The courtyard of the Palazzo dei Conservatori has fragments of a colossal statue of Constantine, the first Christian emperor. When it was intact it stood nearly 12 metres (40 ft) tall.

BELOW: statue of the Nile, outside the Palazzo Senatorio.

TIP

Some of the best views of the city can be seen from the cafés in the Palazzo dei Conservatori and the Vittoriano monument.

that runs underneath the square. From here you can visit the **Tabularium**, Rome's ancient archive (from 78 BC). It was built around the even older Temple of Veiovis, and rose four storeys high, with 10 arches opening on to the Forum, although all but three of them are now bricked up. Memorable views across the Roman Forum can be had from here.

Mamertine Prison

A road winds its way down from the left of the Palazzo Senatorio to the church of San Giuseppe dei Falegnami and the **Carcere Mamertino** ❹ (Mamertine Prison; tel: 06-6792902; summer daily 9am–7pm; winter daily 9am–5pm; donation requested). Defeated kings and generals, having been paraded through the streets in their victor's triumphal march, were imprisoned here before being executed. A small chapel next to a spring commemorates St Peter, who is said to have been incarcerated here, and to have baptised his guards with water from a spring he miraculously created. From the

BELOW: the Vittoriano monument, aka the Typewriter.

prison, the road leads down past Foro di Cesare (Caesar's Forum) to Via dei Fori Imperiali *(see page 79)*.

Piazza Venezia

If all roads lead to Rome, then all roads in Rome seem to lead to **Piazza Venezia** ❺, the hub of the city's road network since 1881. Some 800,000 Romans squeeze their cars through here every day and it's not the best place to be during rush hour. Compared to the grace and majesty of the Campidoglio, the **Vittoriano** monument that dominates the square is a blot on the landscape. In the 19th century, a whole swathe of medieval streets was razed to make way for this hulking white monument erected in honour of Victor Emmanuel II of Savoy, the first king of the newly unified Italy. Romans refer to it irreverently as the typewriter, or the wedding cake. Visitors can climb the monument for wonderful views of the city (summer daily 9.30am–5.30pm; winter till 4.30pm; free) and welcome refreshments in the outdoor café halfway up *(see opposite)*.

Map on page 74

Although the Vittoriano is the most dominant, the **Palazzo di Venezia** is the most interesting building on this square. Built by Cardinal Barbo in 1455 and enlarged when he became Pope Paul II, it was later handed over to the Venetian ambassadors and then the Austrians until Mussolini decided it would make a perfect office and addressed the crowds from its balcony, the very balcony from which Pope Paul II watched the races along the Corso *(see page 98)*.

This palace now holds the **Museo di Palazzo Venezia** ❻ (tel: 06-69994319; Tues–Sun 8.30am–7pm; admission charge), with displays of medieval paintings, sculptures and artefacts, terracotta models (some by Bernini), ceramics, bronze sculptures, and glass, silver and ivory objects. The museum has a permanent collection of Renaissance arts and crafts, and also hosts regular exhibitions dedicated to national and international artists and art movements. Behind the palace is the church of **San Marco** with a lovely mosaic in its 9th-century apse. ❑

RESTAURANTS & BARS

Restaurants

The restaurants and bars in this area are very touristy and not really recommended, but we detail a few places worth visiting, as much for the views and atmosphere as for food and drink.

Vecchia Roma
18 Piazza Campitelli. Tel: 06-6864604, www.ristorantevecchiaroma.com. Open: L & D Thur–Tues. €€€€
At Vecchia Roma you pay for the location, the service and some of the city's finest outdoor seating. The classic dishes are usually good, although occasionally only competent, and the wine is excellent. It's expensive for what you get, but memorable.

Bars & Cafés

The **Caffè Capitolino** (top of Palazzo dei Conservatori, adjacent to Piazza Campidoglio) has one of the most panoramic views in Rome. Outdoor seating under elegant sunshades is expensive but delightful if it's not too hot. Inside, cafeteria-style service is cheaper. Open until 8pm in summer. On the terraces of the Vittoriano monument, the attractive **Caffetterie Museali** (Piazza Venezia) affords splendid views of Rome in all directions. Just off the piazza to the east is a former theatre that attracts a 30-something Roman crowd looking for something slightly different: **Il Centrale Ristotheatre** (6 Via Celsa, www.centraleristotheatre.com) has a bar with a lounge area and restaurant with live music, theatre or cabaret. From 6–10pm you can have one drink and all you can eat from the buffet for a set price.

● ● ● ● ● ● ● ● ● ● ● ● ● ● ● ● ● ● ●
Price includes dinner and a half bottle of house wine .
€ *under €25 ,* **€€** *€25–40,* **€€€** *€40–60,* **€€€€** *€60+*

TIP

Avoid the refreshment stands dotted around the major tourist sites unless you're absolutely desperate for a drink. They're over-priced and prey on thirsty tourists. If you don't want to be ripped off, it's worth stocking up on a supply of bottled mineral water from a grocery store (there's bound to be one near your hotel).

LEFT:
Traffic police on the Piazza Venezia have their work cut out.

ANCIENT ROME

This chapter shows you some of the places where
Ancient Rome thrived, declined and eventually fell.
Here lie the remains of the Fora, the Palatine,
the Colosseum and Nero's Golden House

**Map
on page
74**

By 7.30 in the morning, a traffic jam usually blocks the intersection of Via Labicana and Via dei Fori Imperiali which leads to the Colosseum and the Appian Way. This boulevard, commissioned by Mussolini for the greater glory of the Fascist empire, slices through the heart of Rome's ancient sites. Here, Nero built an artificial lake to grace his palace. Then the Flavians – in a bid to return the tyrant's palace to the people – built the Colosseum. The construction of Via dei Fori Imperiali in 1932 was a relatively recent attempt to use Ancient Rome's monuments to underwrite modern political ambition.

Bulldozers flattened one of the city's oldest medieval quarters to make way for the route, destroying ancient walls, imperial palaces, temples and arches, some dating from the 3rd century BC. Architects ignored the archaeological massacre. When Il Duce ordered the removal of a pile of stones near the Colosseum, nobody pointed out that they marked the Meta Sudans, an ancient spring. Ludwig Curtius, then director of the German Archaeological Institute, said: "It would have been easy while building the street to excavate those parts of the Fora of Julius Caesar and of Trajan still lying underground, and to direct the road over them as a bridge, but the dictator, concerned only for his next demonstration of power, was in a hurry…"

Originally, Mussolini had hoped to excavate the Imperial Fora, which would have served as decoration alongside his new processional road, symbolically connecting his regime with the glory of Roman antiquity. If these plans had been followed, an Archaeological Park would have extended from the excavated Forum area to the ruins of the Baths of Caracalla and on to Via

LEFT: the Arch of Septimius Severus.
BELOW: modern-day chariot rider taking a phone break.

TIP

The simplest way to reach the Foro Romano is to take Metro Line B, or bus nos. 81, 85, 87 or 810, to Colosseo. From Trastevere, the Aventine or Villa Borghese take the ultra-useful tram No. 3. The entrance to Trajan's Markets is only a 10-minute walk away from the Colosseum.

BELOW:
Friends, Romans, countrymen.....

Appia Antica. But the project was never realised and the road became a major thoroughfare. It is unlikely that the ruins beneath it will ever come to light.

The Imperial Fora

The remains of the **Fori Imperiali** ❼ (Imperial Fora; Visitor Center, tel: 06-6797702; 9.30am–7.30pm daily; admission free) lie either side and buried beneath the Via dei Fori Imperiali. As Rome grew in power, its population increased and the original Roman Forum was no longer big enough to serve the city's needs. The Imperial Fora were built by a succession of emperors from Caesar to Trajan. On the south side of the Via are the remnants of the first imperial Forum, the **Foro di Cesare**, built in 51 BC by Julius Caesar when the original Forum became too small for Rome's increasing population. It was dedicated, still unfinished, in 46 BC and completed under Augustus (23 BC–AD 14). Following Hellenistic models, it was square and enclosed by pillars. On its western side stood the Temple of Venus Genetrix, built

because Caesar believed himself to be a descendant of the goddess.

The **Foro di Augusto** (Forum of Augustus) across the street was built to celebrate the emperor's victory over the army of Cassius and Brutus, who had led the conspiracy to assassinate Julius Caesar, his adoptive father. In the centre stood the temple of the war god Mars Utor and in the great apses of the square stood statues of the mythical ancestors of Augustus' family.

The **Foro di Traiano** (Forum of Trajan) was a massive complex of temples, libraries and markets, surrounded by colonnades, that outdid the other fora in size and splendour. It was designed in AD 106 by Apollodorus of Damascus, the best architect of his time. Building it meant removing a small hill between Quirinal and the Capitol. To the northwest, it was bound by the vast Basilica Ulpia, which had five naves. In its western apse, the Atrium Libertatis, slaves were liberated. Trajan also commissioned his architect to build the **Mercati di Traiano** (Trajan's Markets; tel: 06-6790048; summer

Tues–Sun 9am–7pm; winter 9am–6pm; last entry 1 hr before closing; admission charge); the ancient equivalent of a multi-storey shopping mall. Its remains stand behind the Forum on the slopes of the Quirinal, between two libraries (the entrance is at 94 Via IV Novembre). They are remarkably well preserved, and reveal a complex system of streets on various levels, with shops, administrative offices and spaces reserved for the distribution of grain to the public. The magnificent **Colonna Traiana** (Trajan's Column) nearby was erected in AD 113 to celebrate Trajan's victory over the Dacians. The 40-metre (120 ft) column is beautifully decorated with a spiral frieze of bas-reliefs depicting various phases of the Dacian campaigns (AD 101–102 and 105). Originally the reliefs were brightly painted and would have been visible from the balconies of the libraries. In AD 177, a golden urn containing the emperor's remains was buried under the column.

The **Imperial Fora Visitor Center** is located on the Via dei Fori Imperiali between Via Cavour and the Colosseum metro stop. Inside you can find background information on the site, a small exhibition space, and amenities such as a café, a bookshop and toilets.

The Foro Romano: west

The best place to begin a tour of the **Foro Romano** ❽ (tel: 06-699841; summer daily 8.30am–7.15pm; winter daily 8.30am–4.30pm; last entry 1 hr before closing; free) is at the main entrance on Via dei Fori Imperiali, roughly level with Via Cavour. Originally a marshy valley between the Capitoline and Palatine hills, the area was drained by the Cloaca Maxima, the great sewer, and the site became a marketplace that developed into the religious, political and commercial centre of Republican Rome. By the time excavations

began in the 18th century, most of the Forum was buried under rubble, and the place was known as Campo Vaccino (Cow Field), as it was used for grazing cattle.

From the entrance a path leads down to the **Via Sacra** (the Sacred Way), the oldest street in Rome, which ran through the Forum from the Arch of Titus up to the Capitoline. Triumphal processions of victorious generals in horse-drawn chariots parading their prisoners and spoils of war, and followed by their soldiers, would pass along the street to the Temple of Jupiter on the Capitol, where they would make sacrifices to Jupiter, king of the gods.

Walking westwards in the direction of the Capitoline, to the right lie the remains of the **Basilica Aemilia**, an assembly hall for politicians, businessmen and traders dating from the 2nd century BC. It was rebuilt by Augustus after a fire, and then again after another fire in 410, when Alaric and his Goths invaded the city during the conquest of Rome. You can still see the stains left by coins burned into the floor.

Map on page 74

Before working your way around the Forum, and trying to make sense of the ruins, it's a good idea to get an overview of the site. The best vantage point for this is the Tabularium or the terrace behind the Capitol (see page 76). You can also refer to the detailed map of the Roman Forum on the inside back cover of this guide.

BELOW: Trajan's Markets.

Letters in stone, Roman Forum.

BELOW: 1st–2nd century AD porphyry statue in the Curia; some say it portrays Hadrian, others Trajan.

Until 1500, most of the hall was still standing, but Bramante, Rome's chief architect during the High Renaissance, used some of it to build Palazzo Torlonia in the Borgo quarter. On the steps, you can see the remains of a temple to Venus, nicknamed *Cloacina* because the small circular building marks the spot where the **Cloaca Maxima** (the city's main sewer, built in the 1st century BC) empties into the valley of the Forum.

Beyond the Basilica Aemilia is the **Curia**, the ancient Senate House that was the centre of political life in Republican Rome. In the Middle Ages, the Curia was consecrated as a church, but the current building, a replica of Diocletian's, dates from 1937. The bronze doors are copies of the originals, which were transferred in the 17th century to the Basilica of San Giovanni in Laterano *(see page 156)*. In the cavernous inner hall (30 metres/90 ft long, 20 metres/60 ft wide, 20 metres/60 ft high), the 300-strong Senate would gather to control the destiny of the Empire. In front of the Curia is the Comitium where the Popular Assembly met. Even older is the **Lapis Niger** (Black Stone), a pavement of black marble laid to mark a sacred spot; according to legend, the tomb of Romulus, Rome's mythical founder, lies here. The remains of a monument from the 6th century BC have been excavated from under the Lapis Niger and while they do not conclusively prove the existence of the grave, they are evidence that Romulus was already venerated in early Rome.

Behind looms the imposing **Arco di Settimio Severo** (Arch of Septimius Severus). The triple arch is 25 metres (75 ft) wide, 10 metres (30 ft) deep and 20 metres (60 ft) high. It was built in AD 203 to celebrate the tenth anniversary of the emperor's ascent to the throne. The reliefs on the arch depict the victorious campaigns Septimius Severus and his two sons, Geta and Caracalla, fought against the Arabs and the Parthians. In earlier years, the arch was topped by a statue of the emperor in a four-horse chariot. Later, Caracalla had his brother murdered in the arms of

their mother and then placed him under *damnatio memoriae* (exile from memory) by ordering the deletion from monuments of all references to Geta and replacing them with laudatory titles to himself. You can still see the chisel marks on the inscriptions, which were originally inlaid with metal.

Beside the arch is the **Umbilicus Urbis**, a navel-shaped piece of stone that marked the centre of the city. Here, too, stood the **Miliarum Aureum**, a gilded bronze milestone that marked the start (or end) of all the imperial roads connecting the main towns of the empire to Rome. Beside it stood the **Rostra**, the speaker's platform moved here from the Comitium by Julius Caesar. It was once decorated with the prows or beaks (rostra) of ships captured at the Battle of Actium in 338 BC. Trophies from Cleopatra's fleet are reputed to have been displayed here as well.

Behind, to the right, are the remains of the **Tempio della Concordia** (Temple of Concord), a reconstruction by the Emperor Tiberius (AD 14–37) of the sanctu-ary erected to mark the peace accord between the patricians and plebians following the Class Wars of 367 BC.

After their deaths, many emperors were automatically deified and had temples consecrated to them. All that remains of the **Temple of Vespasian** (AD 69–79), erected by his sons Titus and Domitian (both of whom later became emperors) are the three Corinthian columns that rise up behind the Rostra. Emperor Vespasian was one of Imperial Rome's more successful rulers. His reign brought a welcome period of peace and prosperity to Rome. Vespasian was known for his pragmatism. To restore state finances after the disastrous extravagances of Nero (AD 54–69), he levied a tax on the urine that was collected from public urinals as it was a useful raw material for dyeing wool. When asked by one of his sons how he could make money with such a malodorous substance, he replied *pecunia non olet* – money doesn't smell. These taxes helped finance the building of great public works, not least of which was the Colosseum.

Map on page 74

During the Middle Ages, part of the Arch of Septimius Severus, which was half buried in rubble, was used to house a barber's shop.

BELOW: the triple Arch of Septimius Severus.

TIP

Visit the Imperial Fora on Sunday when the road is closed to traffic. You can wander freely between the monuments as Il Duce intended.

BELOW:
the Roman Forum.

In the northwestern corner of the Forum stands the **Tempio di Saturno** (Temple of Saturn), which housed the Roman state treasury. All that remains of this, the most venerated temple of Republican Rome, consecrated in 498 BC, are eight Ionic columns on a podium. Saturn was god of agriculture and ruler of the mythical "Golden Age". Each year in December, the festival of *Saturnalia* (the pagan equivalent of Christmas) was celebrated. Masters and their slaves were briefly deemed equal and gifts were exchanged.

Heading eastwards now along the Via Sacra (with your back to the Capitol), to your left stands the Corinthian **Colonna di Foca** (the Column of Phocus), the most recent of the classical monuments in the Roman Forum. This column was erected in 608 by Smaragdus, the Byzantine Exarch (governor) for Italy, in honour of the Eastern Emperor Phocas who donated the Pantheon to the Church. Next to it, a bronze inscription commemorates one of the sponsors of the paving of the Forum, L. Naevius Surdinus, in

the 1st decade BC. A fig tree, an olive tree and a vine, which used to grow here, together with a statue of Marsyas, symbolised Roman justice.

Between the Column of Phocus and the Rostra is the base of the **Colonna Decennalia**, raised in AD 303 to celebrate 10 years of rule by the two emperors Diocletian and Maxentius. The relief on the base shows the *Souventaurilia*, the ceremonial state sacrifice of a boar, a ram and a bull.

On the other side of the Via Sacra stood the **Basilica Giulia** (Basilica Julia). Started by Julius Caesar in 50 BC and completed by Augustus, it was originally the largest building in the Forum (101 metres/330 ft long and 49 metres/160 ft wide). All that remains of this two-storeyed, marble-faced structure are its pillared foundations. The basilica housed four courts of law, was the seat of the Roman office of weights and measures, and was a meeting place for bankers.

Heading in the direction of the Colosseum, you'll come to the three surviving columns of the

Tempio di Castore e Polluce (Temple of Castor and Pollux), built in 448 BC to commemorate the decisive Battle of Lake Regillus fought between Latins and Romans in 499 BC. The Romans believed victory was secured by the miraculous appearance of Castor and Pollux, Jupiter's twin sons, and built the temple in their honour. A block of marble from this temple was used by Michelangelo as the base for the equestrian statue of Marcus Aurelius he made for the Piazza del Campidoglio.

Behind the pillars is a small marble altar with reliefs of the heavenly twins, and the site of the **Lacus Juturnae** (Fountain of Juturna) the sacred well at which the Dioscuri (the collective name for Castor and Pollux) watered their horses after bringing news of the Roman victory.

On the other side of the temple, at the foot of the Palatine, is the oldest Christian structure in the Forum: the church of **Santa Maria Antiqua** was built in AD 365 on the site of a temple to Augustus.

A path leads away from the church entrance back past the temple of Castor and Pollux to the **Tempio di Cesare** (Temple of Caesar) which occupies the site where Caesar's corpse was cremated after his assassination on the Ides of March in 44 BC. So great was the grief of the people, that they kept his funeral pyre burning for days. After the cremation, his ashes were washed with milk and wine, then buried. The temple was built on the site of the pyre by his adopted son, the Emperor Augustus.

Behind the Temple of Caesar lie the remains of the walls of the **Regia**, the official residence of the Pontifex Maximus, the Chief Priest of Ancient Rome; the title is still held by the Pope today.

The Foro Romano: east

Directly opposite, 20 Corinthian columns surround the remains of the circular **Tempio di Vesta** (Temple of Vesta), goddess of the hearth and patron of the state. Here the Vestal Virgins kept the eternal flame of Rome burning and watched over the

Map on page 74

BELOW: Gladiators in combat before Nero and Agrippina.

Roman Domus

On Clivio di Scauro, south of the Colosseum, and under the Basilica of Saints John and Paul on the Celio Hill, 20 underground rooms dated between the 2nd and 4th centuries AD were recently reopened to the public after extensive restoration work. A series of residences and a private baths built in the 2nd century AD were transformed into a single, luxurious house *(domus)* a century later by a wealthy owner and decorated with frescoes which can be seen today (tel: 06-70454544; www.caseromane.it; Thur–Mon 10am–1pm 3–6pm; admission charge). Entrance to the site is allowed every 30 minutes. Book in advance if you want a guided tour.

Statue of a Vestal Virgin. These high priestesses had seats of honour in the circus and theatre and lived in luxury, but if they broke their vow of chastity, they were buried alive and their lovers strangled.

sacred image of Minerva (daughter of Jupiter and Juno), saved, according to legend, from blazing Troy by Aeneas. The Vestals entered divine service as young girls and lived a chaste life for at least 30 years in the **House of the Vestal Virgins**, the rectangular building next to the temple, a once luxurious building.

Back near the main entrance of the Forum, a broad flight of steps leads up to the **Tempio di Antonino e Faustina** (Temple of Antoninus and Faustina), built in AD 141 by the emperor in memory of his wife. Its conversion into a church saved it from destruction and it is the only Forum building that gives a real indication of just how monumental Roman temples were.

The eastern half of the Forum is dominated by the **Basilica di Massenzio e Constantino**, a three-aisled basilica that was begun by Emperor Maxentius (303–12) and completed by his successor, Constantine (306–30). Only the northern nave remains. The central nave was crossed by cruciform vaults, each resting on eight side pillars, one of which has been outside the church of Santa Maria Maggiore since 1613. Both Bramante and Michelangelo studied its form, using it as a model for the church of St Peter's. In the western apse, a **Colossus of Constantine** was discovered in 1487. Bits of the huge statue, including head, feet and hands, can be seen in the courtyard of Palazzo dei Conservatori *(see page 75)*.

Next to the basilica is the circular **Tempio di Romolo** (Temple of Romulus), dating from AD 309, which now forms the apse of the church of Santi Cosma e Damiano, converted in the 6th century. Beneath the temple are the remains of tiny rooms believed to have been part of a brothel.

With its colourful brickwork, the Romanesque belltower of the church of Santa Francesca Romana will have caught your eye. The present building is 13th century though the facade was added in 1615. Francesca Romana is the patron saint of motorists and on her festival (9 March) the street is congested with cars.

Beyond the church, marking the end of the Via Sacra, stands the majestic **Arco di Tito** (Arch of Titus), the oldest triumphal arch in Rome, built by Domitian to celebrate the capture of Jerusalem in AD 70 by his brother Titus and father Vespasian. Reliefs inside the arch show Titus in his chariot and the spoils of war, including the seven-branched candlestick, being carried in triumphal procession.

Between the Arch of Titus and the Colosseum is the **Tempio di Venere e Roma** (Temple of Venus and Rome), originally built by Hadrian (AD 117–38) and rebuilt by Maxentius in 307 after a fire. At 110 by 53 metres (361 by 174 ft), it was the largest temple in Rome and comprised two shrines placed opposite one another, surrounded by pillared halls in the Greek style. It is well documented that Hadrian was an ardent admirer of Greek culture.

Palatino

From the Arch of Titus, the road goes up to the **Palatino** (Palatine Hill; tel: 06-699841; summer daily

8.30am–7.15pm; winter 8.30am–4.30pm, last entry 1 hr before closing; admission charge), where Rome's imperial rulers lived in luxury. Paths and steps lead up to the **Orte Farnesiani** (Farnese Gardens). These pleasure gardens were laid out in the 16th century for Cardinal Farnese, over the ruins of the Palace of Tiberius. They end at a viewing terrace with a fine panorama over the Forum. A subterranean vaulted passageway leads to the **Casa di Livia** (House of Livia), once part of the Palace of Augustus; the rooms surrounding the atrium contain the remains of some lovely wall paintings and floor mosaics. Also underneath the gardens is a long tunnel built by Nero, possibly a secret route to other parts of the Palatine.

Beyond the gardens, in the southwest corner of the hill, excavations have revealed the oldest traces of a settlement in the city (8th century BC). The story goes that the Iron Age hut known as the **Capanna di Romolo** (Hut of Romulus) was the dwelling of a shepherd who raised Romulus and Remus, after they were suckled by the wolf in a nearby cave.

Map on page 74

TIP

Entrance to the Roman Forum is free but you have to pay to visit the Palatine. There's a ticket office inside the Forum where you can buy a joint ticket which also gives you access to the Colosseum.

BELOW: the Palatine Hill.

South of the gardens lay the **Domus Flavia**, built by Emperor Domitian, who is said to have lined his throne room with mirrors in order to see approaching enemies from any angle. The room with a pattern traced on its floor was the courtyard; behind that was the dining room, and the room to the right was the nyphaeum where diners retired for breaks during banquets.

Next to this palace was the **Domus Augustana** (House of Augustus), private residence of the emperor; the oval building next to it, the vast outline of which can be clearly discerned, was a stadium built for the emperor's private games. To the south are the impressive ruins of the **Terme Severiane** (Baths of Septimius Severus).

The remains of the Palatine palaces overlook the **Circo Massimo** (Circus Maximus). Not much of this 6th century BC stadium remains, but you can make out the track, which was used mainly for chariot races, and there are traces of seating to the south (the tower is a medieval addition).

TIP

You can take a picnic into the Forum/ Palatine area. Officially, it's not allowed, but if you are discreet and tidy, there will be no problem.

BELOW: "The Gladiator's bloody circus stands, a noble wreck in ruinous perfection".

The Colosseum

At the far end of the Roman Forum lie the remains of the majestic **Colosseum** ⓫ (tel: 06-39967700; open summer daily 8.30am–7.15pm; winter 8.30am–4.30pm; last entry 1 hr before closing; admission charge – joint ticket allows entry to the Palatine as well), the most enduring symbol of Ancient Rome. Its monumental grandeur and violent history have enthralled and appalled visitors for over 2,000 years. Work on its construction began in AD 72 under Vespasian, who decided to build it on the site of Nero's artificial lake, and completed by his son, Titus. The vast amphitheatre measured 190 metres (570 ft) long and 150 metres (450 ft) wide, had 80 entrances and could seat between 55,000 and 73,000 spectators. It opened in AD 80 with a three-month programme of games to satisfy a bloodthirsty audience. Christians fought lions, gladiators fought each other and wounded contestants lived or died according to the emperor's whim, expressed by the imperial thumb, which pointed either up or down. Today, the walls of the various dungeons, cages and passageways, gruesome reminders of the centuries-long slaughter that took place here, can be seen through the caved-in floor of the arena. The **Ludus Magnus**, the nearby training ground of the gladiators, complete with its own miniature amphitheatre, was connected to the arena by a tunnel.

Gladiatorial combat was banned in AD 438 and over time the amphitheatre became a quarry supplying material for many of Rome's buildings including Palazzo Venezia and St Peter's. In 1744, Benedict XIV consecrated the arena to the memory of Christian martyrs who died in it (*for more about the Colosseum, see pages 90–1*). Nearby is the **Arco di Constantino** (Arch of Constantine), built in 312 after the victory over Maxentius at the Ponte Milvio.

Nero's Golden House

A short walk uphill from the Colosseum is the **Domus Aurea** (tel: 06-39967700; Wed–Mon 9am–7.45pm, last entry 1 hr before closing, by advance reservation only; admission charge). Work began on **Nero's Golden House** in AD 64 immediately after a fire had devastated a large chunk of Rome. It was made up of a series of pavilions surrounded by a small artificial lake (on which the Colosseum now stands), pastures, woods and vineyards, and originally extended from the Palatine to the Celian and Oppian hills. The enormous complex was filled with Greek statues and monumental fountains.

According to the Latin historian, Suetonius, its vestibule was large enough to contain a statue of Nero 40 metres (120 ft) high, and the house was covered in gold and decorated with precious gems and mother of pearl. There were dining rooms with ivory ceilings from which rotating panels showered guests with flowers, and fitted pipes sprinkled them with perfume. The palace had its own aqueducts to supply water for the fountains and the baths could be filled with sea or sulphurous water, according to Nero's whim. The main building was decorated with shiploads of plundered Greek works of art. But Nero did not have long to enjoy it. He committed suicide in AD 68 after he was condemned to death by the Senate. Almost immediately the house began to be stripped, demolished or built on by his successors. In the early 16th century frescoes belonging to the house were discovered by artists, including Raphael and Michelangelo, but no-one linked these cave-like rooms to the Emperor's outrageous abode until centuries later. Some 30 rooms are open to the public; many more are either off-limits or awaiting excavation. It is hard to get an idea of the opulence and size of the extraordinary 250-room mansion, built on an estate that covered a third of Rome; only the skylit Octagonal Hall gives any real idea of its former architectural grandeur. Visits are on a guided or accompanied basis only, so make sure to book in advance. ❑

An umbrella pine shades the ruins of the Palatine Hill.

RESTAURANTS & BARS

The overpriced tourist restaurants around the Colosseum should be avoided, but if you wander eastwards into the huddle of streets behind it you'll find some good neighbourhood eateries.

Restaurants

Forum Pizzeria
34–8 Via San Giovanni in Laterano. Tel: 06-7002515. Open: L & D daily. €
A large pizzeria, not strong on atmosphere, but serves delicious, thick-crusted pizzas from a wood-fired oven.

Ristorante Mario's
9 Piazza del Grillo. Tel: 06-6793725. Open: L & D Tues–Sun. €–€€
Traditional Roman food (fish is their speciality) and a lovely pergola in the square outside, at affordable prices. Informal at lunch, more elegant at dinner.

San Teodoro
49–51 Via dei Fienili. Tel: 06-6780933. Open: L & D Mon–Sat. €€€–€€€€

Located in a tranquil piazza in what is essentially a desert when it comes to eating options, this elegant restaurant offers traditional food successfully updated and centred on seasonal availability. Staples are fish carpaccios and home-made pasta.

Bars & Cafés

A gay bar (as its name suggests) across from the Colosseum, **Coming Out** (8 Via San Giovanni in Laterano) serving hot food until 2am; karaoke and a lively scene ensure a faithful following, not just from the gay community. At **Oppio Caffè** (72 Via delle Terme di Tito) hi-tech meets Classical Rome. Plexiglass and video screens contrast with ancient brickwork. Outside seating provides stunning views of the Colosseum. Open all day; live music some nights.

● ● ● ● ● ● ● ● ● ● ● ●
Price includes dinner and a half bottle of house wine.
€ under €25, €€ €25–40,
€€€ €40–60, €€€€ €60+

THE GRIM GLORY OF THE COLOSSEUM

"While the Colosseum stands,
Rome shall stand; when the
Colosseum falls, Rome shall
fall; when Rome falls the world
shall fall"

The Colosseum is the city's most stirring sight, "a noble wreck in ruinous perfection" in Byron's words. It was begun by Vespasian, inaugurated by his son Titus in AD 80, and completed by Domitian (AD 81–96). It could seat over 50,000 bloodthirsty spectators who revelled in the spectacle of gladiators fighting to the death. "Bread and circuses" was the judgement of Juvenal, the 1st-century poet, on the way the city's rulers kept the populace happy. With the fall of the Empire, the Colosseum fell into disuse. During the Renaissance, the ruins were plundered of their valuable travertine to build churches and palaces all over Rome. Quarrying was only halted by Pope Benedict XIV in the 18th century and the site dedicated to Christian martyrs.

ABOVE LEFT: the Gate of Life was reserved for victorious gladiators while vanquished gladiators were sent to the Gate of Death. **ABOVE TOP:** Renaissance historians believed that ancient Roman arenas were sometimes flooded to stage mock naval battles, but there is scant evidence to suggest that such a display ever took place in the Colosseum. **ABOVE:** views from the higher tiers down to the arena and a maze of passageways. The moveable wooden floor was covered in sand, to soak up the blood. The subterranean section concealed the animal cages and sophisticated technical apparatus, from winches and mechanical lifts to ramps and trap doors. **LEFT:** trained fighters were pitted against each other and against the beasts.

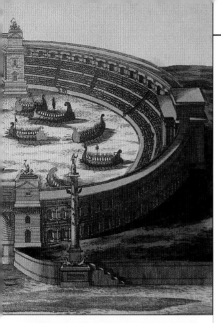

ENTERTAINMENT FOR THE MASSES

The Roman appetite for bloodshed was legendary, with the barbaric *munera*, or blood sports, introduced as a corrupt version of the Greek games. Although supremely public, the Colosseum was a stratified affair. The podium, set on the lowest tier, was reserved exclusively for the Emperor, senators, magistrates and Vestal Virgins. Above them sat the bourgeoisie, with the lower orders restricted to the top tier, and the populace on wooden seats in the very top rows. Shortly before the games began, the Emperor and his followers would enter the amphitheatre, and spectators would show their reverence by clapping, cheering, and chanting their sovereign's honorifics.

A trumpet call started the games and spectacles began with cries of "Hail to the Emperor, those about to die salute thee". If a gladiator tried to retreat into the underground chamber, he was pushed forward with whips and red-hot irons. The gladiators mostly fought to the death. A wounded man could beg for mercy by lifting a finger of his left hand. If the crowd waved handkerchiefs, he was saved. Thumbs down meant death. After the gladiators came the wild beasts, which were made to fight one another or human beings – armed or unarmed. The animals, mostly imported from Africa, included lions, elephants, giraffes, hyenas, hippos, wild horses and zebras. On the arena's opening day, 5,000 animals were slaughtered. In AD 248, the millennium of the founding of Rome was celebrated by gladiatorial contests. Gladiatorial combat was banned in AD 404, while animal fights ended in the following century.

ABOVE: the Colosseum is Rome's top tourist sight. It is floodlit at night when it creates a wonderful spectacle. It has also been used as an arena for crowd-pulling concerts; Simon and Garfunkel played here on their 'Old Friends' tour. **RIGHT:** an 18th-century romanticised view of Rome, by Giovanni Volpato.

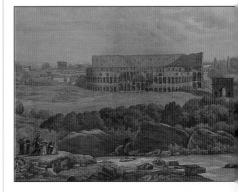

FONTANA DI TREVI AND QUIRINALE

The Quirinal, Rome's highest hill, is synonymous with Italian politics. Its summit is crowned with the President's official residence and at its foot, hidden in a maze of narrow streets, is the Trevi Fountain, one of Rome's most iconic sights

Map on page 94

The Quirinal Hill, the highest of Rome's seven classical hills, is crowned by the Piazza del Quirinale and the imposing presidential palace. The square is somewhat austere but the maze of surrounding streets are worth exploring. A good place to begin a tour of the area is the **Fontana di Trevi ❶** (Trevi Fountain),which rose to fame in Fellini's 1960 classic *La Dolce Vita* when Anita Ekberg plunged provocatively into it for a midnight bathe. Nowadays, if you try to put a foot in the water, a whistle blast from the city police will stop you in your tracks. However, no one will stop you from throwing a coin in the fountain (over your shoulder with your back to the fountain), an old custom said to ensure your return to the eternal city. The steps around the fountain are always packed with tourists tossing coins, eating ice creams and taking endless photos.

The flamboyant rococo-style fountain was designed in 1762 by Nicola Salvi "some sculptor of Bernini's school gone absolutely mad in marble" was Nathaniel Hawthorne's assessment. Its central figure is the sea-god Neptune standing astride a giant shell drawn by winged horses led by Tritons. One horse is placid, the other agitated, symbolising calm and stormy seas.

In the niches on either side are statues of Health (right) and Abundance (left). Above the latter a marble relief shows Agrippa commissioning the aqueduct in 19 BC which supplies the fountain to this day.

The Quirinal

Follow Via San Vincenzo uphill from the Fontana di Trevi then turn left into Via Dataria and follow the steps up to Piazza del Quirinale. In the centre of the square are the colossal statues of the heavenly twins, Castor and

LEFT: the Trevi Fountain. **BELOW:** Piazza del Quirinale.

TIP

Foodies with an interest in the history of pasta should pay a visit to the Museo Nazionale delle Paste Alimentari (Pasta Museum, tel: 06-6991120, www.museo dellapasta.it; daily 9.30am–5.30pm; admission charge), at 117 Piazza Scanderbeg, a coin's throw from the Trevi Fountain.

Pollux with their horses (see page 85). They came from Constantine's baths and were arranged around the obelisk (taken from Augustus's mausoleum) in the 18th century.

The square is dominated by the **Palazzo del Quirinale ❷**, which was the summer palace of the popes until 1870, when it became the palace of the kings of the newly unified Italy. Since 1947, it has been the official residence of the President of the Republic. One section is open to the public (tel: 06-46991; Sept–June Sun 8.30am–noon; admission charge). Across the square the sugary-white **Palazzo della Consulta ❸** houses Italy's supreme court.

Baroque masterpieces

Via del Quirinale runs along the flank of the palace and, on the opposite side, passes two pretty parks, (dotted with shaded benches if you need a rest), and two baroque churches. **Sant'Andrea al Quirinale ❹** is the

work of Bernini whose genius is demonstrated in the elliptical plan, gilded dome and stucco work. Further along is the tiny **San Carlo alle Quattro Fontane ❺**, by Bernini's arch-rival, Borromini. It may be small, but with its concave and convex surfaces it is one of the most original church designs in Rome. The church gets its name, Alle Quattro Fontane, from the **four fountains** at each corner of the busy crossroads, which personify the Tiber, the Nile, Diana and Juno.

From here, Via delle Quattro Fontane leads to **Palazzo Barberini ❻**, the family palace of Pope Urban VIII (1623–44), built by three of Rome's most prominent 17th-century architects, Bernini, Borromini and Maderno. It houses the **Galleria Nazionale d'Arte Antica** (tel: 06-4814591; Tues–Sun 8.30am–7.30 pm; admission charge), which displays works from the early Renaissance to the late baroque, including

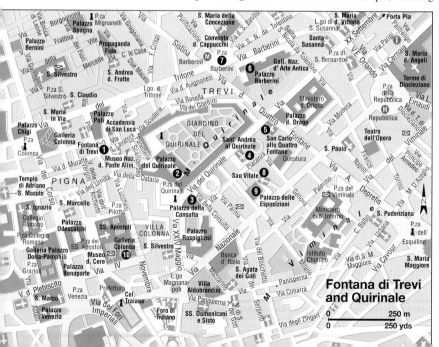

Fontana di Trevi and Quirinale

0   250 m
0   250 yds

The Annunciation by Lippi, canvases by Caravaggio, Raphael's celebrated *La Fornarina*, a Tintoretto, a portrait of Henry VIII by Holbein and a fine ceiling fresco by da Cortona.

Piazza Barberini ❼ boasts two Bernini fountains. The Fontana del Tritone (1632–7) features four dolphins supporting a shell on which the water-spouting Triton sits. The Fontana delle Api (Bee Fountain), on the north side of the square, features the ubiquitous bee symbol of the powerful Barberini family.

From here Via Barberini leads to Largo Santa Susanna and the church of **Santa Maria della Vittoria**, home to Bernini's *Ecstasy of St Teresa*, another masterpiece of baroque sculpture.

The end of Via XX Settembre is marked by **Porta Pia**, Michelangelo's last architectural work.

Via Nazionale

Running parallel to Via del Quirinale, Via Nazionale (laid in 1870 when Rome gained its new status as capital) links Piazza della Repubblica with the Imperial Fora. Towards the southern end are **San Vitale ❽**, built in the 5th century and restored in the 15th century; and the **Palazzo delle Esposizioni ❾** (tel: 06-489411, www.palazzoesposizioni.it; closed for restoration until spring 2006). This huge 19th-century building houses a vibrant cultural centre, with an imaginative programme of art exhibitions and events. Across the road are the impressive **Palazzo Koch**, headquarters of the Banca d'Italia; and the **Villa Aldobrandini** behind which is a small public park (entrance on Via Mazzarino).

Via Nazionale curves around into Via IV Novembre leading to Piazza Venezia, passing Trajan's Market and the **Galleria Colonna ❿** (tel: 06-6784350, www.galleriacolonna.it; Sept–July Sat 9am– 1pm; entrance on Via Pilotta; admission charge), a charming art gallery which includes Raphael's *Putti* and Caracci's *The Bean Eater* among its treasures.

From the palace, **Via della Pillotta**, overhung by four elegant bridges connecting the *palazzo* with the gardens of Villa Colonna, leads back to the Trevi Fountain. ❏

Map on page 94

Decorative detail from the door of Santa Maria della Vittoria. The church is famous for Bernini's rapturous statue of Saint Teresa of Avila in the throes of a mystical experience.

RESTAURANTS & BARS

Restaurants

Al Presidente
95 Via in Arcione. Tel: 06-6797342. Open: L & D Tues–Sun. €€€
A family-run restaurant, with a lovely outdoor area. High-quality food and a good wine list, with a few choice selections to be had by the glass.

Le Tamerici
79 Vicolo Scavolino. Tel: 06-69200700, www.letamerici.com. Open: L & D Mon–Sat. €€€

Innovative cuisine from an all-female team; contemporary décor and a regularly changing menu. This level of refinement does not come cheap.

Vineria Il Chianti
81 Via del Lavatore. Tel: 06-6787550. Open: L & D Mon–Sat. €€
A buzzing, rustic locale with young staff and a Tuscan slant. Hearty soups, quiche with courgette flowers, wild boar fillet; pizzas in the evening and an appetis-ing selection of cheeses served with honey or jam. Stays open late.

Bars & Cafés

Considered by many to be the best in Rome, **Il Gelato di San Crispino** (42 Via della Panetteria, closed Tues) serves ice cream like no other. It comes in paper cups (cones contaminate the taste according to its creators). The signature flavour, Il Gelato di San Crispino, is a basic Italian *crema* made with wild Sardinian honey. **News Café** (72 Via della Stam-peria) takes its name from the racks of newspapers available for customers to read. A good all-day option for salads, soups and pasta. In an anonymous gallery off the street is attractive, olde-worlde **Dagnino** (75 Via V. E. Orlando), a vast Sicilian pastry shop and *tavola calda* serving all-day sweet and savoury specialities.

• • • • • • • • • • •
Price includes dinner and a half bottle of house wine .

€ *under* €25 , €€ €25–40,
€€€ €40–60, €€€€ €60+

PIAZZA DI SPAGNA AND TRIDENTE

Next to the best designer shopping in Rome are the famous Spanish Steps and the former home of John Keats, who was sent to Rome for the good of his health but died there the following year

The Tridente is a mecca for anyone interested in fashion, shopping or art. The area takes its name from the trio of streets built in the 16th century to relieve congestion in Rome's cramped medieval centre. Via del Corso, Via di Ripetta and Via del Babuino emanate like the prongs of a fork from the Piazza del Popolo, for centuries the main entrance to Rome for travellers coming from the north.

Piazza del Popolo

Piazza del Popolo ❶ is one of the most impressive squares in Rome. The paving was allegedly paid for by taxes levied on prostitutes and the piazza was used for executions at one time. In the 19th century, the square was remodelled by Valadier, who added the elegant *pincio* ramps and created the oval form.

The most striking feature of this elegant square is the **obelisk**. Stolen from Egypt by Emperor Augustus, it once decorated the Circus Maximus where it was used as a turning point during chariot races.

Standing at the ends of Via del Babuino and Via del Corso are a pair of churches designed by Rainaldi. Though they appear identical, one is octagonal and the other is dodecagonal. Across the piazza, by Porta Flaminia, is the church of **Santa Maria del Popolo**, built in 1472 over a pre-existing 11th-century chapel. Inside are two fine paintings by Caravaggio, a chapel designed by Raphael and Bernini, an apse by Bramante and frescoes by Pinturicchio.

The Corso

The most important of the trio of streets that fan out from the Piazza del Popolo is **Via del Corso** a long thoroughfare that links the square with the Piazza Venezia, another of Rome's central squares and one of

Map on page 99

LEFT: twin towers of Trinità dei Monti, atop the Spanish Steps.
BELOW: Via del Corso window display.

One of the four lion fountains by Valadier (1823) that grace the Piazza del Popolo. In the background are Rainaldi's twin baroque churches.

BELOW: reliefs on the Column of Marcus Aurelius.

its most terrifying traffic roundabouts. The name "Corso" dates from the 15th century when Pope Paul II introduced horse racing *(corsi)* along its length. Pope Alexander VII straightened the road in the 16th century. The races were imitations of the ancient games (with all their atrocities) and it wasn't only horses that ran: there were races for prostitutes, for children, for Jews and for the crippled. The German poet, Goethe, who lived at No. 19, was one of many visitors to witness the races, which he described in his travel book, *The Italian Journey*. The races were finally banned at the end of the 19th century.

These days, the only people racing along the Corso are politicians being whisked at high speed to **Palazzo Chigi**, the prime minister's official residence, and the neighbouring **Palazzo Montecitorio**, the Chamber of Deputies, on **Piazza Colonna ❷**. This square marks the halfway point of the Via del Corso. The southern half of the Corso between Piazza Colonna and Piazza Venezia is lined with stately palaces, most of which are banks, while the northern half, between Piazza Colonna and Piazza del Popolo is a much more pedestrian-friendly shopping area. In the early evening and on Saturdays, Romans swarm into town to stroll up and down and window-shop on this stretch of the Corso and the surrounding streets *(see opposite)*.

Dominating the Piazza Colonna is the street's only classical relic, the 30-metre (90-ft) **Colonna di Marco Aurelio** (Column of Marcus Aurelius). It dates from AD 180 and the bas-relief around the shaft depicts the campaigns of Marcus Aurelius against the Germanic tribes and the Sarmatians. Stairs lead to the top, where the original statue of the emperor was replaced with one of the Apostle Paul in 1589.

With the exception of some of the churches, the other buildings along the Corso were built over the past three centuries. On the other side of the Corso from Piazza Colonna is **Santa Maria in Via Lata**, which has an impressive façade by da Cortona. In a side street next to the church is one of Rome's "talking" fountains, the *Facchino* (or water-bearer). In the days before freedom of speech the *Facchino* and other "talking statues" were hung with satirical and subversive messages and fulfilled much the same function as a newspaper.

Another noteworthy church is **San Marcello ❸**, further along the Corso towards Piazza Venezia, which has a Van Dyck crucifix in the sacristy.

The palace on the right at the end of the Corso houses the **Galleria Doria Pamphili ❹**, which is included in the Piazza Navona chapter *(see page 118)*. There are several splendid buildings in the city called Doria Pamphili (also spelt Pamphilj), after one of the oldest aristocratic Roman families. One of their mem-

bers, Giovanni Battista Pamphili, became Pope Innocent X (1644–55). The current generation of the family still live in this *palazzo* and their private apartments are sometimes open for guided tours.

The Spanish Steps

The sweeping Spanish Steps combine with the twin towers of the church of Trinità dei Monti on top and the harmonious square with its bizarrely shaped fountain below to form one of the most distinctive of Roman scenes. **Piazza di Spagna ❺** is so-called because there has been a Spanish Embassy to the Holy See here since the 17th century. The French, meanwhile, owned the land around the convent of **Trinità dei Monti** at the top of the steps, so they claimed the right to pass through the square and named part of it French Square. This petty rivalry between the French and Spanish reached a climax with the building of the Spanish Steps. The original design was intended to sing the praises of the French monarchy and there was to have been a huge equestrian statue of Louis XIV. However, the Pope was against this idea, so when the architect de Sanctis finally started building the steps in the 18th century, the only reference made to France was the little fleur-de-lis on the pedestals.

The cascade of **Spanish Steps** is perennially crowded with visitors. In spring, the crowds share the steps with pots of blossoming azaleas. The centrepiece of the square at the bottom of the steps is the fountain by Pietro Bernini, who was aided in its construction by his more famous son, Gian Lorenzo. The so-called **Barcaccia** is a half-sunken boat fed by water from the ancient aqueduct *Acqua Vergine*.

The English Ghetto

The Grand Tourists of the 18th century, most of whom were English

aristocrats, stayed in this area on their visits to Rome (it came to be known as the English ghetto). In the 19th century many illustrious artists, writers and musicians followed in their footsteps: Keats, Tennyson, Stendhal, Balzac, Wagner and Liszt among them. In 1820, Keats spent the last few months of his life in a small room overlooking the Spanish Steps and died of consumption there in 1821, aged just 25. In 1906, the house was bought by an Anglo-American association and turned into a museum and library dedicated to Keats and his fellow Romantics who had made Rome their home. The **Keats-Shelley House** (tel: 06-6784235, www.keats-shelley-house.org; Mon–Fri 9am–1pm, 3–6pm, Sat 11am–2pm, 3–6pm; admission charge) has a collection of personal objects and documents relating to the lives of Shelley and Byron, but the main focus is on Keats – his prints, paintings, books and death mask are on display.

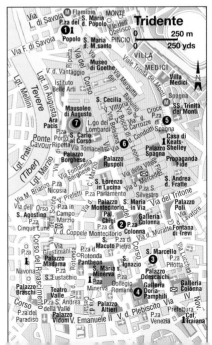

Map
on page
99

*Rome has been called
the city of obelisks –
it has at least 13.
Most were brought
back by triumphant
armies and erected
in public places to
show the power of the
Empire, but some –
such as the one at the
top of the Spanish
Steps – are Roman
imitations of Egypt-
ian originals.*

BELOW:
people-watching on
the Spanish Steps.

Shopping streets

The former artistic enclave is now
the haunt of big spenders and wish-
ful window-shoppers who come to
flex their credit cards in its elegant
and expensive shops. The area
between Piazza di Spagna and Via
del Corso is for dedicated fashionistas. Elegant **Via dei Condotti** ❻ is
designer-label heaven. This street,
plus the parallel **Via Borgognona**
and **Via Frattina**, which are linked
by the equally sumptuous **Via Bocca
di Leone**, are home to all the top
fashion outlets. **Via del Babuino** is
lined with interesting design and
antique shops. Parallel to this is **Via
Margutta**, a pretty, narrow street
with artists' studios, galleries and
workshops. Twice a year, the street
holds a special art show dedicated to
the works of local painters. Matching
the expensive shops in this area are
some of the best hotels in Rome.

Towards the end of Via dei Condotti is the world-famous tourist trap
Caffè Greco, said to have been
opened by a Greek merchant in
1760. The great and the good down
the centuries have frequented this

café, including Baudelaire, Wagner,
Taine, Liszt, Stendhal, Goethe,
Byron, Keats and Shelley.

Monuments to Augustus

The third road in the Trident of
streets, **Via di Ripetta** (*ripa* means
riverbank: a reminder that there was
once a harbour here, back when
ships still plied the Tiber) connects
Piazza del Popolo to the Vatican, via
the Mausoleum of Augustus and the
Ara Pacis, two ancient monuments
dating from the time of Augustus.

The **Ara Pacis** (Piazza Augusto
Imperatore; scheduled to reopen in
autumn 2005) an altar built in 13 BC
to commemorate the era of peace that
followed Augustus's victories in
Gaul and Spain, was painstakingly
pieced together by archaeologists
from original and reconstructed fragments in 1938. The altar is enclosed
by a white marble screen decorated
with reliefs illustrating mythological
and allegorical scenes. It has been
closed to the public for several years.
The current plan is to house the altar
in a new museum complex, complete
with a bookshop and exhibition
spaces, designed by US architect
Richard Meier. The latest date for
completion is September 2005, and
since the bureaucratic and political
wrangling seems finally to be over,
this may actually happen.

Behind the altar is the **Mausoleo
di Augusto** ❼ (accessible by prior
arrangement only; tel: 06-57250410),
which was restored by Mussolini.
The mausoleum was built between 28
and 23 BC – long before it was
expected to be occupied. Covered
with statues and faced with marble, it
was one of the most magnificent
sights in Rome. The emperor was
buried inside the central chamber
while members of his family were
allocated rooms around him. Like
many ancient remains, it served as a
medieval fort and was a theatre for a
while in the 19th century. ❑

Roman Fashion

Italy's fashion industry is revered the world over, and while most of the business is centred on Milan, there are a handful of top designers who have made their base in Rome. The Roma Alta Moda Foundation has also brought back some of the city's sartorial glitz and glamour, showcasing Roman and other big-name fashion designers in various shows and events in January and July. The summer version includes a fashion show which takes place against the dramatic and romantic backdrop of the Spanish Steps. The most famous of these is undoubtedly Valentino, who opened his Roman studio in 1959 and has enjoyed success ever since. His high-profile clients have included Sophia Loren, Audrey Hepburn and Jackie Kennedy.

Two other very important names in international fashion are Laura Biagiotti and Fendi. The former, who has been dubbed the "queen of cashmere", creates luxurious knitwear (coats included), silk separates and loose-fitting dresses. Her headquarters and home are located just outside Rome in the 15th-century castle of Marco Simone, a former medieval fortress. The four towers of the castle form the famous Biagiotti logo.

The second of the two, Fendi, is a company created by a married couple and their five daughters. They first set up their flagship shop on Via Borgognona on the site of a former cinema in the early 1950s. Today, half a century on, the shop is one of the largest in the area and sells beautiful bags, shoes, luggage and ready-to-wear clothes.

More recently the young Gai Mattiolo has been making his mark both at home and abroad. He has his own-name boutique in the ultra-swanky Via Borgognona, and many more in cities throughout the world. Apart from all these designers, two legendary names are still worth checking out: one is Fontana, the other is Capucci.

The heyday of the Sorelle Fontana (Fontana sisters) is associated with the glamorous *dolce vita* of the 1950s and 1960s when droves of aristocratic women and just about all the successful foreign actresses in Rome visited their atelier. You can see their ultra-classic, elegant clothes at Via della Fontanella di Borghese. Roberto Capucci also emerged during the 1950s and is best known for the sculptural quality of his garments that look as good off as on the body. His work has been shown in important design museums in Italy, Vienna, Munich and Paris, and he has a boutique/atelier on Via Gregoriana.

Of course, just about all the other well-known Italian designers, among them Versace, Armani and Trussardi, have shops in Rome as well, mostly around Via Condotti. However, visitors who cannot afford top designer names should not be put off shopping for clothes. All Italian women like to look their best and there are plenty of boutiques selling clothes with far less frightening price tags. Remember, too, that Italy produces stunning shoes, bags and leather accessories and a wide and wonderful selection can be found in the city's shops. ❏

RIGHT: classic couture by Versace.

RESTAURANTS & BARS

Restaurants

Al34
34 Via Mario dei Fiori. Tel: 06-6795091. Open: L & D Tues–Sun. €€
The service is fast, the prices honest, the atmosphere lively and the food classical Italian. Sample the *tonnarelli al granciporro* (pasta with crab) or the fresh fish *misto* (a mix of different fish), and the home-made Neapolitan *caprese* cake, *semifreddo al torronocino* (nougat ice-cream dessert) or pear and chocolate tart.

Dal Bolognese
1–2 Piazza del Popolo. Tel: 06-3611426. Open L & D Tues–Sun. €€€–€€€€
On the theatrical Piazza del Popolo this smart restaurant with paintings on the wall, uniformed waiters and couches on which to sip your apéritif serves good-quality staples from the Emilia Romagna region to a loyal clientele of politicians, film producers and assorted artists and celebrities when in town. Closed 3 weeks Aug.

Da Gino
4 Vicolo Rosini. Tel: 06-6873434. Open: L & D Mon–Sat. €€
Vaulted ceilings and frescoes adorn this trattoria where affordable Roman specialities are served following the traditional weekly calendar, which means fish on Tuesday and Friday. For dessert home-made *crostate* (tarts) and a legendary *tiramisù*. No credit cards.

'Gusto
7 Piazza Augusto Imperatore. Tel: 06-322 6273, www.gusto.it. Open: L & D daily, Br Sat and Sun. Restaurant €€–€€€. Pizzeria €–€€.
Gusto is an empire: a pizzeria downstairs, an upmarket restaurant upstairs, a wine bar on the other side, an *osteria* next to that. There's even a well-stocked cookery store attached. The service is fast and friendly and the general standard is high. An added feature is the outdoor seating most of the year under impressively austere 1930s porticoes that line the square. Booking advisable if you want to be sure of a table. Open late.

Hostaria dell'Orso
25c Via dei Soldati . Tel: 06 68301192, www.hdo.it. Open: D only Mon–Sat. €€€€
Milanese superstar chef Gualtiero Marchesi is at the helm of the new-look Hostaria dell'Orso in a *palazzo* that has been an inn since medieval times. Now a posh but hip restaurant-cum-piano bar-cum-disco, it has an expensive take on nouvelle Italian haute cuisine which can be ordered à la carte or from five different set-price menus *(menù degustazione)*.

Le Pain Quotidien
24–5 Via Tomacelli. Tel: 06-68807727. Open: B, Br, L & D Tues–Sun. €
The first Italian branch of a popular Belgian chain. Ideal for breakfast (their croissants are exquisite) or later, when large salads, quiches and open sandwiches made with fresh stone-ground bread can be washed down with organic wines, teas and fruit juices around large wooden tables. A vast terrace a couple of doors down is a major bonus in summer.

Mangiamoci
6b Via di San Sebastianello. Tel: 06-678 0546. Open: L & D Tues–Sun. €€–€€€
Trendy bar and restaurant with a friendly, colourful atmosphere. Waiters can be seen heading to and from a large open aquarium at the front, full of wriggling eel, crabs and lobsters. Alternatively, you can choose from a more sedate fish counter at the back, or some imaginative vegetarian options.

Margutta Vegetariano
118 Via Margutta. Tel: 06-32650577, www.ilmargutta.it. Open: L & D daily. €€–€€€
This is one of Rome's oldest vegetarian restaurants and offers refined contemporary Italian cuisine and walls filled with modern art echoing its location in the artsy Via Margutta. At lunch there is a set-price buffet and there's a good brunch on Sunday.

Matricianella
2–4 Via del Leone. Tel: 06-6832100. Open: L & D Mon–Sat. €€
Traditional Roman food in a cheerful setting. To start, try their crispy *fritto vegetale* (fried vegetables) and then, if you are a carnivore, the fettuccine with chicken liver and minced beef is a good bet.

Nino
11 Via Borgognona. Tel: 06-6795676. Open: L & D Mon–Sat. €€–€€€
A cordial setting where genuine Tuscan food has been consumed for over 70 years. Sample the leek soufflé, wild boar with polenta ,and pappardelle with hare sauce. The wine list is well thought out and has a good selection of half-bottles. At the upper end of this price scale, and well worth it. Closed Aug.

PRICE CATEGORIES

Price includes dinner and a half bottle of house wine:
€ = under €25
€€ = €25–40
€€€ = €40–60
€€€€ = more than €60

Osteria della Frezza

16 Via della Frezza. Tel: 06-3226273, www.gusto.it. Open: L & D daily. €–€€
Informal but chic, and further proof that anything the 'Gusto team *(see above)* touch turns to gold. Furniture and details have some 1930s' touches and the menu is a skilful combination of traditional and the ultra-contemporary with 400 cheeses, cured meats, deep-fried delicacies, omelettes, soups and good main courses. All served with hearty home-made bread and excellent wines by the glass or bottle from a selection of 1,700 labels.

Otello alla Concordia

81 Via della Croce. Tel: 06-6791178. Open: L & D Mon–Sat. €
Authentically Roman food (*carbonara* pasta, lamb and *tiramisù*) and fresh fish served in a room overlooking a pretty little courtyard, used in summer. Booking recommended.

PizzaRé

14 Via di Ripetta. Tel: 06-321 1468. Open: L & D daily. €
For a simple pizza after a heavy day's spending in the Spanish Steps' clothing mecca, try PizzaRé, maker of the thick and crusty Neapolitan variety and one of the best in the capital. Set-price menus including pasta and grilled meats at lunchtime. All pizzas €6 on Mondays.

Ripa Gauche

158 Via di Ripetta. Tel: 06-68802979. Open: L & D Mon–Fri, D only Sat and Sun. €–€€
Romantic and atmospheric, this restaurant is perfect for lunch as well as dinner. A flavourful *antipasto* is always brought to the table. The menu changes regularly and incorporates meat, fish and soufflés, and there's an appetising set-price menu. Open late.

Bars & Cafés

One of the most appealing wine bars in the area is the **Enoteca Antica di Via della Croce** (76b Via della Croce). It's cosy in winter in its cellar-like interior, and delightful in summer if you can nab one of the few outdoor tables. You can just drink wine, chosen from their lengthy wine list or you can eat here too. Two other buzzing venues are the wine bar in the excellent '**Gusto** complex (23 Via della Frezza, *see previous page*), and a new ultra-modern rival pizzeria-restaurant-café-bar called **Recafé** (Piazza Augusto Imperatore 36). **Buccone** (19 Via de Ripetta) existed long before wine bars became fashionable and hence it is a joy just to take in the sheer authenticity of this high-ceilinged, old-fashioned emporium crammed with bottles of wine and regional specialities. Old-fashioned, artsy hangout **Café Notegen** (159 Via del Babuino) still has plenty of charm, although it is looking a little worse for wear these days. The all-day opening and affable manner are endearing. There are a number of other historic cafés in this area. Long-time rivals **Canova** (16 Piazza del Popolo), pictured below, and **Rosati** (Piazza del Popolo 5) face each other across the grand expanse of Piazza del Popolo. Both are good, but Rosati wins hand down for ambience. Furthermore its cakes are mouthwatering and the cocktails are a cut above the usual offerings. The large **Gran Caffè La Caffettiera** (61 Via Margutta) is in a former 17th-century theatre in the tranquil Via Margutta. It's a little pricey, but let the frescoes and art nouveau details wash over you and you'll soon feel refreshed and relaxed about the prices. The beautiful **Antico Caffè Greco** (86 Via Condotti) with its marble tables and red-velvet chairs is frequented mostly by tourists but the bar out the front makes the most delicious coffee. Drink it standing at the bar, as it's much cheaper than when you are sitting at a table. For the ultimate view of Rome climb up the Spanish Steps and turn left to **Ciampini al Café du Jardin** (Viale Trinità dei Monti), open only in the summer, where you can have light meals, cocktails and an unmissable *aperitivo* as the sun sets over the Eternal City.

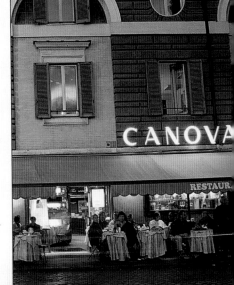

RIGHT: Canova, one of the two rival bars on the Piazza del Popolo.

THE VATICAN AND PRATI

The Vatican City is a shrine to the power and
extravagance of the Catholic Church through
the ages, and to its extraordinary artistic taste

Map
on page
106

The fabulous wealth and extravagance of the Catholic Church through the ages is celebrated without restraint in the Vatican State. The immense basilica of St Peter's with its dome by Michelangelo and an interior sumptuously bedecked with Bernini's glistening creations, is impressive enough. Then there are the Vatican Museums, mile upon mile of rooms and corridors containing historic treasures, and, of course, the Sistine Chapel.

Covering a total area of little more than 40 hectares (100 acres), Vatican City is by far the world's smallest independent sovereign entity. The Lateran Treaty of 1929, concluded between Pope Pius XI and Mussolini, established its territorial limits. The Vatican has its own stamps, currency, media, railway and police force – the Swiss Guards. The city is roughly trapezoidal in shape, bounded by medieval walls on all sides except on the corner, where the opening of St Peter's Square marks the border with Rome.

St Peter's Square

Piazza San Pietro ❶ was laid out by Bernini in 1656–67 for Pope Alexander VII. Its double-colonnaded wings symbolise the outstretched arms of the church, embracing and protecting the congregation. In the centre are

fountains by Maderno and della Fontana, and an Egyptian obelisk, placed here by Sixtus V in AD 37. Between the obelisk and each fountain is a round marble slab, from where the spectator obtains the illusion that each colonnade has only a single row of columns.

At the end of the square, above a triple flight of steps, is the **Basilica di San Pietro ❷** (daily 7am–7pm, until 6pm in winter, no bare legs or shoulders), an undeniably impressive structure, but an unfortunate mixture

LEFT: view of Piazza
San Pietro as seen
from St Peter's Dome.
BELOW:
St Peter's Square on a
rainy day.

TIP

Tours of the Vatican Gardens must be arranged through the Vatican tourist office (tel: 06-69884676; fax: 06-69885100; tours Mar–Oct at 10am on Tues, Thur and Sat; Nov–Feb on Sat at 10am). To visit St Peter's Necropolis, beneath the basilica, contact the Vatican's Ufficio Scavi (Excavations Office, fax: 06-69873017; e-mail: scavi@fsp.va; Mon–Sat 9am–5pm; no phone bookings; no children under 11; children between 11 and 15 must be accompanied by an adult).

of conflicting architectural styles. Built on the site of St Peter's martyrdom in AD 67, during Nero's persecutions of the Christians, the original Constantinian church was of typical basilican form – a Latin-cross with a nave, side aisles and a transept. It was lavishly decorated with mosaics, paintings and statuary, but became so dilapidated that rebuilding became unavoidable. In 1506, Julius II decided on a complete reconstruction and commissioned Bramante whose plan for the new basilica was a Greek cross surmounted by a gigantic dome. On Bramante's death in 1514, the four central piers and the arches of the dome had been completed. Raphael (d. 1520) then took over, and was followed by Sangallo (d. 1546); both men bowed to the clergy's wish for greater capacity by designing a nave and altering the ground-plan to that of a Latin Cross. In 1546, however, before this could be realised, the 72-year-old Michelangelo was sum-

moned by Pope Paul III. He expressed his preference for the original Greek cross and central dome of Bramante; seeing the Pantheon as unambitious, though, he developed his own version of Brunelleschi's Florentine cupola, and substituted Bramante's piers with new ones of tremendous strength. The entire plan was realised after Michelangelo's death in 1564; construction work was continued until 1590, when Pope Paul V decided that the Latin-cross was more appropriate, demanding a nave.

Maderno extended Michelangelo's building to give it its current form, adding the portico in 1614. The building was consecrated in 1626, 1,300 years after the constuction of the original basilica. Seen from the square, Maderno's portico robs Michelangelo's dome of much of its power, though from a distance the cityscape is still dominated by the cupola.

As you pass into the **portico**, the statue on the left of Constantine is by

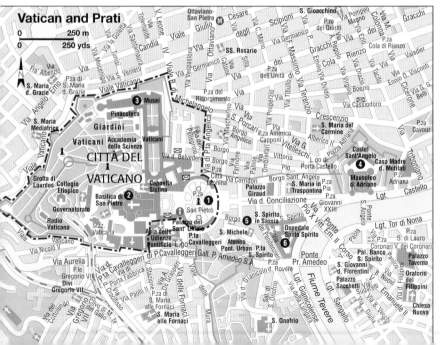

Vatican and Prati

Bernini. Look up, opposite the 15th-century bronze central doors, to see a restored remnant of the original 13th-century mosaic, *La Navicella*, by Giotto. Inside the basilica, turn right for *La Pietà*, Michelangelo's remarkable statue of the Madonna and dead Christ, which he sculpted when only 25. Halfway down the nave the 13th-century statue of St Peter by Arnolfo di Cambio is so widely venerated that its foot, kissed by devout pilgrims for over seven centuries, is almost worn away.

In the centre of the basilica, directly under the dome is the **baldacchino** by Bernini. This huge bronze canopy rises over the holiest part of the church, the legendary tomb of St Peter. The twisted columns are replicas of the ones that Christ apparently leant against in the Temple of Solomon. Bernini added the vine leaves and the bees, symbols of the Barberini coat of arms.

To the right of the baldacchino, stairs lead down to the **grottoes** (daily 7am–7pm; until 6pm in winter; admission free) containing the tombs of several popes, includ-ing that of the recently deceased Pope John Paul II.

On the apse wall, framed by the baldacchino, is another Bernini creation, the **Cattedra di San Pietro** (1665), a gilded bronze throne said to have been the episcopal chair of St Peter. It is supported by statues of the four fathers of the Church, and above it angels and putti surround a halo of gilt stucco with a key to heaven and the dove of the Holy Spirit. Don't miss the ghoulish **tomb of Alexander VII**, to the left of the transept. Just above the door is Bernini's last work, representing a skeletal allegory of death clutching an hourglass, reminding us that death comes to us all.

The entrance to the **dome** (daily 8am–6pm; until 5pm in winter; closed during ceremonies; admission charge) is on the right of the portico. The long climb to the top (there are 320 steps from where the lift stops) is rewarded by extensive views across the city.

The **Vatican Gardens** can be seen from the dome, but if you want a closer look you will have to book in advance *(see tip on page 106)*.

Map on page 106

Swiss Guards caught off guard.

BELOW: Mass on St Peter's Square.

Papal Audiences

Papal audiences are held in the Vatican on Wednesday at 10.30am, except in the height of summer, when they are at his summer residence at Castelgandolfo outside Rome. Apply for free tickets in writing to the Prefettura della Casa Pontifica, 00120 Città del Vaticano, or go to the office on the preceding Monday or Tuesday – it's through the bronze door watched over by Swiss Guards, to the right of the basilica. For more information, tel: 06-69883114. The Pope comes to a window above the piazza on Sunday at noon to give the traditional Angelus blessing.

Pinturicchio's painting of Renaissance pope Alexander VI.

BELOW: *Miracle of the Mass at Bolsena*, one of the Vatican's many works by Raphael.

The Vatican Museums

The **Vatican Museums ❸** (tel: 06-69884947; summer Mon–Fri 8.45am–4.45pm, Sat and last Sun of month 8.45am–1.45pm; winter Mon–Sat and last Sun 8.45am–1.45pm; last admission 90 minutes before closing; closed Catholic holidays; admission charge) are a good 15-minute walk from St Peter's Square; just follow the walls north until you reach the entrance. Expect a long queue especially on weekends and the last Sunday of the month, when the place gets mobbed as admission is free. To help visitors out, the museum authorities have devised four routes marked in different colours lasting from 1½ to 5 hours. All, including the shortest, take in the Sistine Chapel. There are ten collections in all plus the papal apartments. Because different visitors have different tastes and because of the vast amount of exhibits contained in the museums, no single route is described here; only the main highlights *(see also pages 112–113)*; you'll find plenty of detailed information at the entrance.

Sistine Chapel

No visit to the Vatican is complete without a look inside the **Sistine Chapel**. The walls, depicting scenes from the lives of Christ and Moses, were painted by some of the greatest masters of the Renaissance: Botticelli, Perugino, Ghirlandaio and Signorelli. It is Michelangelo's sublime frescoes, however, which have made the chapel universally famous.

To paint the ceiling, Michelangelo worked single-handedly, lying on his back, for four years (1508–12). The frescoes, which underwent a controversial restoration in the 1980s, are much brighter than they once were because several layers of candle-soot, dust, oil, grease and varnish have been removed. The ceiling depicts scenes from Genesis, starting with God dividing light from dark and ending with the drunkenness of Noah (seen in reverse from the entrance). The sides show the ancestors of Christ and, on marble thrones, the prophets and the classical sybils who prophesised Christ's coming. Above these are the *ignudi*, nude figures holding up festoons with papal symbols and medallions. In the four corners are scenes of salvation, including the dramatic hanging of Haman, and Judith swiping off Holofernes's head. A stylistic difference is noticeable between the section of the ceiling nearest the entrance and the rest. Perhaps because Michelangelo had a chance to see the results of his work, or perhaps because the Pope was urging him to finish, he painted the second half with larger, bolder figures and brighter colours.

The ceiling has no fixed point of view, no single system of perspective and no one clear meaning. Critics cannot agree if the ceiling is a neo-Platonic statement or a theological programme devised with the help of religious experts, including, perhaps, Julius II. Some critics say

the overall theme is salvation, reaching its climax in the *Last Judgment* fresco on the end wall (painted by Michelangelo between 1535 and 1541, and beautifully restored in the early 1990s). It depicts a harrowing image of the souls of the dead rising up to face the wrath of God. The good are promoted to heaven, while the damned are cast down into hell. The figure of St Bartholomew is depicted to the right of the beardless Christ, carrying his flayed skin in his left hand. The tragic face depicted on it is Michelangelo's self-portrait; his pained expression reflected the spiritual crisis he was going through and his contemporaries' lack of comprehension.

The Raphael Rooms

The Stanze di Raffaello are four rooms decorated by Raphael in the 16th century at the request of Pope Nicholas V. The first room, the **Sala di Constantino**, was the last to be painted and, since Raphael was on his deathbed, is mainly the work of his pupils. The frescoes depict scenes from the life of Constantine.

The **Stanza di Eliodoro** was decorated by Raphael from 1512–14. The subject matter alludes to events in Pope Julius II's life. *Expulsion of Heliodorus*, with angels chasing a thief out of the temple, refers to Julius's success in expelling the enemy from Italy.

The next room, **Stanza della Segnatura**, was where the Pope's council met to sign official decrees. The frescoes (1509–11) mix pagan and Christian themes. In the *School of Athens* fresco, representing the triumph of philosophical truth, Raphael portrays ancient characters with the features of contemporary heroes. The bearded figure of Plato in the centre is da Vinci; Bramante appears as Euclid in the foreground and the thoughtful figure of Heraclites on the steps is Michelangelo. The *Parnassus* fresco, representing poetic beauty, features Homer, Virgil, Ovid, Dante and Boccaccio.

The last room, the **Stanza dell' Incendio di Borgo**, takes its name from the fresco depicting a terrible fire in the Borgo in 847 that was miraculously extinguished by Leo

Map on page 106

BELOW: Giuseppe Momo's helicoidal staircase (1932).

Map
on page
106

TIP

If you're travelling with children, the Castel Sant'Angelo, with its ramparts, trap doors, prison chambers, drawbridges and cannonballs galore, will keep them amused.

BELOW:
Castel Sant' Angelo from the pedestrian Ponte Sant'Angelo.

IV making the sign of the cross. This room was painted after the first half of Michelangelo's Sistine ceiling was uncovered and direct influences can be seen in the monumentality of the figures.

For information on the other Vatican collections, *see Treasures of the Vatican, pages 112–13.*

Castel Sant'Angelo

Castel Sant'Angelo ❹ (tel: 06-681 9111; Tues–Sun 9am–8pm, last entry 1 hr before closing; admission charge) is approached from across the Tiber by means of the Ponte Sant'Angelo, adorned with statues of saints Peter and Paul and 10 angels sculpted by Bernini and his students *(see page 123)*. Construction of the castle began in AD 123 and 16 years later it became Hadrian's Mausoleum. It has since been a fortress, a prison and the Popes' hiding place in times of trouble, thanks to the *passetto*, the corridor that connects the Vatican palace with the castle. The castle houses artefacts from all periods of Roman history and many of the

rooms, such as the Sala Paolina painted by del Vaga in 1544, are beautifully frescoed. The papal chambers and other rooms are accessible via the spiral ramp inside, which is still in an excellent state of preservation. At the top of the ramp are the terraces and café, both with superb views of the Dome of St Peter's and the rest of Rome. (It was from this parapet that Puccini's heroine, Tosca, plunged to her death.) The gigantic bronze statue of the Archangel Michael that crowns the citadel was placed here in 1753.

The Borgo and Prati

The Borgo refers to the warren of streets east of the Vatican, formerly known as the Città Leonina, after Leo IV who built the fortified walls and connected the Vatican to Castel Sant' Angelo by an overhead passageway. The area is torn in two by Via della Conciliazione, which ruins the effect of Bernini's piazza, but allows for a full view of St Peter's. Across the boulevard is **Borgo Santo Spirito** ❺, where the early Saxons had a school. The church of **Santo Spirito in Sassia**, built for the Saxons in 689, was rebuilt in the 16th century. Next door is the **Ospedale Santo Spirito** ❻, set up by Pope Innocent III in the 13th century as an orphanage for unwanted babies. Inside, there are frescoed rooms and a small museum with an ancient Red Cross carriage and a reconstruction of an old laboratory.

North of the Vatican lies the elegant residential area of **Prati**, composed of grid-like streets and wide tree-lined avenues. It may lack the old-world charm of the Centro Storico, but if you want to get a deeper understanding of the real fabric and rhythm of everyday Roman life, then this is a good neighbourhood to explore. It's also great for shopping; most of the shops are concentrated around the Via Cola di Rienzo and Via Ottaviano. ❏

RESTAURANTS & BARS

Restaurants

Bio Restaurant
53 Via Otranto, Tel: 06-45434943. Open: L & D Mon–Sat. €€
As its name suggests this restaurant is fully organic (*biologico*). It's not only the food and beverages – even the cutlery and tableware are made with products uncontaminated by chemical agents. The food is excellent and varied. Whether you are an unashamed carnivore, or a vegetarian, or prefer sushi, you will eat well in these soothing, earth-toned surroundings.

Clok
21 Via Vittorio Colonna. Tel: 06-3200230. Open: L only Mon, L & D Tues–Fri, D only Sat, Sun. €–€€
One of a trendy new breed of pizzeria-cum-restaurant-cum-wine bar with big windows and minimalist design. You eat downstairs and chill out upstairs in a room with low seating, cushions and candles. Pizzas range from traditional to original (gorgonzola and apple). No fish but good meat dishes and plenty of home-made puddings.

Dante Taberna de' Gracchi
266 Via dei Gracchi. Tel: 06-3213126, www.tabernagrac-chi.com. Open: L & D Tues–Sat, D only Mon. €€–€€€

A relaxing pastel-coloured interior and classic cusine based mostly on fresh fish, and a different soup every day. Try their *bavette ai Gracchi* (flat pasta with courgette flowers, prawns, saffron and ricotta) accompanied with a fine wine from an endless list.

Il Matriciano
55 Via dei Gracchi. Tel: 06-3213040. Open L & D Sun–Fri in summer and Thur–Tues in winter. €–€€
Just around the corner from St Peter's, this restaurant has served genuine local food for over 90 years. Their signature dish is an excellent *spaghetti all' amatriciana* (spaghetti with tomato, onion and cured pork sauce).

La Cava
21 Via Attilio Regolo. Tel: 06-3215532. Open: L & D Mon–Sat; also Sun in summer. €€
With its stark but stylish interior decorated with Travertine marble (hence the name, *cava*, which means quarry) and keen young waiting staff this is a good place to go with a group. The dishes are modern Mediterranean and sometimes a little too inventive for their own good but mostly the chef pulls them off.

Osteria dell'Angelo
24 Via G. Bettolo, Tel: 06-3729470. Open L & D Mon–Sat. €–€€

This neighbourhood *trattoria* with a fixed-price evening menu including house wine is always packed to the gills. Try the *fritti* to begin with and then a flavourful version of the Roman standard *tonnarelli cacio e pepe* (pasta with pecorino and pepper). Booking is advisable. No credit cards. Closed Aug.

Siciliainbocca
26 Via Faà di Bruno. Tel: 06-37512485. Open: L & D Mon–Sat. €€
Come here for a cheerful ambience and good Sicilian food seasoned with the island's flavours: lemons, olives, capers and plenty of sunshine. Their classic ricotta-filled *cassata* is excellent.

Taverna Angelica
6 Piazza Capponi. Tel: 06-6874514. Open: L & D Sun, D only Mon–Sat. €€
Massimo Pinardi's restaurant has only been around a few years but it quickly earned a reputation for high-quality food. Try smoked goose breast with celery, apple and walnuts; pasta with fennel and anchovy; grilled swordfish with pesto; or mango *bavarois* with kiwi sauce. A favourite among the clergy.

Zen
243 Via degli Scipioni. Tel: 06-3213420. Open D only Tues–Fri and Sun, L & D Sat. €€–€€€
High-standard, fresh

Japanese food is Zen's strong point. Pick your dishes as they roll past you on the city's first sushi and sashimi conveyor belt, or order the *tempura* and other heftier dishes à la carte. A room at the back provides a calmer setting.

Bars & Cafés

Pellacchia (105 Via Cola di Rienzo) makes its own ice cream on the premises and is deservedly famous. On an otherwise residential street **Antonini** (21–9 Via G. Sabotino) makes the kind of cakes you bring to dinner parties when you want to impress; perfect for an apéritif. Near St Peter's, **Sora Lella** (Via Porta Cavalleggeri) is a kiosk selling *grattachecca,* the classic Roman crushed-ice drink doused in different fruit- juice flavours. **Bar Bar** (17 Via Ovidio, www.barbar.it) is the first so-called lounge bar in the city; its infinitely long bar counter and sleek furniture give it a New York vibe.

PRICE CATEGORIES

Price includes dinner and a half bottle of house wine:
€ = under €25
€€ = €25–40
€€€ = €40–60
€€€€ = more than €60

TREASURES OF THE VATICAN

Sensory overload, known as "Stendhal's Syndrome", is a natural response to the Vatican's endless artistic riches

The Vatican Museums house one of the biggest and most important art collections in the world. They merit a life-time's study but for those who have only a few hours, there are some sights that simply should not be missed.

The **Sistine Chapel** with Michelangelo's marvelous ceiling, and the four **Raphael Rooms** are the star attractions *(see pages 108–9 for more details)*. The **Museo Pio-Clementino** contains some of the greatest sculptures of antiquity *(see opposite)*. While visiting this museum look out for **Bramante**'s **spiral staircase**, built at the request of Pope Julius II, who wanted it to be navigable on horseback. The **Pinacoteca** picture gallery houses an extensive collection of paintings from Byzantine times to the present, with works by Giotto, Bellini, Titian, da Vinci, Raphael, Caravaggio and many others.

The **Vatican Library** contains a priceless collection of illuminated manuscripts and early printed books. The **Chapel of St Nicholas** has some exquisite frescoes by Fra Angelico; and frescoes by Pinturicchio can be seen in the **Borgia Apartment**. More recent artwork is not neglected, either, and the **Modern Religious Art Collection**, adjoining the apartment, displays works by Paul Klee, Francis Bacon, Max Ernst and Henri Matisse, among others. The **Etruscan Museum**, meanwhile, contains many artefacts found in tombs of the mysterious pre-Roman civilisation *(see pages 290–5 for more on the Etruscans)*. The **Gregoriano Profano Museum** houses finds from the Baths of Caracalla, on the old Via Appia.

ABOVE: Galleria delle Carte Geographiche (Gallery of Maps): This superb barrel-vaulted gallery, also known as the Hall of Cartography, is frescoed with maps of Italy. Most were designed by a 16th-century monk and cartographer. **ABOVE LEFT:** the newly restored Michelangelo frescoes (detail) are controversially colourful. Even a century ago, French writer Guy de Maupassant found them garish and "reminiscent of a fairground".

TOP: Borgia pope Alexander VI (1492–1503) occupied six apartments in the Vatican palaces and had them decorated with frescoes by Pinturicchio and his pupils. The frescoes in the Sala della Vita dei Santi portraying scenes from the lives of the saints, with Lucrezia Borgia in the guise of St Catherine, is the undisputed highlight. **ABOVE:** in 1509, while Michelangelo worked on the Sistine Chapel ceiling, Raphael started to decorate Pope Julius II's apartments. This detail shows the *Battle of the Milvian Bridge* which was completed in 1525 by his pupil, Giulio Romano. **RIGHT:** Known as the Mars of Todi, this 5th-century BC bronze is one of the highlights of the Etruscan art collection. The Etruscans' fluid, expressive statues are believed to have inspired Michelangelo and some of the other great Italian masters.

CLASSICAL MASTERPIECES

The Museo Pio-Clementino houses some of the greatest sculptures of Greek and Roman antiquity. In the **Octagonal Courtyard** of the Belvedere are three masterpieces of classical art: the *Atleta Apoxyomenos*, a 1st-century copy of a 3rd-century bronze, depicts an athlete washing himself after the exertions of a hard-run race. The beautiful *Apollo del Belvedere* , which depicts the Greek sun-god, is another copy of a Greek original, which once stood in the agora in Athens. The action-packed *Laocoön*, a 1st-century copy of a 3rd-century BC bronze sculpture, was found near Nero's Golden House, the Domus Aurea, on the Colle Oppio, near the Colosseum *(see page 89)*. The marble statue depicts a Trojan priest of Apollo and his two sons struggling with two writhing sea serpents.

The remainder of the sculpture gallery is divided up into sections. The **Hall of the Greek Cross** (Sala a Croce Greca) houses porphyry sarcophagi of Emperor Constantine's mother and daughter. The **Circular Hall** (Sala Rotonda) has a huge gilded bronze statue of Hercules and a colossal head of Jupiter of Otricoli, a Roman copy of the Greek original. In the **Hall of the Muses** (Sala delle Muse) there are statues of Apollo and the Muses; in the centre, the *Belvedere Torso* (1st century BC) is a Greek work that was admired greatly by Raphael and Michelangelo.

The **Animal Room** (Sala degli Animali) is particularly worth visiting for its remarkable animal statues by Antonio Franzoni (1734–1818), inspired by Roman originals. The **Gallery of Statues** (Galleria delle Statue) has more Roman copies of Greek originals; and for the **Mask Room** (Gabinetto delle Maschere), intricate 2nd-century mosaics of theatrical masks have been brought from Hadrian's Villa at Tivoli, just outside Rome *(see page 192)*.

PIAZZA NAVONA AND THE PANTHEON

The Pantheon has stood in the heart of Rome for almost 2,000 years, and the foundations of buildings surrounding Piazza Navona are the ruined grandstands of the Stadium of Domitian. Now the area is filled with baroque buildings and churches, along with picturesque alfresco cafés

Map on page 116

The area loosely referred to as the Centro Storico (the Historic Centre) is contained between the great bend of the Tiber to the west and the Via del Corso to the east. In ancient times, the area centred on the Campus Martius (Field of Mars), an army training ground dedicated to the Roman god of war which lay outside the *Pomerium*, the sacred boundary of the city. It was here, in front of the nearby Temple of Apollo (three pillars of which can still be seen next to the Teatro di Marcello), that generals returning from their military campaigns reported to the Senate.

As building space around the central fora became scarce, the city gradually spread beyond the ancient walls and out towards the Tiber. By imperial times the old Campus Martius had all but disappeared, and the area was filled with theatres, baths, porticoes and arenas, and dotted with verdant public parks. All that is left to remind us of the existence of the Field of Mars is an elegant little square and street called Piazza and Via di Campo Marzio.

Rome's population shrank in the Middle Ages due to devastating plagues and the relocation of the empire's capital to Constantinople. Those who remained moved towards the Tiber. The river was good for defence purposes, for water, which there was no access to further inland because so many of the ancient aqueducts had been destroyed, and because it provided a transport route safe from highway bandits. The river current also turned floating mills, which were tied up between the banks.

The ruins in the area also provided building materials for new houses, churches and papal complexes. Some were used as forts or – as with the Pantheon – as

LEFT: Fountain of the Four Rivers, Piazza Navona. **BELOW:** the Pantheon, Piazza della Rotonda.

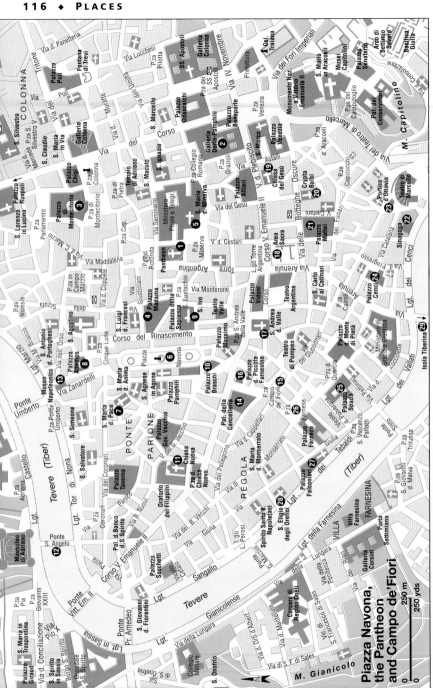

Piazza Navona,
the Pantheon
and Campo de'Fiori

churches. Almost all the major medieval, Renaissance and baroque buildings in the Centro Storico are either expressions of an increasingly powerful church, or reflect the intense competition for power and prestige among Rome's rich and aristocratic families.

But the Historic Centre has more to offer than churches and palaces. Its tangle of streets and alleys has been the home of the craft guilds since medieval times when these quarters were full of *botteghe* (workshops). The type of trades may have changed, but trade is still the lifeblood of the district. In and around Via dei Coronari and Via dell'Orso there are antique shops and fairs, while Piazza della Fontanella Borghese is the site of a print market. One of the most interesting streets is Via dei Cestari (connecting the Pantheon and Largo Argentina), which is lined with shops selling religious raiments and equipment for the Catholic priesthood. Many façades incorporate old guild signs or pieces of ancient marble.

The Pantheon

One of the most memorable and impressive of Rome's many architectural marvels is the **Pantheon ①** (tel: 06-68300230; Mon–Sat 8.30am–7.30pm, Sun 9am–6pm, public hols 9am–1pm; free), the best-preserved ancient building in Rome. Originally built as a temple to all the gods, its subsequent conversion into a church in 609 saved it from being torn down. Only 15 metres (45 ft) above sea level, the Pantheon is now the lowest point in Rome. The ditch around it shows just how much the rubble has raised Rome over the centuries: in ancient times one looked up to the Pantheon, not down.

As the inscription over the portico informs us, the statesman Marcus Agrippa, son-in-law of Augustus, built the original Pantheon in 27 BC in honour of the victory over Antony and Cleopatra at Actium. Agrippa's building, however, was severely damaged by fire in AD 80 and was completely rebuilt by Hadrian (AD 117–38), who has been credited as the building's architect, not just its patron.

Map on page 116

On sunny days, a beam of light pours through the oculus (the all-seeing eye of heaven) and moves around the Pantheon's interior, illuminating the frescoes and tombs.

BELOW: cafés on Piazza della Rotunda.

The portico is stately and imposing: 16 massive Corinthian columns support a roof with a triangular pediment (the notches cut into the portico columns are said to have supported stalls for a fish and poultry market in the Middle Ages). The walls are 6 metres (20 ft) thick and the huge bronze doors 8 metres (24 ft) high. But the most striking aspect of the building is of course the dome, a perfect hemisphere, and a symbol of beauty and harmony that had a profound impact on the architects of the Renaissance, influencing Brunelleschi's cathedral in Florence and Michelangelo's design for the dome of St Peter's. The circular hole (oculus) in its centre is still the only source of light and, sunshine or rain, can create spectacular effects. Originally, the dome was covered in bronze, but the Byzantine emperor Constans II is said to have stripped the outer layer off and taken it to Constantinople in 667. Almost 1,000 years later, in 1620, the Barberini pope Urban VIII had the inner layer melted down to make cannons for Castel Sant'Angelo and Bernini's *baldacchino* in St Peter's. This act of papal vandalism inspired the quip that "what the Barbarians didn't do, the Barberini did".

The Pantheon contains the tombs of painters and kings. The marble floor is an 1873 restoration. Raphael (1483–1520) is buried here. The famous inscription on his tomb by Cardinal Pietro Bembo was translated by Alexander Pope:

Living, great nature feared he might outvie

Her works; and dying, fears herself may die.

A handful of palaces

Another ancient relic that was adapted to modern usage lies in the nearby Piazza di Pietra, east of Piazza della Rotonda. The **Palazzo della Borsa** takes its name from its one-time role as Rome's stock exchange. Prior to that, the building, with its eleven ancient columns, was a customs house, and originally, in the 2nd century AD, it was the Temple of Hadrian, which is how it is mostly referred to now.

Just south of here (off the Via del Corso) is Piazza del Collegio Romano and the entrance to the **Galleria Doria Pamphili ②** (tel: 06-6797323; Fri–Wed 10am–5pm; admission charge), which contains one of the best art collections in Rome with over 400 paintings from the 15th to 18th centuries. The gallery walls are plastered with pictures, including the Velázquez portrait of Innocent X and canvases by Titian, Caravaggio, Lotto and Lorrain. The other gallery on the Corso is in the **Palazzo Ruspoli**, close to Via Condotti, where important temporary exhibitions are held.

Rome is still the centre of Italian government and there are two important government offices in heavily guarded old *palazzi* in this area. Behind Piazza Colonna, **Palazzo di Montecitorio ③** is where the Cham-

TIP

Behind Largo Argentina, south of the Pantheon, you can see the remains of Agrippa's Baths on Via Arco della Ciambella.

BELOW: Palazzo Madama, seat of the Senate.

ber of Deputies has met since 1871. Before that, it was the Papal Tribunal of Justice. Bernini drew up plans for the building in 1650, and Carlo Fontana saw the design and building through to completion in 1697. Virtually all that remains of the 17th-century design is the convex curve of the façade, designed to make the building look even bigger than it is; and the rusticated columns. The Egyptian obelisk in front of the *palazzo* dates from the 6th century BC. It was used by Emperor Augustus for an enormous sundial he laid out in 10 BC. The sundial was discovered in the crypt of the nearby church of San Lorenzo in Lucina.

The Senate has occupied the elegant **Palazzo Madama ❹** between Piazza della Rotonda and Piazza Navona since 1870. It was built for the Medici family in the early 16th century and several of its members lived here before becoming Pope, including Leo X (1513–21) and Clement VII (1523–34). Catherine de' Medici lived here until she married Francis I of France in 1533. The palace gets its name from the Habs-

burg Madama Margherita (1522–86), the illegitimate daughter of Emperor Charles V and the wife of Alessandro de' Medici.

Opposite, is the baroque church of **San Luigi dei Francesi** (closed Thur pm and at lunchtime), the French national church in Rome. It contains works by Giacomo della Porta and Domenico Fontana, but it is the three wonderful Caravaggio paintings in Capella Contarelli, showing scenes from the life of St Matthew, that make a visit very worthwhile.

Southeast of the Pantheon, **Santa Maria Sopra Minerva ❺** is the only truly Gothic church in Rome, It was built in the 8th century on the site of a temple of Minerva. Its present form dates from around 1280 when it was rebuilt by Dominicans. The church houses the tombs of several popes and cardinals, and the relics of St Catherine of Siena (the patron saint of Italy who died in the Dominican convent here in 1380). The church also contains a Michelangelo sculpture and works by Filippino Lippi, Romano and da Sangallo. Outside, the jovial little

Map on page 116

Vaulting in Santa Maria Sopra Minerva.

BELOW: Bernini's elephant bears the heavy load of an ancient Egyptian obelisk.

elephant with an ancient Egyptian obelisk on its back was designed by Bernini in 1667.

Around the corner on Via del Pie' di Marmo is the massive foot of an ancient Roman statue. Beyond this stands the church of **Sant'Ignazio**, built between 1627 and 1685 to honour the founder of the Jesuit order. The interior is a riot of gold embellishments and statuary, but the highlight is Andrea Pozzi's fantastic *trompe l'oeil* views of heaven.

Around Piazza Navona

Piazza Navona ❻ is one of the most animated squares in Rome, invariably full of native Romans and foreign visitors wandering among stalls set up by hopeful artists or relaxing with a coffee in one of the many bars, or stopping for a chat by its gushing fountains. From December until early January, the square hosts a colourful Christmas fair at which all sorts of decorations, toys, sweets, and baroque-style nativity scenes are sold, culminating in a carnival on the night before Epiphany (6 January).

Piazza Navona derives its shape from Emperor Domitian's athletics stadium, the Circus Agonalis, which opened here in AD 86.

BELOW: one of the four allegorical figures in Bernini's Fountain of the Four Rivers.

Piazza Navona was built over the remains of the Emperor Domitian's ancient athletics stadium: the stand forms part of the foundations of the flanking houses and you can see one of the original entrances to the north. The stadium originally measured 50 by 275 metres (150 by 825 ft), with the seats rising to 35 metres (105 ft). It was used for athletic contests and horse races, and was probably still in use when the Goths invaded in the 5th century. However, the plundering of its fabric began under Constantius II (third son of Constantine the Great), who carried off works of art and decorative features in 356 to adorn his new residence in Constantinople, after the seat of the Empire had been moved there.

The piazza owes its baroque appearance to the Pamphili pope, Innocent X (1644–55), who enlarged his family palace and commissioned the square's magnificent centrepiece, Bernini's **Fontana dei Quattro Fiumi** (Fountain of the Four Rivers). The rivers in question – the the Danube, Ganges, the Nile and the Plate – are represented by four huge allegorical figures who in turn represent four continents Europe, Asia, Africa and America. The Nile is blindfolded because the source of the river was then still a mystery. Rising above the statues is an obelisk taken from the Circus of Maxentius. The obelisk is topped by the figure of a dove with an olive branch to show that this once pagan monument has been converted into a Christian one.

To the south of the square is the **Fontana del Moro** (Fountain of the Moor). Its central figure (which looks more like a Triton than a Moor) was designed by Bernini. The **Fontana del Nettuno** (Fountain of Neptune) at the northern end was originally just a large basin. The sculptures were added in the 19th century to create symmetry.

Pope Innocent also commissioned the Borromini façade of **Sant' Agnese in Agone**. Here, it is said, the saint was pilloried and stood naked in the stocks until her hair miraculously grew to protect her modesty. Inside the church there are underground chambers where you can see the ruins of the stadium of Domitian, a Roman mosaic floor and medieval frescoes on the wall.

To the left of the church is **Palazzo Doria Pamphili** (not to be confused with the Galleria Doria Pamphili) designed by Rainaldi in the mid-17th century. It now houses the Brazilian Embassy.

Just off the square is the church of **Santa Maria della Pace ❼**, which was rebuilt in 1482 and then restored in 1656 when the convex, baroque façade was added. The church contains Raphael's frescoes of *The Four Sybils*

The nearby **Santa Maria dell'Anima** is the German-speaking church of Rome and was founded in 1500, although the present building was heavily restored in the 19th century. Apart from a Romano altar-

piece, most of the works of art inside are by pupils and followers of Caravaggio, Michelangelo and Raphael.

Just north of Piazza Navona, on Piazza Sant'Apollinare, is **Palazzo Altemps ❽** (tel: 06-684851; Tues–Sat 9am–7.45pm; admission charge), one of the four sites of the Museo Nazionale Romano which holds the state collection of ancient treasures (the rest of the collection is split between Palazzo Massimo alle Terme, the Terme di Diocleziano, and the Crypta Balbi, *see page 164*).

Full of tranquil rooms and courtyards this beautiful museum contains treasures of classical statuary and art, most of which come from the priceless collection amassed by Cardinal Ludovisi. The prize exhibit is the Ludovisi Throne, a decorative Greek sculpture, thought to date from the 5th century BC, which Mussolini sold to Hitler in 1938, and which is now believed to be one of a pair. The *palazzo* also contains many frescoes and bas-reliefs, a private chapel, and parts of the ancient Roman houses on which the *palazzo's* foundations can be seen.

Map on page 116

Palazzo Altemps, one of the four sites of the Museo Nazionale Romano, and arguably the most beautiful.

BELOW: the Fountain of Neptune, on the north side of Piazza Navona.

East of Piazza Navona, on the parallel Corso del Rinascimento, is the **Palazzo della Sapienza** which housed the headquarters of Rome's oldest university, La Sapienza, until it moved to the Stazione Termini area in 1935. In the square is Borromini's **Sant' Ivo** ❾ (Sun 9am–noon only), a Roman baroque church with a striking, white, spiralling bell tower and unusual façade. On the main altar is a 1661 canvas by da Cortona showing St Ivo and other saints surrounded by angels.

Piazza di Pasquino

Off the southern end of Piazza Navona is **Piazza di Pasquino**. The strange fragment of ancient statue leaning against the wall was found in Piazza Navona and brought here in the 15th century when it became one of Rome's "talking statues". There were several of these across the city, including Marforio in Piazza del Campidoglio. At night, discontented citizens would express their disgust with the status quo by pinning criticisms to these statues. The penalty for this was death,

regardless of rank and including clerics, but there is no record of the penalty being carried out.

The statue leans against a wall of the **Palazzo Braschi** ❿, one of the last papal palaces to be built in Rome, in the 18th century. The *palazzo* is home to the newly renovated **Museo di Roma** (tel: 06-67108346; Tues–Sun 9am–7pm, last entry 1 hr before closing; admission charge), which traces the city's history.

Palazzo Massimo alle Colonne, next to the Braschi, was designed in 1536 by Baldassare Peruzzi for the Massimo family who occupy it to this day. The building is screened by a fine curved portico of Doric columns visible from the Via del Paradiso. Behind the palace, in Piazza de' Massimi, is an ancient column that may have come from the remains of Domitian's stadium.

Further down Corso Vittorio Emanuele II is the 16th-century **Chiesa Nuova** ⓫ (New Church), built for San Filippo Neri, founder of a great spiritual order. St Philip had wished the interior to be plain, but in the centuries after his death

BELOW: Piazza di Pasquino and its "talking statue".

his disciples commissioned da Cortona to paint the magnificent frescoes that decorate the vault, apse and dome. Among the church's other treasures are three altarpieces by Rubens. Next to the church is the **Oratorio dei Filippini**, built by Borromini between 1637 and 1662 as a place of worship for St Philip Neri's fraternity. St Philip was a strong believer in the spiritual benefit of music and instituted the musical gatherings that later became known as oratorios.

In **Piazza della Chiesa Nuova** is a 17th-century fountain that came from the Campo de' Fiori. On the rim of its basin is the inscription: *Ama Dio e non fallire – Fa del bene e lascia dire* (Love God and don't fail – Do good and make sure people talk about it). The nearby **Palazzo del Governo Vecchio** was the residence of the Governor of Rome from 1624 until the mid-18th century.

A little further west along Corso Vittorio Emanuele II is the **Palazzo del Banco di Santo Spirito**. Its façade (1520s) is by Antonio da Sangallo the Younger. From here, Via Banco di Santo Spirito leads to the lovely **Ponte Sant'Angelo** ⓬. The three central arches were part of the bridge Hadrian built in AD 136 to link his mausoleum – now the Castel Sant'Angelo *(see page 110)* – to the centre of the city. Most of the present bridge dates from the 17th century, but it was altered in the late 19th century to accommodate the new Tiber embankment. The glorious angels along the parapet were designed by Bernini in the 1660s.

At the southern end of the next bridge upriver, Ponte Umberto I, is the **Museo Napoleonico** ⓭ (tel: 06-68806286; Tues–Sun 9am–7pm; admission charge). Among the Bonaparte family memorabilia is a cast of the right breast of Napoleon's sister, Pauline, made by Canova in 1805, when he started work on the reclining nude in the Galleria Borghese *(see page 142)*. The nearby **Via dell' Orso** used to be lined with inns and was a favourite haunt of courtesans. Today, the area is better known for its antique shops, especially those along Via dei Coronari, which hosts antique fairs in May and October. ❑

Map on page 116

The eye-rolling, ecstatic expressions of Bernini's ten angels on the Ponte Sant'Angelo have earned them the nickname "the breezy maniacs".

BELOW:
hidden courtyard of the Centro Storico.

RESTAURANTS & BARS

Restaurants

Casa Bleve

49 Via del Teatro Valle. Tel: 06-6865970. L only Tues–Sat, evening buffet Tues–Thur €–€€

Casa Bleve is set against the stunning backdrop of the restored Palazzo Medici Lante della Rovere. An enormous semi-circular counter is laden with all kinds of cold meats, salads and cheeses. Beyond, there's seating in a large, atmospherically lit room. With an exceptional wine list, this is a high-level *enoteca* worth seeking out. Closed Aug.

Cul de Sac

73 Piazza Pasquino. Tel: 06-68801094. Open: L & D daily. €–€€

One of the best-stocked wine bars in Rome. Space may be tight but the atmosphere, prices and array of cheeses, cold meats, Middle Eastern-influenced snacks, hearty soups and salads all hit the right spot. It gets packed so be prepared to queue as bookings aren't taken. Open late.

PRICE CATEGORIES

Price includes dinner and a half bottle of house wine:
€ = under €25
€€ = €25–40
€€€ = €40–60
€€€€ = more than €60

Da Baffetto

114 Via del Governo Vecchio. Tel: 06-6861617. Open: D only daily. €

One of the city's legendary *pizzerie*. Not the best pizza in town, but almost, its typically thin base is always on the right side of crusty. Service is brisk and the turnaround is fast, but if you go early or late, it is more relaxed. No frills, no tablecloths, no credit cards.

Da Tonino

18 Via del Governo Vecchio. No phone. Open: D only Mon–Sat. €

As the weekend queues testify, this is one of Rome's best loved eateries. Stark lighting, basic décor and excellent local food, served in generous portions and at fair prices. Thursday is fresh gnocchi and tripe night; Friday is fish and *pasta e ceci* (pasta and chickpeas) night. No credit cards.

Fortunato al Pantheon

55 Via del Pantheon. Tel: 06-6792788. Open: L & D Mon–Sat. €€–€€€

A place for those who don't want to take risks but want to eat well and be served quickly and efficiently. People keep coming back for the simple classical dishes, such as spinach and ricotta ravioli cooked with butter and sage, grilled squid or veal served with rocket.

Il Bicchiere di Mastai

52 Via dei Banchi Nuovi. Tel: 06-68192228. Open: L & D daily. €€

The right venue for a light (but not necessarily cheap) and memorable meal. Swordfish *carpaccio* with mango and sea bass *carpaccio* with a lemon vinaigrette sauce may be on the menu. For dessert try the ricotta served with plums marinated in armagnac.

Il Convivio Troiani

31 Vicolo dei Soldati. Tel: 06-6869432. Open: D only Mon–Sat, L by request for groups of 8 and over. €€€€

Run by three brothers, Il Convivio is one of the city's foremost gastronomic temples. Equal emphasis is placed on vegetable, fish and meat options but they are always combined with something unexpected. Three elegant rooms and well-trained staff make for a truly rounded gourmet experience.

Il Fico

24 Piazza del Fico . Tel: 06-6875568, www.ilfico.com Open: L & D daily, in winter D only Mon. €€

Set in a small cobbled piazza, this friendly eatery is very reasonably priced for the location. All dishes are made with fresh seasonal ingredients. Try the pasta with mussels and pecorino cheese or the beef fillet with melted Taleggio.

Il Primoli

22 Via dei Soldati. Tel: 06-68135112. Open: L & D Mon–Fri, D only Sat. €€–€€€

In an old *palazzo*, three elegant rooms have been made over in modern minimalist style. The menu is creative though first courses are a bit hit and miss. However, the main courses, desserts and wines compensate for any shortcomings.

L'Altro Mastai

53 Via G. Giraud. Tel: 06-68301296. Open: D only Tues–Sat. €€€€

Foodies and critics alike have high hopes for this new luxury restaurant specialising in Mediterranean haute cuisine. The chef, Fabio Baldassare, trained with Heinz Beck of the superlative La Pergola restaurant *(see page 181)*. The dishes can be sensational, but at an average cost of €100 a head expectations are not always met. Closed Aug.

La Rosetta

8–9 Via della Rosetta. Tel: 06-6861002. Open: L & D Mon–Fri; D only Sat–Sun. €€€€

One of the best seafood restaurants in Rome, where the produce is guaranteed to have been caught that morning and prepared by an experienced chef, with a strong Sicilian bias. But unless you go for the "working lunch" or a set-price *degustazione* (tasting) menu, your bill is likely to tip the €100-a-head mark for a full meal.

Maccheroni
44 Piazza delle Coppelle. Tel: 06-68307895. Open: L & D daily. €€

A lively *trattoria* spread across several rooms and some outdoor tables. It attracts a youngish clientèle drawn by fair prices and competent, typical cuisine. The pasta with black-truffle sauce is worth a try.

Myosotis
3 Vicolo della Vaccarella. Tel: 06-6865554, www.myosotis.it Open: L & D Tues–Sat, D only Mon. €€

A discreet, high-level restaurant. The wine list is exemplary and the handmade *maltagliati* pasta with squid, clams and crayfish, or the tuna fillet served with balsamic vinegar are surprisingly refined. A gourmet experience at an affordable price.

O Pazzariello
19 Via Banco di Santo Spirito. Tel. 06 68192641. Open: D only Tues–Fri, L & D Sat–Sun. €

With an exhibitionist pizza-cook and *simpatico* waiting-staff, this is a sure bet for a fun and affordable evening. The pizzas are thick-crusted and range from small to gigantic. Authentic Neapolitan desserts.

Osteria dell'Ingegno
45 Piazza di Pietra. Tel: 06-6780662. Open: L & D Mon–Sat. €€

Much frequented by politicians due to its location near parliament, this modern *osteria* with art-adorned walls specialises in light, flavourful, inventive dishes. The sweets are home-made and the wines well-chosen. The staff could try smiling a bit more.

Riccioli Café
13 Piazza delle Coppelle. Tel: 06-68210313, www.riccioli-cafe.com. Open: B, Br, L & D daily (10–2am). €–€€€

Riccioli Café was the first oyster bar in the city and serves sushi and sashimi, all beautifully displayed on wooden counters. A recent expansion and extended hours have transformed it into an all-day option but this has not so far meant a downturn in quality.

Vecchia Locanda
2 Vicolo Sinibaldi. Tel: 06-68802831. Open: D only Mon–Sat. €€

In a pedestrianised alleyway this rustic restaurant offers decent if unadventurous food. A nice touch is that you can choose which home-made pasta to go with which sauce.

Bars & Cafés

For a genteel snack lunch or tea with home-made cake head to the delightful **Caffè Novecento** (12 Via del Governo Vecchio) not far from Piazza Navona. A good glass of wine can be had in the friendly and reasonably-priced. **I Spiriti** (5 Via Sant' Eustachio), which stocks 250 labels and spills out on to a *piazza*. The **Tazza D'Oro** (84 Via degli Orfani) serves some of the tastiest coffee in town. Standing room only. For ice-cream, **Giolitti** (40 Via Uffici del Vicario) has been scooping dozens of flavours since 1900. There is an olde-worlde dining room inside. **Cremeria Monteforte** (22 Via della Rotonda) makes some of the tastiest and best-quality ice cream in Rome. The flavours are relatively few, but choosing is still difficult as they are all equally tantalising. Mini-cones are available to try a flavour out before committing to a whole ice cream. **La Caffettiera** (65 Piazza di Pietra) is a smart café where you can enjoy Neapolitan goodies. **Le Coppelle** (52 Piazza delle Coppelle) has a central location and a great line in cocktails. Outdoor seating in summer, and a cosmopolitan vibe.

RIGHT: Giolitti, ice cream connoisseurs since 1900.

CAMPO DE' FIORI AND THE GHETTO

People have lived and worked in this picturesque part of Rome since the Middle Ages. The tangle of cobbled streets and alleys lead to the vibrant Campo de' Fiori market square and beyond into Europe's longest-surviving Jewish community.

The southern part of Rome's Centro Storico is a triangle of tightly packed streets between the Corso Vittorio Emanuele II, Via Arenula and the river, with the lively little market square of Campo de' Fiori at its hub. In ancient times, this area was part of the Field of Mars, a training ground for the Roman army (*see page 115*), until Julius Caesar's reign when the moneyed citizens of Imperial Rome moved in and built great complexes and theatres. By the Middle Ages, the area was a warren of small, dark, narrow streets and few open spaces or *piazzas*. In 1880, the rulers of a newly unified Italy set about putting their mark on the city and built the Corso Vittorio over the ancient tract of Via Trionfale and the winding, medieval Via Papale, destroying beautifully proportioned Renaissance squares and buildings in the process. The resulting avenue had none of the grandeur that was intended and today it's a traffic-choked thoroughfare that disrupts the beauty and harmony of the medieval streets around it.

Set off down the Corso from the Ponte Vittorio Emanuele, then turn right into **Via dei Banchi Vecchi** leaving the busy avenue behind. At No. 22 is the fanciful façade of **Palazzo dei Pupazzi**, built in 1504 and decorated with elaborate stucco

designs by Mazzoni. This street leads to Via del Pellegrino, which winds past artisans' workshops, bookshops and antique dealers to **Palazzo della Cancelleria** , a splendid Renaissance palace built between 1485 and 1527. The architect is unknown but the beautiful courtyard is attributed to Bramante, who also modified the adjoining 4th-century basilica of **San Lorenzo in Damaso**. Bramante had a reputation for destroying medieval monuments (the ancient St Peter's basilica

Map on page 116

LEFT: Campo de' Fiori.
BELOW: a kosher bakery in the Ghetto.

is a prime example), which earned him the nickname *Maestro Ruinante* (Master Ruiner). The palace was built for Cardinal Raffaele Riario, who financed it from the proceeds of one night's gambling, before being confiscated by the Pope and used as the Apostolic Chancery. It is not usually open to the public, but is occasionally used a venue for classical concerts.

Campo de' Fiori

South of the Cancelleria is the lively **Campo de' Fiori** (Field of Flowers), so named because it used to be a meadow that sloped down towards the Tiber. It has been the site of a produce market for centuries and was one of the liveliest areas of medieval and Renaissance Rome, when cardinals and pilgrims would rub shoulders with fishmongers, vegetable sellers and prostitutes.

The Campo de' Fiori is the most secular of Roman squares, for although it is as old as Rome itself, it has never been dedicated to any cult and to this day is free of churches. Its present aspect dates from the end

of the 15th century when the whole area was reshaped. It was surrounded by inns for pilgrims and travellers (there are still plenty of hotels in the area if you don't mind the noise). In the Renaissance, some of these hotels were the homes of successful courtesans, Vannozza Catanei, mistress of the Borgia pope Alexander VI, among them. On the corner of the square and Via del Pellegrino you can see her shield, which she had decorated with her own coat of arms and those of her husband and lover.

With its reputation for being a carnal, pagan place, the square must have seemed a natural spot to hold executions. Of all the unfortunate victims, Giordano Bruno was the most important figure to be burned at the stake here in 1600. A priest and philosopher, he was accused of heresy and found guilty of free thinking, claiming that the Earth was not the centre of the universe but revolved round the sun, a belief which cost him his life.

Today, the Campo flourishes, thanks to a perfectly balanced infra-

Rossini's Barber of Seville *debuted in the Teatro Argentina in 1816. Unfortunately, it was not well received, which led the composer to insult the audience. They, in turn, were enraged and pursued him through the streets of Rome.*

BELOW: Camp de' Fiori has been the site of a produce market for centuries.

structure. It has everything from a butcher's and a baker's shop to clothes boutiques, a cinema and a bustling morning food market. At night, the Campo plays host to hundreds of trendy Romans and visitors who frequent the bars and restaurants or simply hang out under the statue of Bruno, sipping beers until late into the night. Then the Campo has only a few hours to breathe before the market traders arrive to set up their stalls at the crack of dawn.

The streets around Campo de' Fiori still retain the names of trades originally practised in them. Via dei Baullari, the luggage-makers, leads to Piazza Farnese; Via dei Giubbonari, named after the sellers and makers of *gipponi* or bodices, is still lined with clothes shops, which are among some of the cheapest in town. Via dei Cappellari was where the hat-makers congregated, but is now full of furniture restorers, gilders and carpenters practising their trade out on the street.

Turning back up Via dei Baullari to Corso Vittorio, you reach **Palazzo della Piccola Farnesina** ⑯ in Piazza San Pantaleo. Built for a French prelate, Thomas Leroy, in 1523, it is decorated with fleurs-de-lis. When building the Corso, this little palace was cropped and given a new façade overlooking the thoroughfare. The original façade, on Via dei Baullari, is now the entrance to the **Museo Barracco** (closed for restoration; for current status tel: 06-68806848), which houses a collection of Egyptian, Syrian, Babylonian, Greek and Roman sculptures.

Further along Corso Vittorio, the magnificent church of **Sant'Andrea della Valle** ⑰ has the second-largest dome in Rome after St Peter's. Its design is largely by Maderno and the dome is decorated with frescoes by Lanfranco and Domenichino. The church is the setting for Act I of Puccini's much-loved opera, *Tosca*.

The church stands over some of the remains of the **Teatro di Pompeo**, a huge complex that spread from Campo de' Fiori to the temples at Largo Argentina. It was built in 55 BC as part of a plan to introduce some culture to Rome, but the Romans preferred the blood-and-guts entertainment of gladiators, fake battles and animal fights.

Next to the theatre was the **Curia Pompeia** where Julius Caesar was stabbed to death in 44 BC, when it was being using as a meeting place during renovations to the Senate House in the Forum. Remains of the theatre can be seen in the cellars of the surrounding houses, in the Da Pancrazio and Da Costanzo restaurants, and in the breakfast room of Hotel Teatro di Pompeo.

Next stop on Corso Vittorio is Largo di Torre Argentina, one of the busiest crossroads in the city and a major bus interchange. Its architecture – *palazzi,* banks and insurance companies – isn't very exciting. Only **Teatro Argentina**, a state-funded theatre and official home of the Teatro di Roma, radiates any

Map on page 116

Ceiling detail in the Gesù church.

BELOW: Area Sacra, ancient ruin and home for stray cats.

atmosphere. National and international performances, plays and concerts are held here.

The real attractions lie in the middle of the square, several metres underground. During attempts to improve the road system in the 1920s, archaeologists excavated four temples (street levels in ancient times were some 10 metres/30 ft below today's level). The **Area Sacra** ⑱ dates from Republican times, around the 3rd and 4th centuries BC. It is not known to which gods the temples were consecrated, so they are known simply as temples A, B, C and D. Some of the remains, inhabited by Rome's many stray cats, can be seen from above.

East of the square is the large church of the **Gesù** ⑲ more properly called Santissimo Nome di Gesù. Built between 1568 and 1584 with funds provided by the rich and powerful Cardinal Alessandro Farnese, it was Rome's first Jesuit church. The flamboyance of its design and decoration look forward to the baroque churches of the next century. The founder of the Jesuit Order, St

Ignatius Loyola, is buried in the opulent Cappella di Sant' Ignazio di Loyola, built by Andrea del Pozzo in 1696. Above the chapel's altar is a statue of the saint, framed by gilded lapis lazuli columns.

Not far from the Gesù church, at 31 Via delle Botteghe Oscure, is the **Crypta Balbi** ⑳ (Tues–Sun 9am–7.45pm; last entry at 7pm, admission charge), one of the four homes of the Museo Nazionale Romano collection *(see page 162)*. Located on the site of the portico of the Imperial Roman Theatre of Balbus, this museum documents the changing faces of the city from Roman times to the present day.

Just south of here is the scruffy little **Piazza Mattei** ㉑, home to one of Rome's most delightful fountains. The **Fontana delle Tartarughe** (Tortoise Fountain) was sculpted by Taddeo Landini in 1585 and depicts four slender youths supporting four dolphins, from whose mouths water flows into marble shells. The tiny bronze tortoises were added in the 16th century, possibly by Bernini. **Palazzo Mattei** opposite houses the Emeroteca music academy.

BELOW: snapshots of the Jewish Ghetto.

Jewish Ghetto

The area lying between Largo Argentina, the river, Via Arenula and Teatro di Marcello is occupied by the so-called **Ghetto**, Europe's longest-surviving Jewish community. The first wave of Jewish settlers came in the 2nd century BC, and thrived peacefully here until Titus's victory over Jerusalem in AD 70 after which their status changed from free men to slaves (the Colosseum workforce was largely made up of Jewish slaves).

In the centuries that followed, their fortunes and status fluctuated. In the Middle Ages the Jewish population enjoyed relative freedom, and were generally appreciated for their financial and medical skills. But then in 1555, Pope Paul IV's zero-tolerance policy culminated in a papal bull ordering the confinement of the Jewish population into an enclosed area around the Portico d'Ottavia, which became known from then on as the Ghetto. The area was surrounded by high walls with doors that were locked from the outside at night.

The walls of the Ghetto were destroyed in the revolutionary year of 1848. When Rome fell to King Emmanuel's troops in 1870, ending papal dominion over the city, the Jews were finally given the same rights as other Italian citizens. But persecution resumed with the outbreak of World War II when the Fascist regime shipped Jews off to Nazi concentration camps.

Today, the area retains its Jewish heritage and the medieval streets are dotted with kosher shops and restaurants. The **Synagogue ㉒** (tel: 06-68400661; Apr–Sept Sun–Thur 9am–7pm; Oct–Mar Mon–Thur 9am–5pm, Fri 9am–2pm, Sun 9am–12.30pm; guided visits only; admission charge) was consecrated in 1904. Its extreme height was a deliberate message to the Vatican across the Tiber. On 13 April 1986, Pope John Paul II and Rabbi Elio Toaff held an historic meeting here marking the first time that a Bishop of Rome had prayed in a Jewish house of worship. Inside the synagogue (make sure you carry some form of ID, as security is strict) is the

Map on page 116

BELOW: domestic details in the narrow streets of the Ghetto.

Museum of Jewish Culture (same hours as the synagogue).

The church of **Sant'Angelo in Pescheria**, where Jews were once forced to attend penitential services, was built on the ruins of the **Portico d'Ottavia** ㉓, originally the entrance to a colonnaded walkway erected in 147 BC by Augustus to display statues captured from Greece. It was dedicated to his sister, Octavia, the abandoned wife of Mark Anthony.

In the Middle Ages, the ruin was used as a covered fish market and there is a Latin inscription demanding that all the fish exceeding the length marked have to be decapitated and their heads given to Conservatori, as this was considered the best part for making fish soup.

Via del Portico d'Ottavia still has several medieval houses. At the end (No. 1) is **Casa di Lorenzo Manilo**. Lorenzo Manilo had this house built in 1468 and adorned it with a classical plaque. The Latin inscription dating the building employs the Ancient Roman calendar that used the founding of Rome as its starting point. According to this, the year 1468 was 2221. Original Roman reliefs are embedded in the façades, as well as a fragment of an ancient sarcophagus. The shop on the corner is a famous Jewish bakery.

Murder and malice

A short distance west of here is the **Palazzo Cenci** ㉔, the family palace of the infamous Beatrice Cenci, who attracted sympathy for killing her brutal father, but was nevertheless condemned to death for witchcraft and murder, and was beheaded on Ponte Sant'Angelo in 1599. Only parts of the original medieval building remain. The present façade and details are baroque. Note the architectural quirk of an indented balcony on the front facing Via Arenula.

Crossing back over Via Arenula, Via degli Specchi leads to **Palazzo Monte di Pietà**, which was set up as a pawnshop in the 16th century and is still used as an auction house, open to the public every morning. From here, turn left and then right into Via Capo di Ferro. The large building on your left with the façade covered in stucco reliefs by Maz-

Because of its association with the fishing activities of the nearby river port, Sant'Angelo in Pescheria church has numerous aquatic flora and fauna inlays.

BELOW: a coffee break on Piazza Farnese is hard to resist.

zoni is **Palazzo Spada** ㉕. The Spada family bought the palace in 1632 and Borromini restored it, adding the ingenious corridor to the courtyard. Borromini raised the floor and shortened the columns to create a false sense of perspective, making the corridor appear much longer than it actually is. At the end, a statue was placed against a painted garden backdrop. The statue is less than 1 metre (3ft) tall but from afar it seems to be life-size. The *palazzo* is also home to the **Galleria Spada** (Tues–Sun 8.30am–7.30pm; Borromini's *trompe l'oeil* perspective gallery closes at 6.30pm; admission charge), which has a fine collection of paintings, including work by masters including Rubens, Guercino, Tintoretto and Reni.

The end of the street opens into **Piazza Farnese** ㉖, linked by a short street back to Campo de' Fiori. Its twin fountains incorporate two huge basins from the Baths of Caracalla *(see page 159)*. You'll want to linger in this picturesque square and there's an inviting (if overpriced) bar where you can stop for refresh-

ment. The **Palazzo Farnese**, a masterpiece of High Renaissance architecture, was commissioned by Cardinal Alessandro Farnese in 1517 but only completed in 1589. The palace cost so much that for a while even the Farnese finances were strained. The original designs were by da Sangallo, but Michelangelo took over the work. When he died, Vignola and della Porta finished it off. Annibale Caracci frescoed the main salon over the central doorway. In 1874 Palazzo Farnese became the French Embassy, and it is now open to the public only on special occasions.

Via Giulia

The road to the left of the palace leads to **Via Giulia**, named after Pope Julius II who commissioned it as a monument to the Apostolic Church. When Bramante began work on it in 1508, the intention was to make it Rome's most important thoroughfare, connecting the Vatican with Ponte Sisto and the Ripa Grande harbour, and thus the centre of Papal Rome. The centrepiece of

Map on page 116

Mascherone Fountain, Via Giulia.

LEFT: Michelangelo's arch, part of an uncompleted bridge on Via Giulia. **BELOW:** Piazza Farnese.

TIP

A boat service connects the bridges of the River Tiber, starting from Ponte Duca d'Aosta in the north then stopping at Ponte Risorgimento, Ponte Cavour, Ponte Sant'Angelo, Ponte Sisto and finishing at Tiber Island. A one-way trip costs €1 and boats run daily. Guided tours are also offered, but timetables are erratic, so it's best to phone for times. Tel: 06-6789361.

BELOW: on the Ponte Fabricio.

the street was to be the Palazzo dei Tribunali. Bramante started work on this but the building failed to get beyond the foundations stage.

The street became a prestigious address and many high profile people lived in its sumptuous palaces, including Antonio da Sangallo, Raphael and Benvenuto Cellini. The parties in Via Giulia were among the best in Rome and on one occasion wine gushed from the Mascherone Fountain for three full days.

All this is hard to believe now, as the street is quiet and lined with expensive antique shops and art galleries. The elegant arch crossing the street was designed by Michelangelo and was intended to connect Palazzo Farnese with the Villa Farnesina across the Tiber, but the bridge was never built.

Next to the arch is the church of **Santa Maria dell'Orazione e Morte** with a façade by Ferdinand Fuga (1623). The walls and the ceiling are covered with reliefs and mosaics. Grotesque and fantastic arabesques of human bones, children's skulls, collarbones and ribs decorate the walls. The historian Gregorovius commented: "But that Art has here done such a deed, that it has taken that which appears to the living as most gruesome and which the earth should cover in kindly darkness, and made it into pictures and graceful arabesques, is truly too repellent and morbid."

Adjacent to the church is **Palazzo Falconieri** ㉗, which was modernised by Borromini for the Falcone family and is framed by two falcons' heads on female torsos. It is now the Hungarian Academy, and occasionally opens for exhibitions and concerts.

Further down Via Giulia, in Via Sant'Eligio, is the beautiful little 16th-century church of **Sant'Eligio degli Orefici** ㉘, designed by Raphael, with a dome by Peruzzi.

An exception to the refined character of the street is the derelict church of **San Filippo**. In a spectacular plan of Mussolini's, this church was to have been torn down and a panoramic road was to have swept across the river and up to the Gianicolo hill. A little further along is the fortified building of the **Carceri Nuove** (New Prison), built in 1655 to replace the gruesome prisons of Tor di Nona and the nearby torture chambers of the Savella family, who until then were the papal gaolers.

Continuing, past the Palazzo dei Tribunali, you come to several important Renaissance *palazzi*, including da Sangallo the Younger's palace at No. 66 and one of Raphael's houses at No. 85. The street ends with the church of **San Giovanni dei Fiorentini**, built in various stages by Sansovino, da Sangallo the Younger, della Porta and Maderno. The façade was added in the 18th century. Inside, there is a delightful sculpture of St John by the Sicilian Mino del Reame over the sacristy door, and an impressive apse altar by Borromini with a marble group, the *Baptism of Christ*, by Antonio Raggi. Both Borromini and Maderno are buried in the church.

Isola Tiberina

The **Isola Tiberina** 29 is a pretty and tranquil island in the middle of the Tiber. It has long been associated with healing. Legend has it that in 293 BC, the Romans asked the Greeks, their god Aesculapius in particular, for help overcoming a plague. They were sent a shipful of snakes, whose venom was used to cure ailments. The plague was defeated and a temple to Aesculapius duly erected. The church of San Bartolomeo was built on the ruins of this temple in the 10th century. The island is also the site of the Fatebenefratelli (the "do-good-brothers") hospital founded in 1548.

The two bridges linking Isola Tiberina to the shore are among the oldest structures still in use in Rome. The **Ponte Fabricio** (leading to the north bank) was built in 62 BC by the civil engineer Lucius Fabricius, and there's an inscription to prove it. The **Ponte Cestio** was built in 42 BC by Lucius

Cestius and restored in AD 370. The central arch is all that remains from that date; the rest is a late 19th-century reconstruction. This bridge leads into the heart of Trastevere.

Off the eastern end of the island are the remains of Rome's first stone bridge (142 BC), known as the **Ponte Rotto** (Broken Bridge). Most of what remains is from a 1575 reconstruction by Gregory XIII, the rest of which was washed away in 1598. The modern bridge behind it, Ponte Palatino, is sometimes called the English Bridge, because it is the only stretch of road in Rome on which cars are driven on the left.

Back on the mainland, east of the bridge, is the **Piazza della Bocca della Verità**, once the site of the Forum Boarium, the cattle-market of ancient Rome. In the 19th century it was used for public executions. The Bocca della Verità (Mouth of Truth), a stone face with an open mouth, is in the porticoes of the church of Santa Maria in Cosmedin. Tourists enjoy putting a hand in the mouth – the story goes that the hands of liars will be bitten off. ❏

Map on page 116

Bocca della Verità - the 'Mouth of Truth' – an ancient lie detector.

BELOW: Tiber Island, a picturesque route to Trastevere.

RESTAURANTS & BARS

Restaurants

Antica Trattoria Polese
40 Piazza Sforza Cesarini. Tel: 06-6861709. Open: L & D Wed–Mon. €€
Less packed than its rowdier neighbour Da Luigi, Polese has the better outdoor seating in a small *piazza* off Corso Vittorio, and a more refined Roman menu based on what is available at the market that morning. In the evening, pizza is also on the menu.

Ar Galletto
102 Piazza Farnese. Tel: 06-6861714. Open: L & D Mon–Sat. €–€€
A simple *trattoria* with Roman classics such as *spaghetti alla carbonara* or *all'amatriciana*, *abbacchio* (lamb) and *involtini* (meat rolls). The view of Michelangelo' splendid Palazzo Farnese and Bernini's two fountains is unforgettable.

Da Giggetto al Portico d'Ottavia
22 Via del Portico D'Ottavia. Tel: 06-6861105. Open: L & D Tues–Sun. €€

PRICE CATEGORIES

Price includes dinner and a half bottle of house wine:
€ = under €25
€€ = €25–40
€€€ = €40–60
€€€€ = more than €60

It may be very popular with tourists, but don't let that put you off. The standards are reliably high as they take their Roman-Jewish cooking very seriously here, and the service is equally efficient and pleasantly old-fashioned. Try one of the five different good-value menus all of which usually include *carciofi alla giudia* (deep-fried whole artichokes), stuffed courgette flowers or salted cod fillets.

Da Luigi
23–4 Piazza Sforza Cesarini. Tel: 06-6865946. Open: L & D Tues–Sun.
Traditional (and therefore heavy) Roman fare at this always-packed venue on a small square off Corso Vittorio Emanuele. There's a pleasant breeze and a convivial atmosphere on the outdoor patio. Frequented by tourists and locals alike.

Dal Pompiere
38 Via S. Maria dei Calderari. Tel: 06-6868377. Open: L & D Mon–Sat. €€–€€€
Waistcoated waiters dance attendance on customers in the wood-panelled and frescoed rooms of this fine restaurant occupying the first floor of the Palazzo Cenci. The food is Roman–Jewish and consistently good – which means the tables are consistently full.

Der Pallaro
15 Largo del Pallaro. Tel: 06-68801488. Open: L & D Tues–Sun. €
This quintessentially Roman *trattoria* is owned by the jovial Fazi couple and is a reliable favourite for those with big appetites and smaller budgets. There is no menu but for about €20 (house wine and water included) you are served several courses one after another that will leave you more than satisfied. Unsophisticated but tasty; the artichokes are excellent and the desserts home-made. No fish. Open until past midnight. No credit cards.

Ditirambo
74 Piazza della Cancelleria. Tel: 06-6871626. Open: L & D Tues–Sun; D only Mon. €€
The atmosphere is busy but convivial. The varied menu includes numerous and unusually creative vegetarian options, such as ricotta flan with raw artichokes and a pomegranate vinaigrette, aubergine cakes, and wholemeal pasta with red onions and pecorino cheese. There are many good cuts of meat and plentiful fish dishes. The desserts are home-made, fresh and heavenly; the wine list is extensive and the waiters happy to tell you all about it.

Hosteria del Pesce
32 Via di Monserrato. Tel: 06-6865617. Open: D only Mon–Sat. €€€–€€€€
The scrubbed wood and streamlined interior set the tone for this quality restaurant which happily lives up to its pretensions. Pesce serves only the freshest fish, either raw or cooked, combined with vegetables and pasta, and the white-only wine list is judiciously composed.

Il Bacaro
27 Via degli Spagnoli. Tel: 06-6864110. Open: D only Mon–Sat. €€
Located in a small, quiet street behind the Pantheon, the Bacaro oozes charm, and is perfect for a romantic soirée. Its cobbled stone and trellised outdoor area, and tiny internal room are much sought after, so booking is essential.

Il Gonfalone
7 Via del Gonfalone. Tel: 06-68801269. Open: L & D Mon–Sat. €€
This recently renovated restaurant with lovely outdoor seating is an understated gourmet experience. Vegetarians, fish-lovers and meat-eaters are equally well served. The cuisine style is a nouvelle take on Mediterranean. There's a bar and lounge area downstairs where people drink and dance until the small hours.

Il Pagliaccio
129 Via dei Banchi Vecchi.
Tel: 06-68809595. Open:
L & D Wed–Sat, D only Mon
and Tues. €€€
This smart restaurant
has a limited but cre-
ative menu with an
emphasis on beautiful
presentation and quality
ingredients. It's expen-
sive but, as its regular
customers agree, well
worth it.

La Bottega del Vino di Anacleto Bleve
9a Via Santa Maria del
Pianto. Tel: 06-6865970.
Open: until 8pm Tues–Sat. €
A quintessentially
Roman *enoteca* (wine
bar) whose buffet is
loaded with dozens of
delicacies such as
smoked swordfish,
salmon rolls, *sformati*
(flans) and cod carpac-
cio. Locals come here for
the good food, well-cho-
sen wine list and the
simpatia of its husband-
and-wife owners, Tina
and Anacleto. *Aperitivo*
hour starts at 6.30pm.

Renato e Luisa
25 Via dei Barbieri. Tel: 06-
6869660. Open: D only
Tues–Sun. €
A reliable and affordable
trattoria in a rustic, simple setting, serving classical dishes
accompanied by good
house wines. You could
start with *fettuccine* with
pachino tomatoes and
buffalo ricotta, followed
by turkey cooked with
rosemary and honey,
rounded off (hopefully
you've room) with a per-
fect crème brûlée.

Roscioli
21 Via dei Giubbonari. Tel:
06-6875287. Open: L & D
Mon–Sat. €€
This recently opened
deli-cum-restaurant has
received rave reviews for
its authentic produce
and inventive food com-
binations such as their
signature dish,
tonnarelli with groper
fish, pistachios and fen-
nel seeds. Cheerful,
pleasant atmosphere.

Sora Margherita
30 Piazza delle Cinque
Scole. Tel: 06-6874216.
Open: L & D Fri & Sat, L
Tues–Thur and Sun. €
A small (only nine tables)
basic *trattoria* in the
heart of the former
Jewish Ghetto, serving
simple and hearty fare
(much of it vegetarian)
accompanied by bread
from renowned Traste-
vere bakery La Renella.
The sweets are home-
made and the highly
palatable local wine is
from Velletri outside
Rome. No credit cards.

Taverna degli Amici
36 Piazza Margana. Tel: 06-
69920637. Open L & D
Tues–Sat. €€–€€€
A refined alfresco restaurant in an ivy-draped
square of the Ghetto
district. It serves subtly
different versions of
Roman classics as well
as plenty of interesting
vegetarian dishes.

Trattoria Moderna
16 Vicolo dei Chiodaroli. Tel:
06-68803423. Open: L & D
Mon–Fri, D only Sat. €€
A new restaurant with
appealing modern décor.

The owners are experi-
enced Roman restaura-
teurs and the menu is
classical Mediterranean
with some successful
modern touches.

Zio Ciro
1 Via della Pace. Tel: 06-
6864802. Open: D only
daily. €
Succulent, Neapolitan-
style, thick-crusted
pizzas (the Roman ones
have thinner bases) and
a range of pasta dishes
and salads. Excellent
value by Roman stan-
dards, especially in view
of its central location.
Vast outdoor seating
area in summer.

Bars & Cafés

Zi' Fenizia (64 Via Santa
Maria del Pianto) has
been declared the best
takeaway pizzeria in the
city by Gambero Rosso,
Italy's answer to the
Michelin guides. It's all
kosher, and their signa-
ture pizza topping is a
tasty combination of
anchovy and endives.
Il Goccetto (14 Via dei
Banchi Vecchi) has been
serving good wines and
even better cheeses for
over two decades in this
medieval bishop's
palace with frescoed
ceilings. Some 800 dif-
ferent labels are avail-
able for sale, of which
about 40 can be tasted
by the glass.
Award-winning ice cream
maker **Alberto Pica** (12
Via della Seggiola) has
been making *gelato* all
his life and is rather
better at it than most.

People travel from all
over Rome to enjoy his
superlative ice creams in
all the usual and plenty
of unusual flavours.
For a hot or cold drink, or
an innovative cocktail any
time of the day or night
(until 2am) head to the
modern **Lot 87** (87 Via
del Pellegrino) just off
Campo de' Fiori. Feel free
to nurse a drink for as
long as you like, as you sit
at one of their high tables
browsing the papers or
magazines stacked in the
racks by the door.
A kitsch but quintessen-
tially Roman place is
Jonathan's Angels (16
Via della Fossa), which is
bright and full of colour,
and filled with quirky
memorabilia, including
dozens of portraits of
the owner with his
children. It also boasts
the most memorable
toilets in town, complete
with their own fountain.
Sciam (56 Via del Pellegrino) is a laid-back Middle Eastern tea room
with a tempting selection
of sweet and savoury
dishes. You may even be
tempted to take a puff of
the aromatic hookah
pipes. Open till 2am.
Wine Time (15 Piazza
Pasquale Paoli) is a
buzzing oasis of good
wine and good humour.
You can sit at the
counter or at tables, your
drinks accompanied by
delicious cheeses,
salads and desserts.
Just across the river
from Castel Sant'
Angelo.

VIA VENETO AND VILLA BORGHESE

The country estates of wealthy Romans were carved up after Unification and transformed into elegant boulevards lined with imposing *palazzi*. Only the Villa Borghese was saved and turned into a vast public park containing some of the city's finest museums

This chapter takes you from Via Veneto, which leads north from the city centre, up to the Villa Borghese Gardens, Rome's finest park, with a gallery of remarkable paintings and sculptures.

Via Veneto

The southern end of **Via Veneto ❶** begins in **Piazza Barberini**, a busy square with a cinema and fast-food joints. In its centre sits, rather forlornly, Bernini's **Fontana del Tritone** (Triton Fountain). Via Veneto itself, lined with plane trees and pavement cafés, was once the symbol of Roman fashion and style. However, the glorious days of *la dolce vita*, immortalised on screen by Fellini, are long gone. Anita Ekberg now lives in retirement in the Castelli Romani, and the intellectuals have drifted to Piazza del Popolo and the area around Piazza Navona. The long, twisting avenue is now filled for the most part with luxury hotels, embassies and offices, as well as numerous anonymous restaurants with glass-enclosed outdoor seating, hungry for the tourist dollar. Only a few historic cafés – Harry's Bar at No. 150, Café de Paris at No. 90 and the Art Deco Doney's at No. 145 – still bear witness to the street's heyday as the place to be seen in Rome.

For a macabre diversion, examine the remains of 4,000 Capuchin monks in the crypt of **Santa Maria della Concezione** (tel: 06-4871185; www.cappucciniviaveneto.it; Fri–Wed 9am–noon 3–6pm; donation expected) at the southern end of Via Veneto at No. 27. Here, bones and skulls are ornately displayed.

Gardens of Sallust

The **Horti Sallustiani** (Gardens of Sallust) lay between Via Veneto and the Villa Borghese gardens. Gaius

Map on page 140

LEFT AND BELOW:
the Villa Borghese, aristocratic in origin but now a park for the people.

Bernini's Triton Fountain in Piazza Barberini.

Sallustius, an historian and profiteer who made enormous fortunes out of the campaigns of 40–30 BC, embellished his home with magnificent gardens. Soon hailed as one of the wonders of the world, they were quickly appropriated by the Empire. Vespasian and Titus preferred this part of Rome to the Palatine.

Fountains, pools and mosaic floors once drew awed visitors. Now the gardens lie 15 metres (45 ft) below street level, buried by the rubble from collapsed houses and the building activity of the 19th century. Archaeological finds from the gardens include the obelisk at the top of the Spanish Steps and those on show as part of the collection of the Museo Nazionale Romano *(see page 121)*.

The colourful life of the gardens ended when the Goths, under Alaric, stormed the Holy City by the nearby **Porta Salaria** in 410, leaving a trail of destruction

In the Middle Ages, the family of Ludovisi-Boncompagni injected new life into the gardens by planting 30 hectares (74 acres) of vineyards and hosting garden festivals. They lasted until the property boom of the 1880s, which spelt demolition for the gardens.The Società Generale Immobiliare, backed mainly by German and French capital, made an irresistible offer to the Ludovisi princes and the villa was split up. All that remains is the 16th-century **Casino dell'Aurora** in the gardens of the Swiss Cultural Institute.

The other part of the gardens spared by developers is behind the American Embassy, which is housed in **Palazzo Margherita** ❷, completed in 1890. One of the Ludovisi princes had this gigantic building constructed as a substitute for his lost garden, but his money ran out and he had to sell it to the Savoy royal family, who moved the queen mother in. It bears her name to this day.

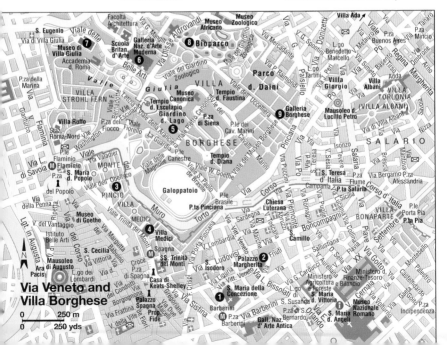

Via Veneto and Villa Borghese

0   250 m
0   250 yds

To the south of the *palazzo*, on the corner of Piazza San Bernardo and Via XX Settembre, stands the church of **Santa Maria della Vittoria** begun by Carlo Maderno in 1605. It contains Bernini's famous baroque Cornaro side-chapel, which uses natural lighting effects to highlight *The Ecstasy of St Teresa*, a sculpture of a Spanish mystic portrayed with open mouth and half-closed eyes at the climax of her vision of Christ. It has prompted many writers and critics over the centuries to suggest that the love she is experiencing may not be divine.

Villa Borghese

At the northern end of Via Veneto, outside the Porta Pinciana, is the **Villa Borghese**, which was founded at the beginning of the 17th century by Cardinal Scipione Borghese Caffarelli, a nephew of Pope Paul V. The family later extended their property by buying some nearby land, so that 100 years ago the park encompassed 75 hectares (190 acres), which the Borghese frequently opened to the public. Property developers cast a greedy eye on the villa in the late 19th century and their plans provoked the first battle to save the Romans' traditional society promenade. Eventually, in 1901, the state bought the villa and, two years later, gave it to the people. The Villa Borghese, along with the Pincio Gardens and the Villa Giulia, is now home to three museums worth visiting, and the city zoo.

The **Villa Borghese Gardens** are laid out over rolling hills with winding paths, little lakes, statues and pretty flowerbeds hidden here and there. On Sunday, the people of Rome take over the park. Every corner is full of picnicking families, strolling lovers, cyclists and joggers, squealing children at play, while their fathers sit with transistors pressed to their ears straining to hear commentary of the match of the day.

A wide *viale* leads downhill from the Porta Pinciana, passing the **Galoppatoio** (horse track) on the left and a statue of Goethe on the right. Veer left at Piazzale Canestre into Viale delle Magnolie and head

Map on page 140

TIP

A good way to get your bearings of the park and the rest of the city is to take a ride on the blue balloon which glides up and down, using a system of ropes and pulleys. At €15 it's not a cheap 15-minute jaunt, but the views of the park and the rest of the city are unforgettable. From 9.30am–dusk daily; tel: 06-3211511, www.aerophile.it

BELOW: the Galleria Borghese, a treasury of artworks.

One of the highlights of the Galleria Borghese collection is the sensual statue of Pauline Bonaparte by Canova. The 19th-century femme fatale, whose conquests in the bedroom matched her brother's on the battlefield, was appropriately sculpted as Venus Victrix. When asked how she could possibly have posed so scantily dressed, she replied "the studio was heated".

BELOW RIGHT: view from the romantic Pincio Gardens.

over the bridge, crossing busy Viale del Muro Torto below, into the **Pincio Gardens** ❸ at the southwest corner of the park. These formal gardens were designed by Valadier in the 19th century. Look out for the fanciful water clock and the **Casina Valadier**, an elegant café visited by the intellectuals of the Roman *belle époque*. Nowadays, it is an expensive bar and restaurant. Outside the café is a stand full of bicycles and pedal-carts for hire - not a bad idea, especially if you plan on visiting the museums across the park. The romantic terrace of the Pincio overlooks Piazza del Popolo and offers a splendid vantage point to view the city. It's a particularly delightful spot for an evening stroll.

Further down the Pincio hillside is the majestic **Villa Medici** ❹. Rebuilt in the 16th century for the Crescenzi family, it was then passed to the Medicis, before being confiscated by Napoleon in 1803 and made the home of the French Academy. It is open for occasional exhibitions and concerts. There are also guided tours of the gardens on

Saturday and Sunday morning (advance booking, tel: 06-67611).

Backtrack and cross the bridge to where a wide *viale* leads up to **Piazza di Siena** on the right. This oval track is the site of the International Horse Show in May – an important social and sporting event. Top-quality show-jumping is spiced up with a cavalry charge by the mounted *carabinieri*.

To the left is the pretty **Giardino del Lago** ❺ with a tiny lake, in the middle of which stands a reproduction of a Greek temple of Aesculapius. Rowing-boats can be hired for a brief paddle. Nearby, you will find the **Fountain of Fauns**, created in 1929 by Giovanni Nicolini.

Two sloping ramps lead to Viale delle Belle Arti and the neoclassical façade of the **Galleria Nazionale d'Arte Moderna** ❻ (tel: 06-32298451; Tues–Sun 8.30am–7.30pm; admission charge). It has a permanent collection of 19th- and 20th-century pieces by Italian and foreign artists (de Chirico, Degas, Cezanne, Kandinsky, Mondrian, Klimt, Henry Moore and others) and

The Galleria Borghese

The Galleria Borghese is housed in an early 17th-century *palazzina* designed by a Dutchman, Jan van Santen. It is divided in two: the sculpture collection on the ground floor is called the Museo, while the art collection on the first floor is known as the Galleria. Between 1801 and 1809 the sculpture collection was severely depleted, when more than 500 pieces were sold to Napoleon; these now make up the Borghese Collection of the Louvre in Paris. But there are still some marvellous pieces, including some of Bernini's best work, such as *David, Apollo and Daphne* and *Pluto and Persephone*, as well as Canova's famous statue of Pauline, Napoleon's sister and wife of Prince Camillo Borghese, posing as Venus. The Galleria is filled with paintings by Italian masters – Perugino, Raphael, Botticelli, Caravaggio and Titian. Within its few rooms are some great treasures: several Caravaggios (including the *Madonna of the Serpent),* three Raphaels, Correggio's *Danae,* Titian's *Sacred and Profane Love* and works by Perugino, Lotto, Domenichino, Giorgione, Dossi and Bassano, as well as by Rubens and Cranach, among others.

Map on page 140

frequently hosts travelling exhibitions of international importance.

Next door, in the Piazza Winston Churchill, is the **Accademia Britannica**, designed by Lutyens and home to visiting scholars. Around the bend, in the beautiful 15th-century **Villa Giulia ❼**, built for Julius II, is the **Museo Etrusco di Villa Giulia** (tel: 06-3200562; Tues–Sun 8.15am–7.15pm; last entry 1 hr before closing; admission charge). Etruscan finds from northern Latium and Umbria are exhibited here, including the 6th-century BC sarcophagus of a married couple – *degli Sposi* – from the excavations in Cerveteri. They form one of the finest collections of Etruscan art in the world, rivalled only by that of the Vatican. Some of the collection is on show in the recently restored, 16th-century Villa Poniatowski nearby. Originally part of the Villa Giulia complex, built for Pope Julius III, it was renovated in the early 19th century by the Polish Prince Stanislao Poniatowski.

The road leading uphill to the left ends at the entrance to the zoo, or **Bioparco ❽** (tel: 06-3608211, www.bioparco.it; Apr–Sept daily 9.30am–7pm; Oct–Mar 9.30am–5pm, last entry 1 hr before closing; admission charge), its official eco-friendly name. In the past the zoo had a reputation for being neglected, but in recent years there have been some worthy and fairly successful attempts to phase out the caging of exotic animals and keep other specimens in more humane, purpose-built environments that more closely resemble their natural habitats.

From here, Viale dell'Uccelliera leads to the **Galleria Borghese ❾** (tel: 06-328101; Tues–Sun 8.30am–7pm, entry every 2 hrs to 5pm; reservations advisable, especially in high season; admission charge), one of the world's largest private art collections. It is housed in the Casino Borghese, built as a summer house for the worldly, pleasure-loving Cardinal Scipione Borghese between 1613 and 1615. The cardinal was a great patron of the arts and laid the basis for the remarkable collection of paintings and sculptures on view today *(see panel opposite)*. The entrance is at 5 Piazzale del Museo Borghese. ❏

Perugino's Madonna and Child *at the Galleria Borghese.*

RESTAURANTS & BARS

Restaurants

Cantina Cantarini
12 Piazza Sallustio. Tel: 06-4743341. Open: L & D Mon–Sat. €€
A high-quality family-run *trattoria* where the price is still right. Dishes are meat-based the first part of the week, fish-based Thur–Sat.

Girarrosto Fiorentino
46 Via Sicilia. Tel: 06-42880660, www.girarrostofiorentino.it. Open: L & D daily. €€–€€€

An island of reliability in a sea of tacky venues. The service is faultless and wall-hangings give it a pleasantly dated look. All the classic Roman dishes are on offer along with some Florentine specialities, including wonderful T-bone steaks.

La Terrazza dell'Eden
49 Via Ludovisi.
Tel: 06-47812752. Open: L & D daily. €€€€
La Terrazza is touted as one of the city's best restaurants, but its pretensions don't quite match up with reality. The dishes, particularly the sweets, are excellent, but the wine list, ambience and service don't quite merit the prices.

Papà Baccus
36 Via Toscana. Tel: 06-427 42808, www.papabaccus.it
Open: L & D Mon–Fri, D only Sat. €€€
Renowned for its attentive service and Tuscan cuisine. Meat features heavily but there are also fish and vegetarian options. A tasty chestnut strudel is top of the dessert menu.

Bars & Cafés

Doney (145 Via Veneto) represents turn-of-the-20th century elegance and is a good bet for everything from breakfast to dinner including cocktails and apéritifs. **Caffè delle Arti** (73 Via Gramsci) is touted as the finest museum-café in Italy and has a beautiful terrace and a fine interior.

● ● ● ● ● ● ● ● ● ● ● ●
Price includes dinner and a half bottle of house wine .
€ *under €25*, **€€** *€25–40*,
€€€ *€40–60*, **€€€€** *€60+*

MARKETS IN ROME

Neighbourhood markets are an essential part of the Roman way of life and are full of local colour

Markets are an enticing invitation to Rome's daily life. The city has about 150 official *mercati rionali* (neighbourhood markets) which run from Monday to Saturday, where there's generally an abundance of the freshest fruit and vegetables, as well as stalls selling meat, fish, cheeses, hams and spices, and others loaded with kitchenware, household linens, clothing and toys. Although supermarkets are competing hard, there are a number of reasons why the tradition of buying from markets will be hard to extinguish. In the city centre a lack of space dictates that the supermarkets that do exist (and most of them have appeared in the past few years) are still comparatively small, and have no convenient parking spaces. Buying from markets, be it for clothing or food, is still often more convenient, both economically and in terms of location. Also extremely important are the personalised service and human contact. Many older people value this highly, and will spend time chatting to stallholders and other customers as they make their purchases. Markets, especially flea markets, also offer the opportunity to do some bargaining, which can be satisfying. Whether you go to buy or to browse, Rome's markets are worth visiting for their atmosphere alone.

ABOVE: an ancient carving on the entrance to Porta Portese, Rome's best-known flea market, where the bead-work (**ABOVE RIGHT**) proves popular with visitors. **RIGHT:** the fresh citrus fruit in Esquilino market shares space with a range of exotic herbs and spices and unusual vegetables.

THE HIGHLIGHTS

The best of Rome's many street markets are listed below. Most of the produce markets are open from Monday to Saturday, 7am–2pm.

Campo de' Fiori (Centro Storico) is Rome's most characteristic fruit and vegetable market. Everything you buy will have been grown by the farmer who serves you.

Mercato dei Fiori, Via Trionfale (Prati). A huge, wholesale flower market that is open to the public on Tuesday morning only. Just south of here, **Mercato Trionfale**, on Via Andrea Doria (Prati), is an enormous, fenced-in market that sells all kinds of produce and more . **Mercato di San Cosimato**, Piazza di San Cosimato (Trastevere) is a small, but popular, fruit and vegetable market. **Nuovo Mercato Esquilino**, Via Ricasoli (Esquilino) is the most multicultural produce market, with exotic herbs and spices, yams, sweet potatoes and okra and lots of other goods as well.

Smaller traditional neighbourhood markets can be found in Trastevere's **Piazza San Cosimato,** San Lorenzo's **Largo degli Osci** (few tourists, low prices), and **Piazza dell'Unità**.

Specialist markets, and those selling goods other than fresh produce, include:

Mercato delle Stampe (Largo della Fontanelle Borghese, Centro Storico; Mon–Sat 8am–sunset), which sells prints and second-hand or antiquarian books.

Mercato di Via Sannio (Piazza San Giovanni in Laterano, San Giovanni; Mon–Fri 8am–2pm, Sat 8am–5pm), sells new and second-hand clothes; the occasional vintage gem can be found here for a bargain price.

Porta Portese (Trastevere; Sun 7am–2pm.). This is the best flea market in Rome. Skill is required to get a real bargain, but it's great fun. Hang onto your bags and look out for pickpockets.

The **Soffitta Sotto i Portici** market (Piazza Augusto Imperatore, under the porticoes; first and third Sun of every month, except Aug, 9am–sunset) is an antiques' and collectors' market.

Borghetto Flaminio (Piazza della Marina, north of Piazza del Popolo; Sun 10am–7pm; closed Aug). All the stallholders here are private individuals, selling heirlooms and clothing, so there is a wide range in quality and price. There's a small admission charge.

ABOVE: Rome's markets have something for everyone and these colourful puppets are guaranteed to entice children who might otherwise find market browsing a chore. **BELOW:** Rome's shoppers have a keen eye and will only buy the freshest and best produce. **RIGHT:** clothes for the fashion-conscious baby.

TRASTEVERE AND THE GIANICOLO

Rome's traditional working-class district "across the Tiber" has always stood apart from the rest of the city. Though it is now the gentrified turf of bourgeois Romans and ex-pats, Trastevere retains its own special charm. Rising behind it the Gianicolo hill offers some of the best views of the city.

Across the river (*trans Tiberium*) from the Centro Storico lies Trastevere. For centuries the working-class district of Rome, Trastevere has a long history as the residence of outsiders. In Roman times, it was settled by sailors and foreign merchants. It was also home to a large Jewish community which later moved to the opposite bank. Over the centuries, Trastevere's separation from the rest of the city resulted in the development of its own unique customs, traditions and even dialect.

But the old *Trasteverini* are a dying breed. The now gentrified district is inhabited by wealthy Italians and foreigners, who are slowly but steadily changing the character of the quarter, resulting in the exodus of its working-class inhabitants. However, Trastevere has kept some of its idiosyncracies, even if many of the old *trattorie* and *osterie* have given way to pizzerias, pubs and trendy wine bars. During the day, it is left to its sleepy self: residents exercise dogs and do their daily shopping, while children play and the elderly sit outside their houses, chatting and chopping vegetables. In the evening, the streets and squares are packed with locals and tourists, who flock here to eat, drink or stroll among stalls selling ethnic jewellery, and fortune-tellers shuffling their cards.

Poets' corner

Like every old quarter of Rome, Trastevere had to make sacrifices when the capital started expanding after 1870. Many historic buildings and streets were destroyed in order to make way for the Viale di Trastevere, a broad boulevard that cuts through the patchwork of Trastevere's little streets. At its northern end, on the banks of the Tiber, is **Piazza G.G. Belli**, named after the much-loved 19th-century Roman dialect poet, Giuseppe Gioacchino

Map on page 148

LEFT: the mellow shades of a Trastevere street. **BELOW:** view from the Gianicolo Hill.

TIP

Rome's most famous flea market is Porta Portese *(see page 144)* held on Sunday from 7am–2pm on Via Portuense and adjacent streets between Via Ettore Rolli and Porta Portese. Go early if you want to get the bargains and avoid the crowds.

Belli (1791–1863) whose statue stands in the square. Behind Piazza Belli is **Piazza Sidney Sonnino** ❶. The Torre degli Anguillara, the last of many towers that once guarded Trastevere, is marked with a plaque commemorating Dante's stay here in 1300. On the other side of the Viale is the church of **San Crisogono**, built over one of the oldest sites of Christian worship in Rome, dating from the 3rd century. The façade is a 17th-century copy of the medieval original and inside are remains of a 5th-century basilica.

Upriver, on **Piazza Trilussa** ❷, is another monument to a popular poet, Carlo Alberto Salustri (1871–1950), known as Trilussa. Among the exhibits in the nearby **Museo di Roma in Trastevere** ❸ (Piazza Sant'Egidio tel: 06-5816563; Tues–Sun 10am–4pm; admission charge), a folklore museum housed in a beautifully restored former convent, is a reconstruction of Trilussa's studio.

Frescoes and fine art

Via della Scala leads from Piazza Sant'Egidio to the **Porta Settimiana**, a gate erected by Emperor Septimius Severus and replaced by Pope Alexander VI in 1498. From here Via Garibaldi winds its way up to the Gianicolo *(see page 150)*. This route was used in the Middle Ages by pilgrims en route to the Vatican, before the building of the "retifili" – the long straight roads built by the Renaissance popes. The longest of these is Via della Lungara, laid out in the early 16th century by Julius II to connect Trastevere with the Borgo. It's a short walk from the Porta Settimiana along Via della Lungara to the **Villa Farnesina** ❹ (tel: 06-68027268; Mon–Sat 9am–1pm; admission charge). This sumptuous villa was built between 1508 and 1511 for the fabulously wealthy papal banker, Agostino Chigi. Renowned for his lavish banquets, Chigi was also a noted patron of the arts and had his

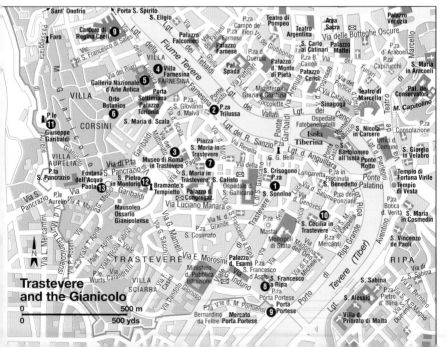

villa decorated with a series of beautiful frescoes by some of the best artists of the time. The highlights of the downstairs rooms are Raphael's sensual *Galatea* and *Three Graces*. Upstairs is a fine *trompe l'oeil* depicting contemporary views of Rome by Peruzzi, and Sodoma's magnificent *Wedding of Roxanne and Alexander*.

Across the road is the **Palazzo Corsini**. Built in the 15th century for a wealthy cardinal, it now houses part of the collection of the **Galleria Nazionale d'Arte Antica ❺** (tel: 06-68802323; Tues–Fri 9.30am–1.50pm, entrance only at allotted times of 9.30am, 11am and 12.15pm; Sat–Sun 8.30am–1.50pm; admission charge), which includes works by Rubens, Van Dyck, Caravaggio and Reni (the rest of the collection is in Palazzo Barberini, *see page 94*).

Behind Palazzo Corsini is the **Orto Botanico ❻** (tel: 06-6864193; Mon–Sat 9.30am–6.30pm in summer, until 5.30pm in winter; admission charge). Original part of the palace grounds, the botanical gardens are now open to the public. There are about 7,000 plants on display, including a scented garden for the blind and a collection of medicinal herbs. On the slopes up to the Gianicolo is a series of tiered fountains.

Three piazzas

Follow the road back to Piazza Sant' Egidio, and through to **Piazza Santa Maria in Trastevere ❼**, the heart of the neighbourhood. This cobbled, square is one of the most charming in Rome. There's a steady ebb and flow of tourists and locals whiling away their time in the cafés or sitting on the steps of the fountain (1692) around which musicians perform in summer.

The piazza is named after the **basilica** on its eastern side, one of the oldest churches in Rome. Its present appearance dates from the 12th century, although the portico (which has been cleaned and treated to protect it

from the ravages of pollution) was added in 1702. The 12th- and 13th-century mosaics, both inside and outside the church, are spectacular and it is worth taking a pair of binoculars to enjoy their details. *The Life of the Virgin* series is by Cavallini (1291).

The atmosphere is more brisk and business-like in **Piazza San Cosimato**, where the daily food market is surrounded by food shops, bars, restaurants and a hospital. On nearby Piazza di San Francesco d'Assisi, the church of **San Francesco a Ripa ❽**, contains a powerful late work by Bernini, the *Blessed Ludovica Albertoni*. Her ecstatic expression is reminiscent of his more famous statue of St Teresa in Santa Maria della Vittoria *(see page 141)*.

The church is not far from **Porta Portese**, **❾** a gateway built by Urban VIII on the site of the ancient Porta Portuensis. Rome's cheap and cheerful fleamarket is held here on Sunday mornings *(see pages 144 and 148)*

South of Viale Trastevere

Nestling in a quiet and secluded part of Trastevere is the church of **Santa**

Map on page 148

The altar in Santa Maria in Trastevere.

BELOW: a busy café in the Piazza Santa Maria in Trastevere.

Map on page 148

Giuseppe Garibaldi's monument in Piazzale Garibaldi.

BELOW: Bramante's Templetto.

Cecilia in Trastevere ⑩ (daily 9.30am–12.30pm, 4–6.30pm; admission charge for crypt), dedicated to the martyr St Cecilia, condemned to death for her faith in 230. She was to have been executed by means of suffocation, but when this failed, an executioner was despatched to behead her. She survived three strokes of the axe, living for a further three days and converting 400 pagans before she finally died. In 1599, her tomb was opened and her body, in a semi-foetal position, was found in a miraculous state of preservation. The artist, Maderno, made a beautiful statue of the saint which can be seen beneath the high altar. Her sarcophagus can be seen in the crypt (Mon–Sat 10.15am–12.15pm, Sun 11.30am–12.30pm; admission charge).

The Gianicolo

The **Gianicolo** (Janiculum Hill) is climbed from Trastevere by the long and winding Via Garibaldi. After the liberation of Rome from papal rule in 1870, this hill became a gathering place where anticlerical citizens of Rome could honour Giuseppe Garibaldi. An equestrian monument to the freedom-fighter stands on **Piazzale Garibaldi** ⑪ and, a little further north, is another for his wife, the intrepid Anita. Views from the terrace are magnificent. Also on the hill is **San Pietro in Montorio**, with works by Vasari, del Piombo and Bernini. **Bramante's Tempietto** ⑫, one of the gems of the Renaissance, was erected in the courtyard in 1502 *(see box below)*.

Via Garibaldi continues uphill to the **Fontana dell' Acqua Paola** ⑬, a fountain commissioned in 1612 by Pope Paul V to grace the end of an ancient aqueduct built by Trajan.

South of Gianicolo Hill is a small park, full of statuary and shady trees, the **Villa Sciarra**. Larger green expanses lie further west in the biggest public park in the city, the **Villa Pamphili**, where much of the natural landscape remains unspoilt, making it a peaceful place for a walk or a picnic *(see page 180)*. It was laid out in 1652 by Camillo Pamphili, nephew of Innocent X, who also financed the summer residence in the park, the **Casino del Bel Respiro**. ❏

Bramante's Tempietto

When the centre of the Renaissance shifted from northern Italy to Rome at the end of the 15th century, the atmosphere of the Eternal City injected a fresh impetus for the architects of the day to rediscover the styles and motifs of antiquity. Donato Bramante had learned his trade in the north and moved to Rome in 1499. The Tempietto di San Pietro in Montorio (1502) was almost his first commission in Rome, but it bears little resemblance to anything he had produced in Milan. This is the first monument of the High Renaissance style. Set in an Early Renaissance courtyard, the Tempietto possesses a gravity all of its own – not suprising, considering its location: it marks the spot that was believed to be the site of St Peter's crucifixion. On closer inspection, visitors will see that there is very little surface decoration and that the style of the colonnade – Tuscan Doric – is also unadorned. Too small to fit a congregation (5 metres/15 ft in diameter) the circular temple supports a classical entablature, which lends further weight and severity. These features, combined with the perfect classical proportions, make the Tempietto a brilliant homage to antiquity.

RESTAURANTS & BARS

Restaurants

Alberto Ciarla
40 Piazza San Cosimato. Tel:
06-5818668 www.albertocia-
rla.com. Open: D only
Mon–Sat. €€€€
Friendly staff, sophisti-
cated décor and six set-
price gourmet fish
menus or à la carte. One
of the top fish restau-
rants in the city.

Antico Arco
7 Piazzale Aurelio. Tel: 06-
5815274. Open: D only
Mon–Sat. €€€
Excellent restaurant on
the Gianicolo hill; some
traditional dishes, some
more innovative. The spe-
ciality is risotto with a
Piedmontese cheese.

Asinocotto
48 Via dei Vascellari. Tel: 06-
5898985. Open: D only
Tues–Sat, L & D Sun. €€€
Small, typical Trastevere
trattoria offers refined
and creative cusine
(gnocchi with peppers
and mint, veal liver in
raspberry vinegar). Gay-
friendly and gay-owned.

Checco er Carettiere
10 Via Benedetta. Tel: 06-
5800985, www.checcoercaret-
tiere.it. Open: L & D Mon–Sat,
L only Sun. €€–€€€€
A pleasant outdoors
section and a steadfast
Roman menu of fish and
meat make this a sure
bet. Sweets and ice
cream are home made.

Dar Poeta
45–46 Vicolo del Bologna.
Tel: 06-5880516. Open:

D only daily. €
Pizzas made with a blend
of yeast-free flours which
creates an incomparably
fluffy base. No smoking
and no reservations.

Enoteca Ferrara
41 Piazza Trilussa. Tel: 06-
58333920. Open: D only
daily. €€€
Minimalist décor and cre-
ative menu (with organic
ingredients), comprehen-
sive wine selection (850
labels). Light snacks or
full meals. Reservations
essential at weekends.

Il Ciak
21 Vicolo del Cinque. Tel: 06-
5894774. Open: D only Tues–
Thur, L & D Fri–Sun. €€
Game hanging in the
windows testifies that
this is a meat-eating
venue. Dishes based on
hearty Tuscan recipes
and served with the
house Chianti.

La Fraschetta
134 Via S. Francesco a Ripa.
Tel: 06-5816012. Open: D
only Mon–Sat.
Simple pizzeria and trat-
toria menu served with
house wine in a jovial
atmosphere.

Le Mani in Pasta
37 Via de' Genovesi. Tel: 06-
5816017. Open: L & D
Tues–Sun. €–€€
Inviting and friendly
restaurant serving meat
and fish carpaccios;
home-made pastas are
cooked in a myriad
different ways. No menu
but the prices are
reasonable.

Panattoni
53 Viale Trastevere. Tel: 06-
5800919. Open: D only
Thur–Tues. €
Not the most inspiring of
interiors but a Rome
classic for its thin crusty
pizzas, large antipasti
buffet, low prices and its
quicker than lightning
brusque Roman service.
No bookings.

Paris
7a Piazza San Calisto. Tel:
06-5815378. Open: L & D
Tues–Sat; L only Sun.
€€–€€€
At the upper end of this
price scale with elegant,
slightly dated décor and
reliably excellent tradi-
tional Roman-Jewish cui-
sine : golden deep-fried
vegetables and coda alla
vaccinara (braised oxtail
with tomatoes, celery
and white wine). Small
outdoor eating area.
Closed in August.

Spirito Divino
31b Via de' Genovesi. Tel:
06-5896689. Open: D only
Mon–Sat. €€
History permeates this
restaurant which stands
atop the remains of a
synagogue and an
ancient Roman house.
Classic dishes, many
based on recipes used in
Ancient Rome. The wine
list is international and
has won plaudits.

Bars & Cafés

The perfect place for a
pre-dinner cocktail or a
post-dinner drink is

Ombre Rosse (12 Piazza
Sant'Egidio). In a scenic
piazza it offers a good
atmosphere and is open
all day every day (except
Sunday morning). **Trasté**
(76 Via della Lungaretta)
has low seats and tables
and lots of cushions and
serves all kinds of teas,
fruit and milk shakes and
alcoholic beverages. **Bar
San Calisto** (3–4 Piazza
San Calisto) is small and
plain but nevertheless
pulls in an incredibly
mixed crowd. Their choco-
late ice cream and hot
chocolate in winter are
deservedly famous. **Star-
dust** (4 Vicolo de' Renzi)
is open late, and attracts
an arty crowd, Live jazz
and talented local singers
some nights. On the
scenic Gianicolo Hill, the
Caffè del Gianicolo (5
Piazzale Aurelio) is a simple bar where light snacks
and fruit shakes can be
consumed indoors and
out. The best-priced café
in lovely Piazza Santa
Maria is **Caffè di Marzio**
(15 Piazza Santa Maria in
Trastevere). Friendly staff
and excellent opportuni-
ties for people-watching.

PRICE CATEGORIES

Price includes dinner
and a half bottle of
house wine:
€ = under €25
€€ = €25–€40
€€€ = €40–€60
€€€€ = more than €60

AVENTINO AND TESTACCIO

The most southerly of Rome's hills, the Aventine has always been a tranquil and sought-after residential area. It is also home to a number of religious shrines. Testaccio, once a busy working river port, is still one of the city's most down-to-earth and genuinely Roman districts

Map on page 154

BELOW:
a far-reaching view from the Aventine Hill.

The Aventine Hill is now one of the most desirable places in Rome to live; a tranquil oasis conveniently close to the city centre. Considered the "Sacred Mount" in ancient times, it is the site of pagan temples and of some of Rome's earliest Christian churches.

For centuries, the Aventine lay outside the city walls. It remained virtually uninhabited until 494 BC when the plebeians retreated here to organise the first general strikes against patrician rule. During the latter years of the Republic, it was the residence of foreign merchants and nouveau riche plebeians. By the Imperial era, the hill had moved right up the social scale. The aristocracy moved in and built magnificent temples and luxury villas on it. In subsequent centuries, several churches were built on the ancient sacred sites. Today, the Aventine remains a well-to-do neighbourhood.

High on the hill is the **Parco Savello**, laid out in the 1930s with orange trees and a view over the river

towards the Vatican. The gardens flank the early Christian basilica of **Santa Sabina ❶**, skilfully restored to its near original state in 1936. It was built in the 5th century by a priest from Dalmatia, Peter of Illyria, on the site of the house of a martyred Roman matron called Sabina. The broad nave is lined with elegant Corinthian columns, relics of a temple which once stood here. The west door is as old as the church; its carved wooden panels depict biblical scenes, including the earliest known representation of the Crucifixion.

Next door, the church of **Sant' Alessio ❷** has a fine Romanesque *campanile* (bell tower). A pretty courtyard leads into a baroque interior with a gilt-covered relic of a staircase, beneath which St Alexis is said to have lived and died.

From here, Via Santa Sabina leads into **Piazza dei Cavalieri di Malta ❸**. The square is named after the ancient chivalric order founded in 1080 as the Hospitallers of St John to run a hospital for pilgrims in Jerusalem. The Hospitallers developed into a powerful military order,

based in Malta until they were expelled by Napoleon in 1798. The Knights of Malta have been based in Rome ever since.

The square was designed by the 18th-century engraver Piranesi and has heraldic symbols containing allusions to the military prowess of the Knights. Piranesi was also responsible for the monumental gate to the **Priorato di Malta**, the residence of the Grand Master of the order. Peek through the keyhole for the famous view of the dome of St Peter's framed by a tree-lined avenue.

Down the hill and to the northeast is the church of **Santa Prisca ❹**, said to occupy the site of a 3rd-century house belonging to Prisca and Aquila, who invited St Peter to dine here. Beneath the church are the remains of a *mithraeum*, a grotto to the ancient god Mithras.

Further down the hill you come to the Viale Aventino, which divides the main Aventine Hill from the smaller one known as *Il Piccolo Aventino*. On the right are remnants of the city walls dating from the 4th century BC.

A Maltese Cross in Piranesi's Piazza dei Cavalieri di Malta.

BELOW:
the Piramide di Caio Cestio, Testaccio.

Rome's team colours: the inhabitants of Testaccio are said to be the most loyal supporters of the Roma football team.

Across Piazza Albani, Via San Saba leads to the pretty 10th-century church of **San Saba ❺** founded in the 7th century by exiled Palestinian monks. A selection of ancient sculptural fragments is displayed in its portico, and the interior has some Cosmatesque work and remains of a 13th-century fresco of St Nicolas.

Porta San Paolo

Originally the Porta Ostiense, because it marked the beginning of the road to Ostia, **Porta San Paolo ❻** is one of the best preserved of the ancient city gates. It was renamed after St Paul who entered Rome through it. Impressive though the gateway is, it is overshadowed by the nearby **Piramide di Caio Cestio ❼**, the tomb of a vainglorious Roman officer, Gaius Cestius, buried here in 12 BC. Adjoining the pyramid is Rome's **Cimitero Acattolico** (tel: 06-5741900, Mon–Sat 9am–5pm; admission free) known in English as

BELOW: post-war urban housing in Testaccio.

the Protestant Cemetery. The Italian Communist Party founder, Antonio Gramsci, poets Shelley and John Keats (who died in a house overlooking the Spanish Steps), and the son of the German writer, Goethe, are buried here.

Testaccio

Testaccio, the area west of Porta San Paolo, doesn't feature on most tourist itineraries, but it's worth a visit if you want to experience a genuine Roman working-class district, before it goes the way of Trastevere and trendification changes its character for good.

The heart of the district is the 35-metre (105-feet) high **Monte Testaccio ❽**, or 'Hill of Shards', which gets its name from the broken bits of amphorae that can be found here. Testaccio was basically an ancient landfill site. The amphorae used to transport oil and wine were dumped here once their contents had been unloaded in the warehouses of the

Republican port which lined the Tiber between Ponte Testaccio and Ponte Aventino. Today the mound is closed to the public, though visits can be arranged (tel: 06-57250410). Views of the Tiber valley from the top are splendid.

By the middle Ages Testaccio had largely been abandoned and wasn't developed into a residential area until the end of the 19th century when rows of low-cost tenement blocks with characteristic internal courtyards were built to house the workers. Many of these so-called *case popolari* are still publicly-owned rent-controlled working class residences.

Testaccio is now one of the most culturally active areas in Rome, with theatres, a cinema, a music school and some of the liveliest nightlife in town. Many of the old wine cellars have been transformed into clubs, discos and late-night bars.

Despite the advent of trendy boutiques and bars, Testaccio manages to preserve an authentic working-class appeal. The boisterous daily produce market in **Piazza Testaccio** ❾ is a testimony to this.

To the south lies **Via Galvani**, home to some trendy minimalist restaurants serving fusion cuisine. Galvani heads towards Monte Testaccio, which is circled by **Via di Monte Testaccio**, an uninhabited and almost rural lane that is best visited at night when its clubs, bars and restaurants, housed in unlikely-looking warehouses and low buildings, really get going.

Between Monte Testaccio and the river lies the **Mattatoio** ❿, the city's former slaughterhouse dating from 1891, when the cattle market was moved here from Piazza del Popolo. For decades, the Mattatoio was the main source of revenue for Testaccio, but in 1975 it was pensioned off when a modern "meat centre" was built outside the city. There are plans to convert all the buildings to house exhibition spaces, the university's architecture department and other art-related activities; for the moment it is used in part by the city's contemporary art gallery, MACRO, and by Villaggio Globale, a left-wing arts venue with live acts and clubbing nights in a large outdoor tent. ❑

The walls in Testaccio are covered with graffiti, proclaiming various affinities.

RESTAURANTS & BARS

Restaurants

Checchino dal 1887
30 Via di Monte Testaccio. Tel: 06-5743816. www.checchino-dal-1887.com. Open: L & D Tues–Sat. €€€
Typical Roman cuisine, excellently prepared. Known throughout the city. Booking advisable. Closed Aug.

Da Oio a Casa Mia
43 Via Galvani. Tel: 06-5782680. Open: L & D Mon–Sat, €€ Well-made Roman specialities

(pasta classics and lots of meat and offal) in a friendly trattoria.

Doc
9 Via Benjamin Franklin. Tel: 06-5744236, www.osteriadoc.com. D only Mon–Sat.
€€ A refined but informal interior sets the tone for this small restaurant specialising in fish, though meat-eaters and vegetarians are well catered for.

Ketumbar
24 Via Galvani. Tel: 06-57305338. Open: D only daily. €€–€€€

Sleek, minimalist interior. Sushi, *nasi goreng* and braised tuna fillets with parmesan wafers. Music gets louder as the evening wears on.

Letico
64 Via Galvani. Tel: 06-57250539. Open: D only Tues–Sun. €€
Modern and inviting restaurant that does interesting and lighter versions of traditional regional cuisine.

Remo
44 Piazza S. Maria Liberatrice. Tel: 06-5746270: Open: D only Mon–Sat. €
One of the best pizzerias

in the area, with good starters. No booking.

Bars & Cafés

Oasi della Birra (38 Piazza Testaccio) is a popular meeting spot for young Romans. More than 500 beers from all over the world. For a cappuccino or light lunch head to trendy **Il Caffè del Seme e la Foglia** (18 Via Galvani).

● ● ● ● ● ● ● ● ● ●
Price includes dinner and a half bottle of house wine.
€ under €25, €€ €25–40, €€€ €40–60, €€€€ €60+

CELIO AND SAN GIOVANNI

The Lateran, on the eastern extremity of the
Celio Hill, was the centre of the Catholic Church
until the seat of the papacy was transferred to
the Vatican in the 14th century. Slightly off the beaten
track, this area is filled with striking ancient
monuments and churches steeped in history

Map
on page
157

BELOW: the 18th-
century facade of San
Clemente in the
Lateran district.

When the Lateran Palace was the seat and residence of the popes (from the 4th century until the papacy's temporary move to Avignon in 1309), the Lateran was the centre of the Catholic Church. On the return of the papacy to Rome in 1377, the Pope's official residence was moved to the Vatican, but the Lateran remained an important centre for the Church – popes were still crowned there until 1870.

At the heart of the Lateran district is **Piazza di San Giovanni**, flanked by the **Palazzo Lateranense**  (Lateran Palace). The original papal residence, founded in the 4th century, was severely damaged by fire and fell into ruin. In 1586, Pope Sixtus V commissioned Domenico Fontana to build a new palace as a papal summer residence, though it was never used as such. Fontana's baroque palace now houses the offices of the diocese of Rome (of which the Pope is bishop). It was the site of the historic meeting that led to the 1929 Lateran Treaty, which established the current boundaries of the Vatican and stabilised its relationship with the Italian state.

San Giovanni in Laterano

Next to the palace stands the mighty **San Giovanni in Laterano** ❷ (tel: 06-69886433; daily 7am–7pm; free), the "mother of all churches" and the first Christian basilica in Rome, founded by Constantine the Great. The church has stood here since 313, but it has burnt down twice and been rebuilt several times. As a result, it is a hotch-potch of building styles from the exquisite 4th-century baptistry to the majestic baroque interior.

The east façade, through which you enter, is the work of Alessandro Galilei (1732–35), but Fontana designed the north façade when he was rebuilding the Lateran Palace. The central doorway has the original bronze doors taken from the Roman Curia of the Forum (see page 82). The façade is crowned by 15 huge statues of Christ and the apostles, visible for miles around. Most of the marble-clad interior is the result of remodelling by Borromini (1646), but some of the works of art and church furnishings are far older. They include a fragment of fresco attributed to Giotto (1300) and a 14th-century Gothic *baldacchino* from which only the Pope is allowed to celebrate Mass. The nave's gilded wooden ceiling was completed in 1567. Other features of note include the baroque frescoes and reliefs of the transept, and the peaceful 13th-century cloisters.

The **Battistero Lateranense** ❸ (Baptistry; daily 8.30am–12.30pm, 4–7pm; free) was part of the original complex, but was rebuilt in its present octagonal shape in the 5th century. In the earliest days of Christianity, all Christians were baptised here. The chapels of St John the Evangelist and Santi Rufina e Secunda (the original entrance) contain exquisite 5th-century mosaics.

Standing 30 metres (100 ft) high, the **obelisk** on the square is the tallest and oldest in Rome; it honours the Pharaoh Tutmes III and once stood in the Circus Maximus.

Churches and chapels

Across the street from the Lateran Palace is the entrance to the **Scala Santa** ❹ (Holy Staircase; daily 6.30am–noon, 4–6.30pm, mass at 6pm; Oct–Mar 3–6pm; free), said to be the stairs that Christ ascended when he was tried by Pontius Pilate. Brought to Rome from Jerusalem by Constantine's mother, Helena, they are protected under a layer of wood, but you still have to mount them on your knees, and the devout (who arrive in bus loads) do so slowly,

The gilded wooden ceiling of San Giovanni in Laterano.

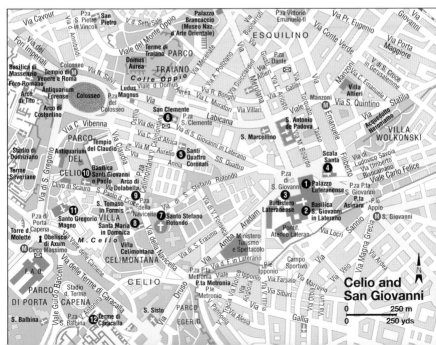

Celio and San Giovanni

0 — 250 m
0 — 250 yds

The ancient Arco di Dolabella was incorporated into Nero's aqueduct.

BELOW: refreshing shade in the Parco del Celio.

stopping on each of the 28 steps to pray. You can cheat and walk up one of the side staircases to the **Sancta Sanctorum** (Holy of Holies; tel: 06-7726641, Mon–Sat 7am–noon, 3.30–6pm; admission charge), where there is a painting of Christ, said to be the work of St Luke and an angel.

West of the basilica lie two more important churches. The **Santi Quattro Coronati** ❺, originally part of the fortress that protected the Lateran Palace, belongs to a community of silent Augustine nuns. The present church, built over the remains of a larger, 4th-century edifice, dates from the 11th century. You'll have to ring a bell to summon a nun, who will give you the key to the 12th-century cloisters or to the **Chapel of San Silvestro**. This 13th-century chapel contains an endearing fresco illustrating the conversion of Constantine to Christianity by St Sylvester (who was Pope at the time). You can see the emperor suffering from what looks like the advanced stages of a skin disease, then travelling to Rome to be cured

by the Pope. A mosaic depicts St Helena's discovery of the True Cross, which she found at the same time as the Scala Santa.

The basilica of **San Clemente** ❻ (tel: 06-7740021; admission charge for excavations) is one of Rome's most fascinating churches. It is in fact two churches, one built on top of the other, beneath which there lie still earlier remains. The present church dating from the 12th century is built in basilica form with three naves divided by ancient columns. It features a beautifully detailed mosaic depicting the Cross as the Tree of Life nourishing all living things. In the **Chapel of St Catherine** are some early Renaissance frescoes of the life of St Catherine of Alexandria by Masolino (1383– 1447) and Masaccio (1401–28).

To the right nave a staircase leads down to a 4th-century church, with fine 11th-century frescoes of miracles being performed by St Clement, the fourth pope.

An ancient stairway leads deeper underground to a maze of corridors and chambers. Down here is the earliest religious structure on the site, a 2nd-century **Temple of Mithras**, dedicated to the Persian god whose cult spread to Rome in the 1st century BC. The cult, which offered hope of an afterlife, was extremely popular with Roman soldiers, and was a powerful rival to early Christianity.

The Celio Hill

The Celio Hill, incorporated into the city in 7 BC when the defeated citizens of the rebellious city of Alba lived there, is one of the seven classical hills of Rome. Today, it's home to Villa Celimontana, surrounded by the pleasant **Parco del Celio**, sprinkled with ancient ruins and some fine early medieval churches. One of the most notable is the circular, mid-5th century **Santo Stefano Rotondo** ❼. The soft natural light that filters

through its 22 windows reveals gruesome 16th-century frescoes of martyred saints by Pomarancio.

On the other side of Via della Navicella, is the 9th-century church of **Santa Maria in Domnica ➑**. It has a magnificent mosaic of the Virgin and Child surrounded by saints and angels in a garden of paradise – the man on his knees at the Virgin's feet is Pope Paschal I, who commissioned the mosaic.

Turn left outside the church to reach Via di San Paolo della Croce which is straddled by the 1st-century **Arco di Dolabella ➒**, part of Nero's great aqueduct *(see page 89).* Next to the arch, the gateway of **San Tommaso in Formis** is decorated with a 13th-century mosaic showing Christ with two freed slaves, one black and one white. The road leads to the church of **Santi Giovanni e Paolo ➓**. The first church here was built in the 4th century, but the present one is mainly 12th-century, with an early 18th-century interior. The 13th-century belltower was built into the remains of a Temple of Claudius.

Another noteworthy church in this area is the 17th-century **San Gregorio Magno ⓫**, founded by St Gregory in the 6th century.

The Baths of Caracalla

A short walk south are the **Terme di Caracalla ⓬** (tel: 06-5758626; Apr–Sept Tues–Sun 9am–7.15pm, Oct–Mar Tues–Sat 9am–4.30pm, Mon 9am–2pm all year, last entry 1 hr before closing; admission charge), in AD 212 the most luxurious baths of ancient Rome and the city's largest until the completion of the Baths of Diocletian a century later. In their heyday, these baths could accommodate 1,600 people. Visitors could enjoy the use of libraries and lecture rooms, a gymnasium and a stadium, gardens and shops, quite apart from the complex of saunas and pools.

The interior was sumptuously decorated with marble, gilding, coloured mosaics and magnificent statues. The unearthed statues are now scattered among various collections and only patches of mosaic survive, but the buildings are still impressive, their vaults rising 30 metres (100 ft). ❏

The remains of the *caldarium* (hot room) in the Terme di Caracalla are used to stage an annual outdoor opera and ballet festival in July and August.

RESTAURANTS & BARS

Restaurants

Ai Tre Scalini
30 Via dei SS Quattro. Tel: 06-7096309. Open: L & D Tues–Sun. €€
Modern, inviting décor and close to the Colosseum. Equally strong on meat, fish and pasta.

Crab
2 Via Capo d'Africa. Tel: 06-77203636. Open L & D Tues–Sat, D only Mon. €€€–€€€€
A reputable but expensive seafood restaurant

with the best oysters in town, as well as every kind of crustacean and mollusc imaginable.

Isidoro
59a Via San Giovanni in Laterano. Tel: 06-7008266. Open: L & D Sun–Fri, D only Sat. €–€€
Fifty pasta first courses, mostly suitable for vegetarians, although on Fridays many of them are fish-oriented. You can ask to try several different varieties of pasta on one plate.

La Tana dei Golosi
220 Via San Giovanni in Laterano. Tel: 06-77203202, www.latanadeigolosi.it. Open: L & D Tues–Fri, D only Mon & Sat. €€
A different regional Italian cuisine every two months. High-quality and often organic ingredients and a refined ambience. Fixed-price cheaper lunch menu.

Le Naumachie
7 Via Celimontana. Tel: 06-7002764. Open: L & D daily. €–€€
Warm brick interior and a solid menu of pasta, pizza, grilled meats and

salads. Very reasonably priced for the area.

Bars & Cafés

Shamrock (26d Via Capo d'Africa) offers Guinness on tap and reasonable pub food. For wine try the sleek but reasonably priced **Divinare** (4 Via Ostilia) for a good selection by the glass and light, interesting meals.

● ● ● ● ● ● ● ● ● ● ● ●
Price includes dinner and a half bottle of house wine .
€ *under €25 ,* **€€** *€25–40,*
€€€ *€40–60,* **€€€€** *€60+*

MONTI AND ESQUILINO

The sprawling area covered in this chapter centres on the Esquiline and Viminal hills that lie between the Colosseum and Stazione Termini. Wander the streets of bohemian Monti and multicultural Esquilino, take in the artworks and mosaics of their many fine churches, and visit a stunning collection of Roman antiquities.

Map on page 162

In ancient times Monte Esquilino, the largest of Rome's seven hills, was the site of communal burials for slaves and executed prisoners. Emperor Augustus transformed the area into an aristocratic residential zone with palatial villas and idyllic gardens. Maecenas, a rich *bon vivant* and Augustus' lifelong friend, built himself a luxury villa on the hill, and Virgil and Horace also had homes here. Nero built his magnificent Domus Aurea *(see page 89)* on the Oppian hill (Colle Oppio), which was later incorporated into the foundations of Trajan's Baths. On the site of what is now Termini Station stood Pope Sixtus V's magnificent villa. While the wealthy lived in luxury on the breezy summit, the foot of the hill was occupied by the slums of the densely populated Suburra district.

Many of the ancient palaces and villas of the area were cleared or built over to make way for the boulevards flanked by stately *palazzi* built after Unification in 1870. These days traffic thunders along Via Nazionale and Via Cavour, two characterless thoroughfares intersecting the area, but between the lower end of them is a cluster of pretty, narrow, cobbled streets lined with bars, restaurants, and boutiques, which make up the heart of the trendy bohemian Monti

district. To the east, centred around the faded splendour of Piazza Vittorio, lies the Esquilino quarter, now the capital's prime multicultural district, where the majority of shops and restaurants are owned and run by North Africans, Indians and the Chinese.

Monti

The western side of the Esquiline hill known as Rione Monti or simply Monti, is now a district popular with artists, artisans and boutique owners.

LEFT: urban transport in the Monti neighbourhood. **BELOW:** wisteria arch at the Baths of Diocletian.

TIP

The Museo Nazionale Romano's collection of classical Roman art and statuary is contained in four different sites: the Terme di Diocleziano and Palazzo Massimo alle Terme near the station, Palazzo Altemps by Piazza Navona and Crypta Balbi near the Jewish Ghetto. A museum card, valid for seven days, covers all four sites.

This neighbourhood boasts a number of notable churches.

According to legend, in August of AD 352, following a vision of the Virgin Mary, Pope Liberius witnessed a snowfall on the summit of the Esquiline hill and built the basilica of **Santa Maria Maggiore ❶** to commemorate the miracle. If you happen to be in Rome on 5 August, go to the church to see the spectacle of white flower petals being showered through a hole in the ceiling in an annual simulation of the miraculous event.

The church is one of Rome's four great patriarchal basilicas. The 18th-century baroque façade gives no indication of the building's true antiquity, but step inside and its venerable origins become apparent. The gilded coffered ceiling and elaborate chapels are relatively new additions, but the magnificent mosaics tell another story. The apse mosaic is a 13th-century replica of the original, but the mosaics that decorate the triumphal arch and the panels high up on the nave walls are the original 5th-century ones.

Just south of Santa Maria Maggiore, lies **Santa Prassede ❷**, built by Pope Paschal I in the 9th century-who commissioned mosaic workers from Byzantium to decorate the apse, the triumphal arch and the side chapel of San Zeno, reintroducing an art that had not been practised in Rome for three centuries.

From Piazza dell'Esquilino, which lies before the rear façade of Santa Maria Maggiore, the busy Via Cavour descends the hill towards the Forum. Halfway down, a steep flight of steps leads to Via delle Sette Sale and **San Pietro in Vincoli ❸**. The church of St Peter in Chains was founded in the 5th century as a shrine for the chains said to have bound St Peter during his imprisonment in Jerusalem. They are preserved in a bronze and crystal

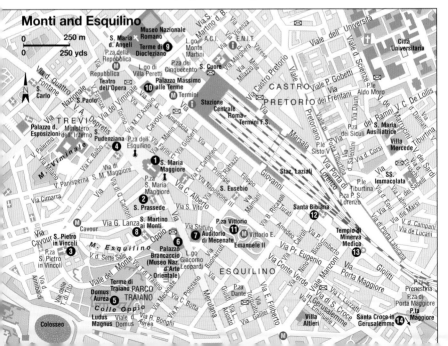

reliquary beneath the high altar. The church is also home to Michelangelo's monumental *Moses*, part of the unfinished tomb that the artist was preparing for Pope Julius II.

On the north side of Via Cavour, Via Panisperna is lined with artisans' shops and restaurants. Just off it is the beautifully restored Piazza degli Zingari, where gypsy (*zingari*) caravans once congregated. From the square, Via Urbana leads to the church of **Santa Pudenziana ❹**, built over a house where St Peter allegedly stayed. Dating from the 4th century, its apse is decorated with one of the earliest known Christian mosaics.

The Oppian Hill

The **Colle Oppio ❺**, site of Nero's legendary Golden House (*see page 89*), is now an ill-kempt park strewn with rubbish and stray cats, but there are some lovely views of the Colosseum from up here. Cutting through this area is the busy Via Merulana. On the right of it, the 19th-century **Palazzo Brancaccio ❻** houses the Museo Nazionale d'Arte Orientale (tel: 06-4874415; daily 8.30am– 2pm except 1st and 3rd Mon of month; until 7.30pm on Tues, Thur and Sun; admission charge). In the gardens are remains of Nero's water cistern, the Sette Sale, built for his private house and used to feed Trajan's Baths.

Further along Via Merulana is the **Auditorio di Mecenate ❼** (visits must be booked in advance on tel: 06-67103819; admission charge), dating from 30 BC and believed to be the *nymphaeum* of Maecenas' villa. Inside are the remains of frescoes depicting garden scenes, birds and small figures.

Follow Viale del Monte Oppio downhill to the 8th-century **San Martino ai Monti ❽** (ask the sacristan for the key), a damp, dark church dotted with mosaic remnants and classical statuary.

Esquilino

At the northern end of Piazza della Repubblica are the remains of the **Terme di Diocleziano ❾** (Baths of Diocletian; tel: 06-39967700; Tues– Sun 9am–7.45pm; admission fee), one of the four sites of the Museo Nazionale Romano. Early in the 4th century, these baths – then the largest and most beautiful of the city's 900 bath houses – were a buzzing centre of social activity. They fell into ruin after the aqueduct that fed them was destroyed by invading Goths. In the 16th century, the church of **Santa Maria degli Angeli** was built inside the *tepidarium* (warm bathroom) to a design by Michelangelo. The interior exploits the massive vaulting of the ancient building. Highlights include a painting by Domenichino of the Martyrdom of St Sebastian and an elaborate sundial on the nave floor.

The splendid **Aula Ottagona** (Octagonal Hall; Tues–Sat 9am– 2pm, Sun 9am–1pm; free) round the corner is an integral part of the immense structure of the baths and now houses sculptures from the museum collection.

Map on page 162

Detail of the beautifully delicate wall frescoes from the Villa di Livia, displayed in the Palazzo Massimo alle Terme.

BELOW: a stone vessel outside the Baths of Diocletian.

Map
on page
162

Dionysius – a fresco detail in the Palazzo Massimo alle Terme.

BELOW: the sleek interior of the Stazione Termini.

On Piazza dei Cinquecento, the imposing **Palazzo Massimo alle Terme ⑩** (tel: 06-48020; Tues– Sun 9am–7.45pm, last entry 7pm; admission fee), the main site of the Museo Nazionale Romano's museum quartet, houses the most important part of its vast collection of Roman antiquities. There's a stunning array of statues on the ground floor from the Republican Age (2nd–1st century BC) to the late-Imperial Age (4th-century AD), but best of all are the splendid floor mosaics and wall paintings from the houses of wealthy Romans, seen at their best in the delicate frescoes from Villa di Livia, the house of Augustus's wife that once stood on the Via Flaminia. The frescoes decorated the dining room and depict a garden paradise.

Central Station

On the other side of extensive Piazza dei Cinquecento is one of the few successful pieces of post-war architecture, the graceful ticket hall of **Stazione Termini** designed by Angiolo Mazzoni. Its undulating roof echoes the remains of the Servian

Walls which are visible through long glass windows. Uncovered during the building of the first station in 1867, they are believed to date from the reign of Tullius Servius (6th century BC). The revamped station now offers a vast selection of services including a shopping centre, an art gallery, a gym, restaurants, a post office, a church and a medical centre.

Towards Porta Maggiore

Directly south of the station is **Piazza Vittorio Emanuele II ⑪**, built in the late 19th century to accommodate government ministries. Until recently the square hosted a huge food market that has moved to Via Ricasoli (Mon– Sat 7am–3pm). Several blocks east is the church of **Santa Bibiana ⑫**, one of Bernini's first architectural projects. Heading south towards Porta Maggiore, you pass the remains of the 4th-century **Tempio di Minerva Medica ⑬**.

Porta Maggiore is a wonderfully preserved 1st-century gate, which also served as an aqueduct. You can still see the channels that carried the water. In 1917, a 1st-century underground basilica was discovered here (tel: 06-6990110 or ask at a tourist information point to arrange a visit).

South of Porta Maggiore, along Via Eleniana, is the splendid white façade of **Santa Croce in Gerusalemme ⑭**, established in AD 320 by St Helena, Emperor Constantine's mother, to house fragments of the True Cross that she acquired on a visit to the Holy Land. Next door, the **Museo Nazionale degli Strumenti Musicali** (Tues–Sun 8.30am– 7.30pm, www.museostrumentimusicali.it; admission charge) has some 3,000 pieces documenting musical history from antiquity to the 19th century. Surrounding the church and the museum are the remains of the 3rd-century **Anfiteatro Castrense**. The section along Via Castrense is particularly well preserved. ❏

RESTAURANTS & BARS

Restaurants

Africa
26 Via Gaeta, Termini. Tel. 06 4941077. Open: L & D Tues–Sun. €
Stewed dishes from Ethiopia and Eritrea which you scoop up with flat bread. Some vegetarian options.

Agata e Romeo
45 Via Carlo Alberto. Tel: 06-4466115. Open: L & D Mon–Fri; closed Sat–Sun. €€€€
Despite their weekend closing and the fact that the kitchen shuts down at 10.30pm, this is still one of the city's best dining experiences. Highly creative dishes (for example, Irish cod served in four different ways and trench-seasoned cheese soufflé with pear sauce). Huge wine selection from their renowned cellar. Booking essential.

Alle Carrette
14 Vicolo delle Carrette. Tel: 06-6792770. Open: D only daily. €
Tucked away in a little side street, close to the Forum is what many consider the best pizzeria in the area. There's a beer tavern feel to it and some outdoor seating.

F.I.S.H.
16 Via dei Serpenti. Tel: 06-47824962, www.f-i-s-h.it Open: L & D Tues–Sun. €€€
A trendy fusion and sushi restaurant done up in hi-tech style. The menu is fish-based only and divided into four sections – Mediterranean, Oriental, oceanic and sushi/sashimi. The results are mostly very good. Limited dessert options. At the lower end of this price scale.

Hang Zhou
33c Via San Martino ai Monti. Tel: 06-4872732. Open: L & D daily. €
One of the better of the many Chinese restaurants, Hang Zhou offers a fixed menu or à la carte. Particularly good are the steam-cooked vegetable ravioli and the chicken with ginseng. The fried ice cream is a nice closing touch.

Hasekura
27 Via dei Serpenti. Tel: 06-483648. Open: L & D Mon–Sat. €€€
A small, streamlined interior makes a classic Japanese setting for sushi, sashimi and tempura. At lunchtime you can choose from one of many degustazione menus priced from €15–€35.

Hosteria degli Artisti
6 Via G. Sommeiller. Tel: 06-7018148. Open: L & D Mon–Sat, L only Sun. €€
In an anonymous part of town where there are few shops or restaurants you will find this heavily decorated trattoria, a temple to the cuisine of Campania. Run by a husband and wife team who have given it their own unique slant. Flavours of anchovy, mozzarella di bufala and fish and seafood dominate an enjoyable experience. Neapolitan music on Friday and Saturday nights.

Il Guru
4 Via Cimarra. Tel: 06-48904656. Open: D only daily. €€
To satisfy your need for something not pizza or pasta-based go to Guru, one of the most welcoming Indian restaurants in town. Choose various dishes from the classic tandoori or curry options or one of three fixed menus – vegetarian, fish, meat.

La Piazzetta
23a Vicolo del Buon Consiglio. Tel: 06-6991640. Open: L & D Mon–Sat. €€
A popular and cosy restaurant which gets packed as it is small. Fish and large portions of perfectly cooked pasta are polished off with enthusiasm, and the in-house sweets are excellent. Some seating in the medieval lane outside in summer.

Trattoria Monti
13a Via San Vito. Tel: 06-4466573. Open: L & D Tues–Sat, L only Sun. €€
The owners are from the Marches region and the menu reflects this: home-made vegetable lasagne, chicken or rabbit in potacchio (with tomato, onion, garlic and rosemary), roast turkey with balsamic vinegar. There is fish on Friday and the menu changes almost daily in this long and narrow elegant trattoria.

Bars & Cafés

Il Palazzo del Freddo di Giovanni Fassi (65–7 Via Principe Eugenio) is a Roman institution. Its huge, kitsch interior is filled with local people at all times of the day and night (it's open till midnight) queuing to get their hands on some of the tastiest ice creams in the city. Their speciality is gelato al riso (rice ice cream). Sublime! For a decidedly more contemporary experience, which is worlds away from the multi-cultural area in which it stands, try the first-floor chill-out bar of the luxury **es hotel** (171 Via Filippo Turati). Here you can sip a cocktail as you lounge on leather sofas and look out onto the streamlined spectacle of Termini Station below.

PRICE CATEGORIES

Price includes dinner and a half bottle of house wine:
€ = under €25
€€ = €25–€40
€€€ = €40–€60
€€€€ = more than €60

THE APPIAN WAY

Via Appia, named after Appius Claudius Caecus under whose magistracy the road opened in 312 BC, was an important part of Christian Rome and is, therefore, home to many interesting sites

Map on page 168

BELOW: Porta San Sebastiano, the best-preserved ancient gateway in the Aurelian Wall.

I n classical times, Via Appia began at the Circus Maximus, just south of the Colosseum, and passed the Baths of Caracalla on its way to the city gate of Porta Appia (now Porta San Sebastiano) in the Aurelian Walls. Today, only the section of the road outside the ancient Porta Appia is known as Via Appia. The stretch between the Circus Maximus and the Porta San Sebastiano is called Via di Porta San Sebastiano and passes through the **Parco degli Scipioni** ❶. At No. 9 is the **Sepolcro degli Scipioni** (closed for restoration work), the mausoleum of the powerful Scipio family. The first family member entombed here was L. Cornelius Scipio, a consul in 298 BC. By the middle of the 2nd century BC, the square tomb was full and an annexe was dug adjacent to it. Nearby is the 1st-century AD Columbarium of **Pomponio Hylas** (also closed to visitors), which stored the cremated remains of those too poor to build their own tombs. Rich Romans often had *columbaria* built for their freemen, but this was probably a commercial venture in which people bought a slot, much as they book graveyard plots today. To go inside, make an appointment at the Museo delle Mura *(see below)*.

Porta San Sebastiano

Porta San Sebastiano is the entrance to the **Museo delle Mura** ❷ (tel: 06-70475284; Tues–Sun 9am–2pm; last entry at 1.30pm; admission charge), where there's a detailed account of the building of the Aurelian Walls, once almost 20 km (12 miles) long with 381 towers. In AD 403, their height was doubled – to 12 metres (40 ft). They were then 3.5 metres (12 ft) thick and had 18 gates.

Older buildings, such as the Pyramid of Cestius, the Porta Maggiore,

the Praetorian barracks, the aqueducts, the Castrense amphitheatre and Hadrian's Mausoleum, were incorporated into the walls. A walk along the top gives an idea of the view the imperial legionaries had as they watched for barbarian armies. Today, however, there are concrete blocks in every direction, except towards Via Appia, where the Campagna is almost in its original state.

When Via Appia was extended outside the city walls to Capua by Appius Claudius Caecus in 312 BC, it followed an existing route to the Alban Hills and was the major campaign path for the conquest of southern Italy. In 190 BC it was extended via Benevento to Brindisi, connecting Rome with the eastern Mediterranean. When the Empire fell, the road decayed and was not used again until the time of Pius VI.

A small minibus, the Archeobus, leaves daily from Piazza Venezia (opposite the church of San Marco) and goes the length of the Appian Way with the option of getting on and off (daily 9am–7pm; 10am-5pm in winter). Alternatively, on Sunday when traffic is restricted, bikes can be hired at 42 Via Appia Antica.

Via Appia Antica

Beyond the gate is Via Appia Antica (Old Appian Way). The first part, with the main monuments and sights, is not an entirely pleasant walk due to unrelenting traffic. Half a mile down, on the left, is the church of **Domine Quo Vadis** ❸ ("Lord, where are you going?"), where the Apostle Peter, after escaping from a Roman prison, is said to have met Jesus. Jesus replied to Peter's question "To let myself be crucified a second time." Jesus is said to have left his footprints on the road and you can see them, preserved, inside the church.

To the left of the church is the little **Via della Caffarella**, which leads into the valley across Via Latina. Bear right at Domine Quo Vadis and head along Via Ardeatina, on which the mausoleum and memorial of the **Fosse Ardeatine** ❹ are located. Here, 335 Italians were murdered on 24 March 1944, in revenge for a partisan attack in which 32 Nazi sol-

The church of Domine Quo Vadis, built on the spot where St Peter is said to have met Jesus.

BELOW: the Tomb of Cecilia Metella.

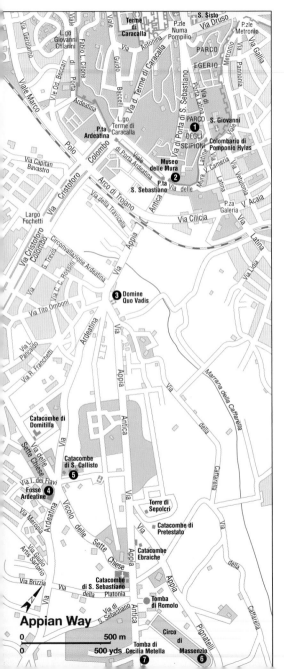

Appian Way

0   500 m

0   500 yds

diers were killed. The victims had nothing to do with the attack, but were rounded up, shot and buried in a mass grave. After the war, their bodies were retrieved and reburied in sarcophagi in the mausoleum, each tomb bearing the name, age and occupation of the occupant. On the way back to Via Appia are the **Catacombe di San Callisto** ❺ *(see page 171)*. In the **Cripta dei Papi** (Crypt of the Popes), inscriptions of at least 10 bishops of Rome from the 3rd and 4th centuries have been discovered. Among them is the first documented use of the title "Pope" for the Bishop of Rome (dating from 298).

Also open to the public are the **Catacombe di San Sebastiano** *(see page 171)*, the first of the underground burial sites to be so called due to its proximity to a cave (from the Greek *kata*, near, and *kymbas*, cave); and the **Catacombe di Domitilla** *(see page 171)*, among the largest catacombs in Rome. Contrary to popular belief, the catacombs were not used for worship, nor for hiding in during times of Christian persecution; the excavated rooms were used for simple funeral ceremonies. They were built outside the city because the law forbade burials within city limits, and they tended to be in the grounds of wealthy Christians or their sympathisers.

Among the rows of shelves for the dead, you can see a lot of little "tombs", used for the tragically high number of infant deaths, and some particularly large or imposing ones, usually belonging to martyrs who were reburied in Roman churches in the Middle Ages. Further along Via Appia, at No. 119A, are the Jewish catacombs of Vigna Randanini. They are not usually open to the public, but permission can be sought from the Comunitá Ebraica in Rome.

Also worth seeing are the **Circo di Massenzio** ❻ (Circus of Maxentius; tel: 06-7801324; Apr–Sept Tues–Sun

9am–7pm, Sun 9am–1.30pm; Oct–Mar Tues–Sun 9am–5pm; admission charge) and the **Mausoleo di Romolo** (Mausoleum of Romulus, son of Emperor Maxentius; opening times as above), from 309. The Circus was used for chariot races and could seat 10,000 spectators. Maxentius's imperial palace, **Villa di Massenzio**, is nearby (opening times as above).

The **Tomb of Cecilia Metella** ❼ (tel: 06-7802465; Tues–Sun 9am–7.15pm; until 5pm in winter, last entry 1 hr before closing; admission charge) was built for the daughter of Quintus Metellus Creticus, conqueror of Crete. She was later the wife of Crassus, son of the famous member of the Triumvirate of Caesar's time. During the 14th century the tomb was used as a fortress by the Caetani family, relatives of the Pope, who used to boost the family coffers by extracting tolls from passers-by.

Beyond this, Via Appia is far more walkable, sparse and quiet with overgrown ruins, private gated villas, shady trees and, in some parts, the original Roman flagstones. The roadside has the remains of many Republican tombs, built by the great families of Rome because of the ban on burials within the city. Some still have their original inscriptions and portraits of the dead in marble relief.

Beyond the crossing with Via Erode Attico, the ancient remains in the middle of farmland to the left are those of the 2nd-century AD **Villa dei Quintilli** (access at 1092 Via Appia Nuova; Tues–Sun 9am–7.15pm, until 4.30pm in summer, last entry 1 hr before closing). If you look closely, you can see a *nymphaneum*, the arches of aqueducts and other buildings. Finally, where Via Appia joins the road that leads back to Via Appia Nuova, there is the domed **Casale Rotondo**, a late 1st-century BC tomb, with fragments of relief stuck to its sides and a farmhouse and garden built on top. ❑

RESTAURANTS

L'Archeologia
139 Via Appia Antica. Tel: 06-7880494, www.larcheologica.it. Open: L & D Wed–Mon.
€€–€€€
Set in a 16th-century house with a beautiful outdoor area and ancient Roman ruins on view. Fresh fish is on offer every day and the excellent wine cellar is located in an old catacomb.

Cecilia Metella
125–9 Via Appia Antica. Tel: 06-5136743. Open: L & D Tues–Sun. €€€
Just across from the catacombs of San Sebastiano this could easily have been a tourist trap but luckily it isn't. The ingredients and the cooking are good, and the plant-covered terrace is delightful.

● ● ● ● ● ● ● ● ● ● ● ● ● ● ● ● ● ●
Price includes dinner and a half bottle of house wine .
€ under €25 , €€ €25–40,
€€€ €40–60, €€€€ €60+

The entrance to the catacombs of St Calixtus.

BELOW: children pay a visit to the Catacombs of St Calixtus.

RELICS OF THE CATACOMBS

"A desert of decay, sombre and desolate; and with a history in every stone that strews the ground" (Charles Dickens)

The catacombs are the place for spiritual pilgrimage, pleasurable terror, or romantic musings on mortality. For health reasons and habit, the Romans buried their

dead outside the city walls; the Appian Way is lined with the tombs of Romans, Christians and Jews – and, for the less wealthy, catacombs, whose labyrinthine galleries contain niches *(loculi)* built into the tufa rock on different levels.

While Christian and Jewish practice was burial of the body, Romans believed in cremation, with the ashes buried in an urn. Christian bodies, embalmed or shrouded in linen, were placed on ledges in the walls, sealed beneath marble slabs on the floor or interred in family vaults *(cubicula)*.

The Christianisation of Rome led to the cult of the early martyrs with pilgrimages and renewed interest in the catacombs. The relics of St Peter and St Paul may have been hidden here during the 3rd century. The frescoed interiors are adorned with Christian symbols or graffiti, from a dove, fish or anchor to acanthus leaves and vines.

While some are mossy and mouldering, the weather-worn tombs make an impressive proclamation of faith. It was not Roman practice to desecrate the tombs of any sect but in the course of time some have suffered from relic-mongers. Today, Via Appia is an inspired or desolate scene, depending on one's mood.

RIGHT: the Last Supper fresco in the cubiculum of the sacraments in the catacombs of San Callisto. Callisto was born a slave and became Pope before dying as a Christian martyr in 222. These catacombs were only rediscovered in 1850.

ABOVE: this chamber, called the Hypogeum, is part of an underground tomb or *ipogeo*. These were often frescoed, depicting pagan scenes such as funerary feasts or blood sacrifice. Although Charles Dickens found it "so sad, so quiet, so sullen", Henrik Ibsen enjoyed lying among the tombs – "and I do not think this idling can be called a waste of time". **ABOVE RIGHT:** this fresco, a particularly delicate tomb decoration, is in the catacombs dedicated to the Roman soldier who became a Christian martyr. **RIGHT:** many Jews converted to Christianity, but those who kept their faith were buried separately in the Jewish Catacombs. **FAR RIGHT:** Underground Rome has more to offer than catacombs. This 1st-century Temple of Mithras, dedicated to a polytheistic Persian cult, lies below San Clemente. In a relief, Mithras is depicted slaying a bull, the symbol of fertility.

SUBTERRANEAN SCENE

Three of the largest Roman underground burial sites are to be found in the vicinity of the Appian Way:

Catacombe di San Callisto (110 Via Appia Antica; tel: 06-51301580; Mar–Jan Thur–Tues 8.30am–noon, 2.30–5.30pm, until 5pm in winter; admission charge). Rome's first official Christian cemetery encloses the crypts of many early popes and saints.

Catacombe di San Sebastiano (132 Via Appia Antica; tel: 06-7850350; Mon–Sat 8.30am–noon, 2.30–5.30pm, until 5pm in winter; admission charge). Three exquisitely preserved mausoleums and miles of subterranean galleries unfold over four levels.

Catacombe Domitilla (282 Via delle Sette Chiese; tel: 06-5110342; Feb–Dec Wed–Mon 8.30am–noon, 2.30–5pm; admission charge). One of the earliest images of Christ as the Good Shepherd features among its sublime frescoes.

Leaflets identifying the area's many tombs are available from any tourist information booth.

The following are in the northeast of Rome:

Catacombe Priscilla (430 Via Salaria; tel: 06-86206272; Feb–Dec Tues–Sun 8.30am–noon, 2.30–5pm; admission charge). In the third and fourth centuries, these catacombs found favour among the fashionable upper classes as the resting place of choice. They have retained their dignified stucco decoration.

Catacombe di Sant' Agnese (349, Via Nomentana; tel: 06-8610840; closed holidays in the morning; Mon 9am–noon, Tues–Sun 9am–noon, 4–6pm; admission charge).

FURTHER AFIELD

Even outside the city centre, Rome offers plenty of
ancient Roman sites, bombastic urban planning,
striking architecture, huge parks and some
really memorable museums

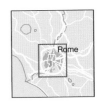

I f you have time to spare after visiting the many sights in the city
centre, you will find the outlying
areas have a lot to offer.

Mussolini's legacy

When we think of Roman architecture, we think mainly of Ancient
Rome and the Renaissance, but
Mussolini's Fascist regime in the
1920s and 1930s has left its imprint
as well. Whole areas of the city are
dominated by massive, obtrusive
buildings with white, rectangular
columns and plain, reddish-brown
façades, decorated with statues of
naked athletes and grim-faced
women holding ears of corn or
bunches of grapes. This style even
continued after the war, when Mussolini's regime had collapsed.

Some of the most impressive
examples are Stazione Centrale di
Termini, the Città Universitaria in the
San Lorenzo district, and the former
air ministry. Another is the building
to the south of the Circus Maximus,
now occupied by the Food and Agriculture Organization of the United
Nations, but originally intended as
the administrative centre of the
African empire of which Mussolini
dreamed. And then there is the
church of Santi Pietro e Paolo, to the
south of the Aurelian Walls, with a
dome resembling a spiked helmet.

However, the most prominent examples of Fascist architecture can be
seen in the area of southern Rome
known as EUR (pronounced *ay-oor*),
and at the Foro Italico across the
Tiber *(see page 177)*.

Some of these projects involved
large-scale demolition; for example,
a huge swathe was cut through the
Fora to build Via dei Fori Imperiali
as a route for military parades. And
the construction of Via della Conciliazione, at the entrance to the
Vatican, built as a symbol of recon-

Map on page 184

LEFT: the Palazzo della
Civiltà del Lavoro.
BELOW:
a modern Olympian at
the Foro Italico.

ciliation between the Holy See and the Italian State, involved demolishing the Spina, a row of suburban houses several hundred metres long. Partly as a signal of the city's expansionist intentions, however, EUR was built on the outskirts of the city, in a largely undeveloped area.

EUR

The rather clumsy acronym **EUR** stands for the Esposizione Universale di Roma (Universal Exhibition of Rome), which was to have been held in 1942 to mark the 20th anniversary of Mussolini's accession, but because of the war it never took place. The slightly hilly site, then over 3 km (2 miles) outside the built-up area of Rome, was intended to form an impressive entrance to a new town extending all the way to Ostia. But by the time the Fascist regime was over, only two palaces on either side of Via Cristoforo Colombo had been built. A start had been made on Palazzo della Civiltà del Lavoro (Palace of the Civilisation of Labour), which soon became popularly known as the "square Colosseum". Today, with its six storeys and plain arcaded windows, it has become a symbol of EUR.

After the war, the city continued the work begun by the architect Marcello Piacentini, and began building housing in the empty fields between the Aurelian Walls and EUR. Today, only a small dip on either side of Via Cristoforo Colombo remains undeveloped.

The idea of a town in the countryside, with a new interpretation of the use of space, is mingled in Piacentini's plans, with a monumental grandeur and a repetitive motif: square pillars, square ground plans and square roofs. The buildings radiate a cold beauty that is all the more striking because, in the city's centre, nothing is rarer than a straight line. The streets are named to honour the ideals of the time: agriculture *(agricoltura),* industry *(industria),* humanism *(umanesimo),* technology *(tecnica)* and arts *(arte).* Where plans were completed before the war stopped work, there are statues and mosaics glorifying workers, soldiers and miners.

TIP

EUR has two excellent *gelaterie* (ice-cream parlours): the traditional Giolitti (Casina dei Tre Laghi, 90 Viale Oceania) and Chalet del Lago, next to the lake.

BELOW: Mussolini's macho statuary at EUR.

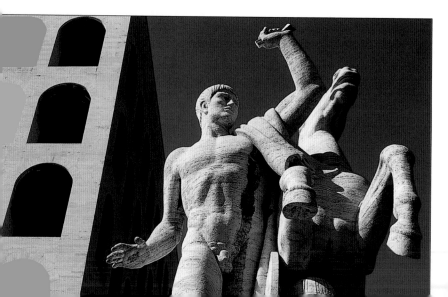

EUR was one of the main focal points of the 1960 Olympic Games and the multi-purpose Palazzo dello Sport (also known as Palalottomatica, since its expensive renovation and facelift, courtesy of lottery giant Lottomatica) was built at the top of the second hill to the south. The sports hall holds up to 20,000 people, and is used for major concerts, sports events and for party and trades union conferences. A water tower with a viewing platform and restaurant was built to the west, giving a unique view of Rome. In the depression between the two main hills, a three-section artificial lake was built, surrounded by beautiful greenery, with huge fountains that are only occasionally switched on.

By the time these buildings were erected, Mussolini-style architecture was passé, giving way first to glass façades and reinforced concrete, and then to post-modernism. The result is a largely unplanned mish-mash of styles. Via Cristoforo Colombo, which runs straight through the centre, is lined with government buildings and a large conference centre, **Palazzo dei Congressi**; this is bureaucracy writ large. It was originally intended that the whole of the government district should be located here, but the main ministries wanted to remain in the centre of the city. A new, futuristic conference centre, the Centro Congressi Italia, is to be built to a design by Massimilano Fuksas in a vast area between Via Cristoforo Colombo and Viale Shakespeare, though financial problems have been plaguing the project and construction remains on hold for now.

It is not all modern. There is a reminder of Ancient Rome in the form of the **Abbazia delle Tre Fontane**, the 8th-century abbey on the northeast slope of the EUR hill, reached by a path from the sports ground on Via delle Tre Fontane. This is where St Paul was reputedly beheaded: his head is said to have bounced three times and each time a spring welled up from the ground. As a result, three churches were built.

Culture in the EUR

Museums are EUR's main attraction. The **Museo Nazionale Preistorico-Etnografico Luigi Pigorini** (tel: 06-549521; Tues–Sun 9am–8pm; admission charge) on Piazza Guglielmo Marconi houses a large number of prehistoric artefacts from Africa, Asia, Australia and America. Next to it is the **Museo Nazionale delle Arti e Tradizioni Popolari** (tel: 06-5926148; by appointment only; admission charge), a lively portrayal of Rome's social history, including puppets, costumes, historic tools, votive objects and even an original Venetian gondola.

Opposite is the **Museo dell'Alto Medioevo** (tel: 06-54228199; Tues–Sun 9am–8pm; admission charge), where valuable medieval collections reflect a time when occupied Rome had little political significance, but achieved a high standard of prosperity and produced high-quality arts and

Map on page 184

TIP

The Cistercian monks who now live in the Abbazia delle Tre Fontane distil a powerful spirit from eucalyptus, and sell it in a small shop open daily (closed at lunchtime).

BELOW: classical athletes in mosaic.

crafts. The most interesting of the museums is the **Museo della Civiltà Romana** (tel: 06-5926041; Tues–Sun 9am– 2pm; admission charge), behind the grand colonnade, which chronicles every aspect of life in Ancient Rome. The exhibits include entire temple frontages; the spiral reliefs from Trajan's Column, originally more than 150 metres (500 ft) long and now broken into pieces; Diocletian's famous emergency prices edict, a means of dealing with rampant inflation in the 3rd century; and a 20 x 20 metre (65 x 65 ft) model of Rome at the time of Constantine. This can be viewed from the surrounding balustrade and gives an impression of the size of the city at the time. The vast, high-ceilinged building also houses the **Planetarium** (Tues–Fri 9am–2pm, Sat–Sun 9am– 7pm; shows every 1½ hrs from 9.30am; tel: 06-82077304 for info and bookings, morning only; admission charge) featuring a starry vault where spectacular light, sound and image shows about astronomy take place. There's also an astronomy museum, and a library. Visitors first pass through a series of rooms representing the earth, the moon and solar system, the planets, and extra-planetary space. The planetarium's exit is reached through a dark, constricted corridor representing a black hole.

Wealthy suburbs

If you start from EUR and go along Via Cristoforo Colombo away from the city centre, passing the junctions with Viale dell'Oceano Atlantico and Viale dell'Oceano Pacifico, you come to an odd stretch of road, 25 km (15 miles) long. There are few buildings along it, but this six-lane highway looks like a cross between a major city street and a long-distance *autostrada*. Street lights have been placed in fields for no apparent reason and the road ends by a swimming pool on the beach at Ostia.

The reason for the road's existence is that a whole town was originally intended to be built between EUR and Ostia. It never happened, and the residential areas that grew up to the southwest in the 1970s and 1980s wisely stayed well away from the road. The result is an expensive dis-

BELOW:
Roma's team colours are worn with pride.

Sport: a National Obsession

Sport, particularly football, plays an important part in the lives of the Italian people. When there's a football match in progress, Romans of all ages have radios pressed to their ears, eager to hear the latest result. If the home team wins, the peace of the afternoon will be broken by honking car horns and a great deal of shouting.

If you like football, going to an Italian match is an experience that should not be missed, for several reasons: the quality of play, the excitable crowds and the electric atmosphere. Rome has two teams: Roma and Lazio, who play at the Stadio Olimpico on alternate Sunday afternoons. Seats can be difficult to come by; the best places to buy tickets are shops by the Lazio Point on 34 Via Farini (near Termini) or the AS Roma Store at 360 Piazza della Colonna.

Aside from football, Rome hosts major events on the men's and women's international tennis circuits. Both events are known as the Italian Open and they take place at the Foro Italico during May. You will never see another tennis event like it – unlike Wimbledon, it's not a case of polite clapping at appropriate moments – the crowd clap and jeer to their heart's content.

trict in which white-collar workers live in atrium apartments and bungalows surrounded by tall hedges and walls, their tranquillity disturbed only by the occasional roar of a jet engine from Fiumicino Airport to the north.

Flaminia

To see the other major example of Fascist-era architecture, you need to go to the city's northern suburbs. Northern Rome is connected to the city by the Via Flaminia, which begins at Piazza del Popolo and continues in a straight line. The first sight you'll see is the **Foro Italico** ❷ sports complex, designed in the late 1920s by prominent architect, Enrico del Debbio. As you cross the Ponte Milvio, you will see a square obelisk bearing the words "Mussolini Dux". Most of the buildings are rectangular with reddish-brown façades and white columns but some, such as the great swimming-pool, have softer, rounded edges, and there are more informal areas such as the tennis courts and lawns.

This district was formerly dominated by the **Stadio dei Marmi**, built by Mussolini's architects in the style of a Greek stadium and surrounded by 60 marble figures of athletes in heroic poses. Today, it is dwarfed by the **Stadio Olimpico**, the huge football and athletics stadium immediately behind it, designed by Pier Luigi Nervi, with capacity for 80,000 spectators. This is where the opening ceremony of the 1960 Olympics took place and when the World Cup was held here in 1990, the stadium was extended into the Monte Mario behind it; the stands have since been roofed over. It now hosts football matches most Sundays during the winter and is the venue for much passion and excitement, and also, unfortunately, violence, when there is a derby, when the two home teams, AS Roma and SS Lazio, play each other. The youth hostel near the stadium was once part of the Olympic Village.

The foreign ministry, the Farnesina, stands on an empty patch east of the stadium, with Viale Macchia di Farnesina running behind it. A little further up Via Flaminia is what promises to be the city's most

Map on page 184

BELOW: a cyclist at the Stadio dei Marmi.

The hill of Monte Antenne got its name from Ante Amnes, meaning "before two rivers" – the Tiber and the Aniene.

BELOW: a decorated facade in the Quartiere Coppedè.

exciting cultural area. Since 2002 Rome has acquired a much-needed, state-of-the-art auditorium designed by Genoese architect Renzo Piano, the **Auditorium-Parco della Musica** (Viale Pietro de Coubertin 30; tel: 06-80241281, www.auditorium.com) set in open parkland. With a 7,600 seat capacity spread over three concert halls, including a large outdoor amphitheatre, and covering an area of 55,000 sq metres/65,780 sq yards, it is the largest complex of its kind in Europe. It even incorporates a ruined Roman villa within its boundaries. Just across Via Flaminia, west of the auditorium is the **Museo Nazionale delle Arti del XXI Secolo**, or MAXXI (6 Via G. Reni; tel: 06-3202438, www.maxximuseo.org; Tues–Sun 11am–7pm; admission charge), a centre for contemporary arts that will open mid-2006. The site is currently being transformed under a project by architect Zaha Hadid. Part of the state collection of contemporary art and architecture will be transferred here, and the site will also host temporary shows. Exhibitions can already be seen at an adjacent pavilion.

Northeast of the city

To the northeast, **Via Salaria** crosses the suburbs and leads out to the Sabine Hills. This old Roman road is named after the salt *(sale)* which was transported into Rome from these hills. Just before the Salaria Bridge (1874) is the hill of Monte Antenne, where the Sabine settlement of the Antemnae is said to have stood and from here, the Romans, under Romulus, are supposed to have kidnapped the Sabine women. Via Salaria was an important street and, in the early years of Christianity, many churches and catacombs were built here.

At No. 430 is the entrance to the **Catacombe di Priscilla ❸** (tel: 06-86206272; Feb–Dec Tues–Sun 8.30am–noon, 2.30–5pm; admission charge), begun in the 1st century in the gardens of Priscilla Acilii's estate and greatly extended in the 4th century. Some popes were buried here, which is why there are good-quality frescoes and stucco decorations. The catacombs extend under the park of Villa Ada, now the Egyptian Embassy but formerly Vittorio Emanuele II's hunting lodge. It is surrounded by a beautiful park which is open to the public.

On the other side of the Villa Ada is the chic residential area of Parioli, where the main attraction is Rome's first mosque. Built in 1992, it serves a Muslim population of 100,000.

To the east of Via Salaria, either side of Via Po, is the fashionable area known as **Quartiere Coppedè** after the Florentine architect who designed many buildings here. Of particular interest is Piazza Mincio, a square with an unusual fountain of frogs that Gabriele d'Annunzio described as "a genuine disgrace to Rome". Coppedè, whose buildings were the last notable architecture of pre-Fascist Rome, intended this square to show a harmony between the individual details of each house

and the great tradition of Florentine craftsmanship.

At the beginning of Via Salaria, close to the bustling **Piazza Fiume**, in the former Peroni brewery, is the **Museo di Arte Contemporanea di Roma** (MACRO; 54 Via Reggio Emilia; tel: 06-671070400, www. macro.roma.museum; Tues–Sun 9am–7pm; admission charge). The site is being expanded and connected with glass walkways to other buildings behind it. The bigger venue will be ready in 2007 but the current one shows much of the city's collection of modern and contemporary art, as well as hosting temporary art shows.

Via Nomentana

Further east, on Via Nomentana, is **Villa Torlonia ❹**, the last great villa built in Rome. The Torlonia family contracted French architect Valadier to design the villa, which had a small lake, guest house, sports field and Temple of Saturn. It later became one of Mussolini's private residences. Now, the buildings are in a state of neglect, but the gardens are still open to the public. Beneath the villa, the Jewish Catacombs, two cemeteries dating from the 3rd and 4th centuries, extend for about 9 km (6 miles), but they are in bad repair and closed to the public. Make sure you visit the **Casina delle Civette** (Owl House), in the park at 70 Via Nomentana. It was built in 1840 and restored in the 1920s in the Art Nouveau style with stained-glass windows featuring idyllic scenes of flora and fauna.

Continuing down Via Nomentana, you come to the church of **Sant'Agnese fuori le Mura** at No. 349, built over a complex of catacombs (tel: 06-8610840; Mon 9am–noon, Tues–Sun 9am–noon, 4–6pm; admission charge) next to the circular mausoleum built for Constantine's daughters, Costanza and Helen. The interior vaulting of

the mausoleum is decorated with exquisite 4th-century mosaics depicting scenes of the *vendemmia* (grape harvest). In the apses of the chapels are 7th-century mosaics representing biblical scenes.

The neighbouring church, built over the catacombs where St Agnes was buried, dates from the 4th century, although it was rebuilt in the 7th century and has been restored several times since. The relics of St Agnes, martyred in AD 304, are housed in the high altar. Every 21 January, the saint's day, two lambs are blessed and shorn to make woollen robes for the Pope.

Eastern suburbs

To the east of the city centre, on the other side of the railway tracks beyond the ancient Porta Tiburtina, the **San Lorenzo** quarter, known as the student area of Rome, is actually very close to the centre but feels like a separate town. The streets, named after the Italic and Etruscan tribes, are full of bars, cheap *trattorie* and pizzerias. San Lorenzo has also recently aquired interesting gourmet

A fountain in the garden of the Villa Torlonia, the last great villa built in Rome.

BELOW: the Good Shepherd mosaic in the Catacombe di Priscilla.

TIP

To visit Meier's Tor Tre Teste church, take No. 14 tram from Via Giovanni Amendola, close to the railway station, get off at the Togliatti/Gelsi stop and take bus No. 556 which will drop you off at the church – the Tovaglieri/Ermoli stop (9 stops in all). The journey should take just under an hour and requires one public transport ticket.

BELOW: designer chic and urban expression in San Lorenzo.

restaurants and original artisans' boutiques. The Città Universitaria, on Viale dell'Università, was constructed in the 1930s in typical Fascist style: big, white and imposing.

The area takes its name from the ancient basilica of **San Lorenzo fuori le Mura ❺** (St Lawrence outside the Walls), one of Rome's first Christian places of worship, made up of two churches joined together. The raised apse is the nave of the Constantinian basilica erected in 330 (rebuilt in the 6th century with beautiful Corinthian columns); the 5th-century basilica next door creates the present nave. The two were joined together in the 8th century. The interior is decorated with early mosaics and some beautiful Cosmatesque work. To the right is the entrance to the pretty cloister and underneath lies a labyrinth of catacombs. There has been much restoration since severe World War II bombing.

Rome's isolated eastern suburb of **Tor Tre Teste** has a church designed by Richard Meier which was inaugurated in 2003 (pictured on page 53). The **Chiesa di Dio Padre Miseri-cordioso** on Via Francesco Tovaglieri stands somewhat incongruously but majestically in the centre of a triangular site with a public park on one side and several scattered 10-storey apartment blocks on the others. Its three striking white shells of graduated height curve up and over the main body of the church. The endless white of the walls, a Meier trademark, creates a sensation of space and light. enhanced and amplified by the dizzying array of skylights and the walls of glass in the front and back.

West of the city centre

Southwest of Trastevere and behind the Gianicolo hill lies the green and well-heeled **Monteverde Vecchio** residential area, built in the late 19th and early 20th centuries, and one of the most desirable places in Rome to live. Here also is the vast **Villa Pamphili ❻** park, the largest in Rome, with undulating terrain, fields, picturesque walkways, pine forests, fountains, lakes and gardens, as well as an ice rink and pony hire. Underneath it are the **catacombs of San Pancrazio** (Mon–Fri

10am–noon, 4–6pm; admission charge) attached to the basilica of San Pancrazio, on the site of St Pancras' tomb. Not far to the east is another park, far smaller but beautifully designed – the Villa Sciarra.

South of the centre

This area is filled with late 19th- and early 20th-century blocks of workers' housing. The **Via Ostiense** area is a lively and at times alternative area for nightlife. The former Mercati Generali (Food Market) is being transformed into shops, boutiques, cafés and galleries. A large FNAC (music and books megastore) is set to open here in late 2004 and a science museum will be built on the land around the *gazometro*, the natural gas silo that has become the area's trademark and featured in many films shot in Rome.

In a former electricity power plant, a 10-minute walk from the Piramide di Caio Cestio, what began as a temporary solution to the overcrowding of the Capitoline museums has become a delightful landmark museum, the **Centrale Montemar-**tini (Via Ostiense 106; tel: 06-5748042; Tues–Sun 9.30am–7pm; admission charge). Four hundred pieces of Roman sculpture are on permanent display and the juxtaposition of statues with gleaming machinery, tubes and furnaces, make this a highly unusual venue, well worth a detour.

Between Via Guglielmo Marconi and the Tiber stands **San Paolo fuori le Mura 7** (186 Via Ostiense; daily 7am–7pm) one of Rome's four patriarchal basilicas and its second-largest church (if you are coming by Metro get out at San Paolo Station). The church was built on the site of St Paul's tomb by Constantine the Great in the 4th century, and was later extended by Theodosius. In 1823, it was almost completely destroyed by a fire (apart from the apse), but was faithfully restored. The entrance portico was added by Calderini in 1892, the façade is by Vespignani and the gold mosaics by Agricola. Inside, there are 80 monolithic granite columns, and the arches are covered in mosaics. There is also a beautiful, early 13th-century monastery courtyard. ❏

Map on page 184

RESTAURANTS

Al Ceppo
2 Via Panama, Parioli. Tel: 06-8419696. Open: L & D Tues–Sun. €€–€€€
A class act with impeccable and imaginative food, a vast wine list and home-made sweets, sorbets and ice creams.

Arancia Blu
55–65 Via dei Latini, San Lorenzo. Tel: 06-4454105. Open: D only Mon–Sat, L & D Sun. €€
An upmarket vegetarian restaurant which offers consistently tasty food.

Formula Uno
13 Via degli Equi, San Lorenzo. Tel. 06-4453866. Open D only Mon–Sat. €
Genuine buffalo mozzarella on the pizzas and the fried *baccalà* (salt cod) is excellent.

Uno e Bino
58 Via degli Equi San Lorenzo. Tel. 06-4460702. Open: D only Tues–Sun. €€€
A welcoming but discreet location offering an outstanding and affordable gourmet experience.

Tram Tram
44 Via dei Reti , San Lorenzo. Tel: 06-490416. Open: L & D Tues–Sun. €€
A small, cosy *trattoria*. Pugliese specialities such as *linguine* with squid and *porcini*.

La Pergola del Cavalieri Hilton
101 Via A. Cadlolo, Monte Mario. Tel: 06-35092152; Open: D only Tues–Sat. €€€€
German superstar chef Heinz Beck has made this a place worth making a detour for. Enviable views, attentive staff and ultra-refined food.

Da Franco ar Vicoletto
1–2 Via dei Falisci, San Lorenzo. Tel: 06-4957675. Open: L & D Tues–Sun. €
A real neighbourhood *trattoria* with no frills, just lots of good and fishy food. Pick the set-price menu and the waiters will bring out dish after dish of seafood served with pasta or salad, or simply grilled, roasted or fried.

● ● ● ● ● ● ● ● ● ● ● ●
Price includes dinner and a half bottle of house wine
€€€€ *€ 60 plus*, **€€€** *€ 40–60*, **€€** *€ 25–40*, **€** *under € 25*

Further Afield

0 | 10 km

0 | 10 miles

EXCURSIONS FROM ROME

The countryside around Rome offers such a variety of
landscapes that it is worth a holiday in itself

I t is surprising that so few of the more than 12 million tourists who pour into Rome every year find their way into the provinces, the "hinterland romano" – to the Etruscan graves near Cerveteri; the lakes of Bracciano, Albano, Nemi; the remains of the pre-Roman shrine in Palestrina; the fountains of the Villa d'Este; or the Byzantine Greek Orthodox abbey in Grottaferrata. And there's more to Frascati than a light white wine: a former summer residence for Roman nobility, this region offers glorious scenery and, for the energetic, long country walks.

The fertile, hilly area immediately south of Rome is known as the Campagna. Now thronged with billboards featuring Asterix and Obelix, it was here that Rome fought to establish supremacy over Latium. After the defeat of Veio (396 BC), the Agro Romano was, at last, Roman. Soon, the small farms were displaced by *latifundia* (large agricultural estates), which used cheap slave labour to work the fields. Shortly before the fall of the Empire, the Campagna blossomed once more, because everyone who had a chance fled the city. Most of the ruins turned up by farmers' ploughs today date from this time. After the Empire's collapse, the Campagna decayed into a malaria-ridden marsh.

The "Bonifica" of the Campagna was one of the first actions undertaken by the new Italian government before the turn of the century. Earlier appeals to the popes to have the Campagna drained and cultivated had failed. At first, only a stretch of some 10 km (6 miles) around the city was drained – this area has long since been built upon. The rest of the area, which was drained after World War I, is where Mussolini built his *borgate* (satellite towns).

Despite these inroads made by the city, the Campagna still feeds most Romans. Dairy farming, market gardening, strawberries, wine, carnation growing and arable farming flourish. In spring, the fields are bursting with the bright yellow of rape-seed in flower; in autumn, whole groves of olive trees blossom. ❏

PRECEDING PAGES: archaeological site of Ostia Antica.

OSTIA ANTICA

The wonderful ruins of the Roman town of Ostia, surrounded by Roman pines and flat coastal plains, make a great excursion from the dusty hustle and bustle of Rome

Rome
Ostia Antica

Maps on
pages
184/187

BELOW LEFT: walls and columns still stand at an Ostia Antica bath complex.
RIGHT: a lively mosaic at the Baths of Hercules.

King Ancus Marcius, according to legend, founded a port town in the 7th century BC and named it **Ostia 8** (tel: 06-5635 8099; Apr–Oct Tues–Sun 9am–7.30pm; Nov–Mar 9am–5pm; last entry 90 minutes before closing; admission charge) after the *ostium* or mouth of the Tiber. However, the archaeological evidence dates only to the second half of the 4th century BC, when fortifications were built around the town. Rome was very dependent on this one connection with the sea, because all its essential commodities – especially grain – were transported from Ostia along the **Via Ostiensis**.

Rome's dependence on Ostia was good news for the port's inhabitants. Imported goods from both the West and East, which Rome devoured, were traded here, and the population consequently enjoyed a luxurious standard of living. The town even had special status, with the male inhabitants being freed from military service. There was also money

to be made from holidaymakers. On hot summer days, when the stone streets of Rome practically blazed, Romans fled to the seaside resort.

However, when Emperor Augustus moved the Roman naval base to Misenium, Ostia felt the loss of the free-spending sailors and all the associated trade. For a while, it remained the unloading point for the grain ships and, in AD 41–54, Claudius had new docks built, but the beginning of the end of Ostia was already evident – the harbour was silting up. Not even a new harbour basin – now the airport of Fiumicino – that was dug on the orders of Trajan (AD 98–117) could stop this process. The coastline gradually moved west and today Ostia is several kilometres from the sea.

Mass exodus

At the height of Ostia's prosperity in the early 2nd century, its population was around 500,000, but its decline was steady and relentless. Emperor Constantine's decision to move the capital of the Empire to Constantinople in the 3rd century, continual pirate attacks and, in the early Middle Ages, the threat of Saracen invasions, meant that Ostia's population was forced to leave their homes. Soon, the only inhabitants left were malarial mosquitoes.

At that time, the coastline was about 4 km (2 miles) further inland than it is today. Luckily for archaeologists, the city has never been repopulated and it has been very well preserved under a bed of sand. Although the ruins were quarried for building materials in the Middle Ages, about two-thirds of the Roman town can now be seen, thanks to extensive archaeological excavation. Since the 19th century, this archaeological treasure house has been systematically laid bare. The better finds are on display in Rome's museums.

Today, many Romans still flee the heat of the city to spend the day at the beach of **Lido di Ostia**. The wealthy, however, have moved a bit further south, to **San Felice Circeo** and **Terracina**.

At the entrance to Ostia, visitors follow the **Decumanus Maximus**, the same main road used by the Ancient Romans, which leads through the city centre. Worthwhile noting en route are the **Terme di Nettuno** (Baths of Neptune), named after their glorious mosaic floor, and the **Teatro** (theatre), which warrants a visit for the splendid views offered by its upper tiers. Underneath these tiers, there would have been taverns and shops. Beside the theatre, three large masks have been mounted on tufa – originally, they were part of the theatre's decoration. In summer months, the theatre is used to stage plays and concerts.

Also well worth looking at are the stalls in the **Piazzale delle Corpo-**

Intricate geometric mosaic in Ostia Antica.

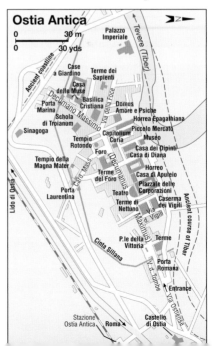

Maps on
pages
184/187

TIP

Next to Fiumicino Airport is the Museo delle Navi (tel: 06-6529192, closed for restoration until 2006, call ahead to check status), containing four ancient Roman vessels in an archaeological park. You can see the remains of Claudius's artificial harbour which, like Ostia, soon silted up.

BELOW: a young visitor at the Piazzale delle Corporazioni.

razioni (Square of the Guilds), where lovely floor mosaics preserve the insignias of the various guilds – most of which were associated with fitting and supplying the ships.

The Decumanus Maximus leads to the **Forum**, where citizens met to gossip and justice was dispensed by city officials, and the **Capitolium Curia**, Ostia's largest temple, which was dedicated to Jupiter, Juno and Minerva. Beyond is the **Schola di Traianum** (School of Trajan), formerly the headquarters of a guild of merchants, and the **Basilica Cristiana** (Christian Basilica).

The workers of Ostia lived in **insulae**, blocks of flats three or four storeys high. The **Casa di Diana** (House of Diana), near the Forum, is one of the smarter ones and is well preserved. It had a balcony on the second floor, its own private bath house and a central courtyard where there was a cistern to collect water. An interesting insight into the sort of housing used by ancient Romans, it also incorporates a tavern on the ground floor, complete with a marble counter on which customers

were served their sausages and hot wine (sweetened with honey), as well as ovens, storage facilities, and a beer garden for outdoor drinking.

A few miles away, the tombs on **Isola Sacra** (Sacred Island) give a good impression of ancient burial customs in the 2nd to 4th century AD. The dead of Ostia were buried in layered tombs, which can be seen outside the city, but within the fence of the excavated zone.

Medieval Ostia

Before heading either to Rome or to the beaches of Ostia, you shouldn't miss the opportunity to visit the medieval town of Ostia.

Developed around the ruins of Gregoriopolis, a fortified citadel built on the orders of Pope Gregory IV between 827 and 844, Ostia was a medieval village within defensive walls; its inhabitants worked in the nearby salt pans. After it had been destroyed by invading forces in 1408, Martin V built a defensive tower against the barbarians and Saracens. This tower became the centre of a castle built by Pontelli later in the same century for the future Pope Julius II, then a cardinal. However, the attacks continued and, together with the silting-up of the river and a huge flood in the 16th century, drove the inhabitants away.

You can visit the **Castello di Giulio II** (16 Piazzale della Rocca; tel: 06-56358099; Tues–Sun 9am–1.30pm, also 2.30–4.30pm Tues and Thur; admission free) as the castle is now known. It has some interesting features, such as scarped curtain walls, which were innovative at the time, but became commonplace in the 16th century. You can also see the fortress's museum; its church, Santa Aurea; and the Palazzo Episcopale, official residence of the Bishop of Ostia. The latter houses some notable frescoes by Peruzzi. ❑

Beaches

Lido di Ostia, just half an hour by train from Piramide metro station (get off at the Cristoforo Colombo stop for the marina proper), and the surrounding beaches are the most popular and locals start descending on them at weekends in their hundreds of thousands from late May or early June. This cannot be attributed to the cleanliness of the water or the charm of modern Ostia, but to its convenience as the nearest seaside resort to Rome and the fact that it is packed with *stabilimenti* – amenities, and a rather chaotic nightlife.

It is worth bearing in mind that Italian beaches are organised around *stabilimenti balneari*, bathing establishments, which increasingly offer far more than clean toilets, deckchairs, sunloungers and umbrellas for hire. Since many holidaymakers spend their whole day there, the complexes have increased their services and many now offer sporting equipment for hire, host children's activities, put on courses for adults and children, and have cafés which may include full-blown restaurants.

If Lido di Ostia sounds too hectic, head some 10 km (6 miles) south of Ostia to the sand dunes of Capocotta. A once-infamous nudist beach (a small, respectable and predominantly gay section, known as Il Buco, remains, just beyond the gates, going towards Torvaianica), it has totally cleaned up its act and is now run by a Rome city council-backed consortium which offers the perks of a *stabilimento* for free. Located behind several gates, which close at about 7.30pm, this stretch of coastline is clean, well-kept and of some natural beauty, since it is located next to the Italian president's hunting reserve, Castel Porziano, and within the protected Parco del Litorale Romano. Take the Roma–Lido di Ostia train from Piramide metro station but get off at the Cristoforo Colombo railway station, the last stop. Here you can hire a bike and pedal down the coast, or wait for the "Mare 2" shuttle bus which leaves every 10 minutes.

Further south, Anzio and Nettuno are two nostalgic port towns whose hotels, restaurants, seafront cafés and boutiques cater to a more demanding clientele, and also to aficionados of sailing and yachting. For a heady mix of antiquity and sunbathing, head to the beach at Villa di Nerone, to which you can walk or cycle with ease from the centre of Anzio, and which is located under the town's lighthouse. Here you can sunbathe in full view of the beautiful remains of Nero's palace and find shade inside the Grotte di Nerone, Roman warehouses that hark back to the town's ancient port days. Trains to Anzio and Nettuno leave regularly from Roma Termini.

The Riserva Naturale di Tor Caldara (Thur, Sat and Sun), about 6 km (4 miles) north of Anzio, is a beautiful 43-hectare (106-acre) nature reserve and, sadly, all what is left of the ancient Nettuno forest. The yellowish colour of the earth testifies to the sulphur-rich deposits in the ground and in the water. Tor Caldara can be reached by walking from the Villa Claudia railway station (two stops before Anzio).

For the first really clean water and large sandy beaches south of Rome you will have to go a bit further, to Sabaudia (direct buses leave from the EUR Fermi metro stop). ❏

RIGHT: awaiting the weekend crowds.

TIVOLI

Travel through vineyards and past sulphurous springs to reach Tivoli, a small town pressed against a hillside that has three famous villas and was home to Roman emperors, Borgias and Habsburgs

Tivoli is one of many towns set in the hills outside Rome that has long served as a getaway for Romans – both ancient and modern – in the hot summer months. Three famous villas (which are UNESCO World Heritage Sites) make Tivoli a popular attraction and a worthwhile day trip. To reach Tivoli: you can either drive or take a bus (journey time approximately 45 minutes) from the Ponte Mammolo station of Metro line B.

Villa d'Este

The primary attraction is **Villa d'Este ❾** (tel: 0774-312070; Tues–Sun 8.30am–1 hour before sunset; call in advance for exact times; admission charge), which is justly famous for its wonderful fountains and waterworks. Originally a Benedictine convent, the building was converted into the Governor's Palace in the 13th century. In 1550, Cardinal Ippolito d'Este, son of Lucrezia Borgia and grandson of Pope Alexander VI, was elected governor. He then began to renovate the villa and its gardens into something befitting his aspirations to the papacy. He never became Pope, but he did leave a memorial to himself in the fountains, which have delighted visitors for centuries and served to inspire waterworks all over Europe. After the decline of the Este family, the Habsburgs inherited the villa, but they were poor caretakers. After World War I, the Italian State took it over and restored it.

A walk through the terraced gardens, beautifully laid out by Ligorio and Giacomo della Porta, is a delight. The **Viale delle Cento Fontane** (Avenue of a Hundred Fountains) has a row of close-set pipes that spray water into the air. Set in the middle of the road is the **Fontana dei Draghi**, made in hon-

Map on page 184

LEFT: a fresco in the Villa d'Este.
BELOW: fountain in the Villa's gardens.

our of Pope Gregory XIII, who was once a guest here and whose emblem included a dragon.

Located at the end of the Viale, on the right-hand side, is the **Fontana dell'Ovato**, decorated with eight nymphs. The **Fontana dell'Organo Idraulico** (Fountain of the Hydraulic Organ) no longer plays music, as it once did, but it isn't hard to imagine how lovely it might have sounded.

Tivoli's watery attractions don't all flow in the Villa d'Este. The town is full of ancient remains of temples and other buildings – some (such as the Temple of Vesta) are extremely well preserved, while others have been incorporated into medieval churches. Not far from the Temple of Vesta is what will become the new entrance to **Villa Gregoriana**, a dramatic and steep wooded park set in a rocky gorge and created in 1835 at the request of Pope Gregory XVI. It is due to reopen in mid-2005 after lengthy restoration work. Here, the River Aniene plunges into the famous **Grande Cascata**, over 100 metres (300 ft) high. Steep paths will lead

down to the villa's galleries, terraces and belvederes, from which visitors will be able to admire the waterfall and the nearby grottoes, both natural and artificial. About 15 km (10 miles) further on, you reach the area where the spring for the **Acqua Vergine** rises. It feeds the aqueduct restored by the popes that leads into the Fontana di Trevi in Rome. Carry on past the **Bagni di Tivoli**, sulphurous medicinal springs that have been popular since Roman times.

Hadrian's Villa

Even more impressive than the Villa d'Este are the ruins of **Villa Adriana** ❿ (Hadrian's Villa; tel: 0774-530203; daily 9am–1 hour before sunset; call in advance for exact times; admission charge), the most magnificent country villa of imperial times. Even today, after centuries of despoilment and decay, it exudes an atmosphere of wealth and leisure.

When the Roman Empire flourished, **Tivoli** (ancient Tibur), in the foothills of the Sabine Hills, was a favoured retreat for poets and wealthy citizens. Among the guests

Roman columns at Tivoli, where there are many well-preserved remains.

BELOW: there are numerous lovely cascades in the Villa d'Este's gardens.

Map on page 184

at the splendid villas were Horace, Catullus, Maecenas, Sallust and Emperor Trajan. In AD 117, Emperor Hadrian started to build a luxurious refuge for himself at the foot of the hill on which Tivoli stands. His plan was to rebuild the monuments that had most impressed him on his travels, particularly in Greece and Egypt. He demanded more than mere copies of the originals: he wanted to create aesthetically pleasing edifices that would contrast dramatically with functionalism and practical common sense. A notable feature of the villa was Hadrian's idea, a new concept at the time, of scattering the individual buildings over the 60 hectares (148 acres) of the park, rather than grouping them in a central complex. To protect against the weather, all the buildings were connected by covered walkways and underground passages (cryptoportici).

Beautiful imitations

The beautifully painted colonnade, Stoa Poikile, which Hadrian had seen in Athens – and is here called the **Pecile** – is one of the most noteworthy buildings. The mighty surrounding wall, 230-metres (760-ft) long, has survived on the north side, as has a basin in the centre. On the inner side stood a covered, pillared entrance. Excavations, first carried out to obtain marble, have turned up more than 300 statues since the 15th century; they are now on display in museums all over the world.

Well worth closer inspection is the **Teatro Marittimo** (Maritime Theatre), a circular construction surrounded by a moat, and reached by two wooden swing bridges. Passing the olive grove, you see the **Ninfeo** (nymphaeum), a flat area between two walls that was originally thought to be a stadium. The **Terme** (baths), consisting of the Small

Baths and the Great Baths, show the high architectural standards that were employed.

Next to the baths is the most ambitious of Hadrian's replicas, the **Canopo** (Canopus), a copy of the famous Temple of Serapis near Alexandria in Egypt; the 15-km (10-mile) canal, lined with luxury residences and statues, led from the River Nile to the Temple. Hadrian tried to imitate the scenario by creating a 119-metre (390-ft) long canal, by the side of which stood marble architraves and copies of Egyptian statues. The southern bank was originally occupied by a copy of the Serapis shrine, but all that remains is a large niche in the rock and a big chunk of rock lying in the water basin.

Hadrian's eclectic collection of statuary has helped archaeologists restore the originals. For example, Phidias's *Amazon*, now in the villa's museum, is a copy of the original from Ephesus's Temple of Diana.

Hadrian didn't enjoy his collection for long – he died only four years after it was completed. ❑

Caryatids in the park of Hadrian's Villa.

BELOW: the Teatro Marittimo at Hadrian's Villa.

CASTELLI ROMANI

This group of small towns to the southeast of Rome has been known since the Middle Ages as the Castelli Romani and it has always been a popular retreat for the city's inhabitants

For a leisurely country drive through towns and villages famous for their food and wine, you could do no better than hire a car and tour the Castelli Romani. Alternatively, take a bus from the Anagnina Metro stop on Line A, or a train from Termini Station (journey time 30–50 minutes).

Thirteen towns in the Alban Hills are known collectively as the "Castelli Romani" (Roman Castles). The name stems from the fact that they grew up around the feudal castles of Roman patrician families who sought refuge here when anarchy ruled in Rome. During World War II, some towns in the Castelli were badly damaged by Allied bombing. Frascati, seat of the German High Command and Queen of the Castelli Romani, suffered particularly heavy bombardment.

Frascati

Frascati ⓫ has long been an attractive place to visit. Poet and critic Arthur Symons, who came here in 1903, wrote: "Frascati, as one turns in and out of its streets, opening on vague glimpses, as if cut by the sides of a frame, is like a seaside village; and one cannot help imagining the wash of waves; instead of the grassy plain of the Campagna, at the end of those coiling streets."

One of the best times to visit is in October, when the grape harvest begins; a *frasca di lauro*, a laurel twig, is displayed; the smoke of the first wood fires mixes with the sweet scents from the vineyards; and a fat, fresh *porchetta* (whole-roast pig stuffed with aromatic herbs, for which the region is justly known) lies on the counter of every *alimentari* (local grocery).

Frascati, which takes its name from the thatch (*frasche*) used to roof its huts, became a town in 1197,

Map on page 184

LEFT: the Greek Orthodox abbey in Grottaferrata.
BELOW: Frascati makes a lovely setting for a wedding.

TIP

A secret lies hidden in the vineyards south of Frascati. In Via Enrico Fermi, Bruno Touschek, a young Jewish physicist exiled from Austria, invented the first electron accelerator. This broke new ground and paved the way for other research establishments, such as CERN in Geneva and DESY in Hamburg, in the discovery of quarks, the basic building blocks of matter.

BELOW:
the remains of one of Castelli's old castles.

when the ancient city of Tusculum was destroyed and its population settled here. Later, it became the favourite resort of the affluent.

The town's trademark is its wine – a light, quaffable wine with a faint, refreshing prickle – which is a product of the rich volcanic soil. In Italy, Frascati is drunk mostly by the *Frascatani* themselves. Much of the stuff on sale in supermarkets bears little relation to the drink served in *cantinas* (wine shops or bars), which ranges from pale to dark yellow. Much of the exported wine comes from neighbouring towns and villages rather than Frascati itself, but the reason it is so poor is that most is based on the rather bland Trebbiano grape; only the better producers – Fontana Candida and Colli di Catone (especially Colle Gaio) – use Malvasia.

Begin with a walk around town, starting at **Piazza San Pietro**. From here, go through the little *galleria* (walkway) to **Piazza del Mercato**, where you can get a good sandwich bursting with *porchetta*. Go left past the market and you will find several

wine shops and bars in **Via Regina Margherita** that allow customers to bring *cibo proprio* (their own food).

Frascati is not only famous for its wine, but also for its many palaces and their gardens. Next to the bus station, is the park of **Villa Torlonia**, originally part of a 16th-century estate that was bombed to the ground in World War II. Now only the gardens remain and the striking Teatro delle Acque (Theatre of the Waters) fountain designed by Carlo Maderno. Above the town rises the **Villa Aldobrandini**, built in 1602 for Pietro Aldobrandini, a nephew of Clement VIII. The most beautiful feature, and the only area that may be visited (Mon–Fri 9am–1pm 3–5pm; permits are available from the tourist office on nearby Piazza Marconi; tel: 06-9420331; admission free), is the park. It contains a wonderful water display with Atlas balancing a "globe with a hundred thorns" on his head, and behind him a grove of oddly shaped oak trees.

Tusculum

The way to **Tusculum**, where Cicero wrote *Tusculanes,* lies uphill, along about 5 km (3 miles) of asphalt road. (There are no easily accessible footpaths, but you may still be able to find your way along the unmarked woodland paths.)

The ancient city of the Latins (founded, according to legend, by Telegonus, son of Circe and Ulysses) was a monarchy before it came into Rome's sphere of influence in the 6th century BC. Later, in 340 BC, the city participated in the revolt against the Romans. From the 10th to the 12th centuries, the Counts of Tusculum ruled over it – as well as Rome. In 1191, the Romans destroyed the town as an act of revenge for its subjugation, and its inhabitants fled to Frascati. The town has never been rebuilt, so all that remains are ruins.

Grottaferrata

It's only a few kilometres from Frascati to **Grottaferrata**, known for its Greek Orthodox **Abbazia di San Nilo**. The abbey was founded in 1004 by Nilus, a monk from Calabria fleeing north to find a site safe from attack by Saracens. Under Byzantine rule, southern Italy had a large Greek minority, whose descendants survive today in a few remote areas. The monks built the monastery on the remains of a sepulchre dating from Republican times. The abbey church, **Santa Maria di Grottaferrata**, has some beautiful frescoes by Domenichino in the Cappella dei Santi Fondatori. After visiting the abbey, you could try the brothers' own wine, which is on sale. On Sunday morning, Mass is celebrated according to the Greek Orthodox rite – it's worth making a special visit just for this because the chorales are unrivalled.

From here, you can see the cross atop the hill at **Rocca Priora ⓬**, the highest town in the Castelli at 768 metres (2,520 ft), which is often covered in snow in winter.

Rocca di Papa

The town of **Rocca di Papa** ("The Pope's Rock") lies a few miles away, steeply uphill, on the northern flank of the **Monte Cavo**, the highest peak of the Alban Hills (949 metres/3,114 ft). This attractive medieval town has a *quartiere bavarese*, named after the Bavarian mercenaries who were stationed here by Emperor Ludwig III in the 1320s. Rome is only a few miles away and yet the city, whose lights twinkle like glow worms below, couldn't seem more distant. The wine of Monte Cavo is excellent and a particularly delicious local speciality, the *sfogatelli* mushroom, is worth seeking out.

From Rocca di Papa, you may want to climb to the peak of **Monte Cavo**, following Via Sacra through the oak woods. The summit is a little disappointing because it is covered in hundreds of TV antennae. Although an alternative site is being looked into, for the moment these cover the remains of the ancient shrine of Jupiter, worshipped by the 47 federated Latin cities, and a more

Map on page 184

A coin from the time of Julius Caesar, discovered in the region.

BELOW: the Villa Aldobrandini is set in parkland.

recent monastery. Despite the antennae, the view is fantastic. In the distance, beyond Rome, are the **Tolfa Hills**, where the ancient Etruscans discovered iron ore, and the Etruscan plain around **Lago di Bracciano**. You can recognise Rome's charter airport, **Ciampino**, and St Peter's if it is clear, but in high summer the city is too smoggy to see anything. Further inland, looking northwards, you might just see **Terminillo**, a 2,200-metre (7,200-ft) mountain popular with winter skiers, only an hour's drive away.

Further east lies the massif of **Gran Sasso d'Italia**, another skiing spot. To the south and southwest, beyond Lago di Albano and Rocca di Papa, lie the former Pontine Marshes, where mozzarella cheese (traditionally made from buffalo milk) is produced.

Marino

On the site of the ancient fortified citadel of Castrimoenium lies **Marino ⓭**. In the main square, **Piazza Matteotti** (named after the Socialist leader murdered by Mus-

solini), stands the Fountain of the Moors, built in honour of the *condottiere* (mercenary admiral) of the papal fleet, Marcantonio Colonna, Prince of Marino, the victor of the sea battle of Lepanto in 1571. The **Madonna del Rosario** church is well worth a visit. Built in 1713, probably by Sardi, it is the most beautiful rococo church in Lazio. Dominican nuns, living in a closed community, are responsible for its excellent state of preservation.

Popes' summer residence

The Popes' summer residence at **Castel Gandolfo ⓮** is beautifully situated 400 metres/1,300 ft above the crater rim of Lago di Albano. This was the site of Alba Longa, the city founded by Aeneas. After a long struggle between Alba Longa and Rome, the latter won. Alba Longa was destroyed as a punishment for treachery, but the temples were spared. They are said to have occupied the exact spot of the papal villa.

The Holy See acquired Castel Gandolfo at the end of the 16th century, and in 1628 Pope Urban VIII

BELOW: guards at Castel Gandolfo, the Popes' summer residence.

commissioned Maderno to design a villa here. Completed by Bernini, the **Papal Palace** is linked by bridges and loggias to the other two pontifical villas, Villa Barberini and Villa Cybo. The gardens are closed to the public for security reasons. In summer, the Pope holds the Angelus prayer at midday on Sunday on the **Loggia della Benedizione**.

Stendhal, Goethe and Gregorovius all had a high opinion of Castel Gandolfo and modern Romans love it, too, particularly because it is so close to **Lago di Albano**. The clean water of this volcanic lake invites boating and swimming, but in the middle, where it is 170 metres (558 ft) deep, there are dangerous currents. There is a delightful footpath, 10 km (6 miles) long, around the lake. On Sunday, it is as crowded as the seaside.

To the southwest of the lake, the supposed tombs of the Horatian and Curatian families can be seen in **Albano Laziale** on the right-hand side of **Via Appia Nuova**, if you are travelling in the direction of **Aricia**. The local park has remains of the **Villa of Pompey**.

Genzano

Further along Via Appia Nuova, the foundation of a medieval castle also provided the starting point for the town of **Genzano**, on the southeastern edge of the little lake of Nemi. This town has been famous since the 16th century for its elm-lined roads and is also known for the *Infiorata* (Flower Festival) on the first Sunday after "Corpus Domini". The main street to the church of **Santa Maria della Cima** is decorated with magnificent holy pictures made with 5 tonnes of flower petals.

Nemi and Oasis di Ninfa

A 30-minute walk along the **Lago di Nemi** leads to the town of the same name. **Nemi ⓯** is famous for its *fragole di bosco* (wild strawberries). Set on a cliff, the little town takes its name from the goddess Diana, in whose honour Caligula built huge boats over 70-metres (230-yards) long. Discovered in the 1920s they were exhibited in the local museum until this was destroyed in World War II. One-fifth scale models are on display in the nearby **Museo delle Navi Romane** (tel: 06-9398040; daily 9am–7pm, until 5pm in winter; admission charge). Follow the path to the right, under the sleepy **Palazzo Cesarini**, to a small garden watched over by a statue of Diana. This is a pleasant place to rest, and the café sells excellent vanilla ices.

The beautiful **Oasi di Ninfa** (visits on 2 days a week Apr–Nov; information and tickets from the entrance lodge of Palazzo Caetani in Rome, 32 Via delle Botteghe Oscure, Mon–Fri), lie in the southeast of the Castelli Romani, about 60 km (38 miles) from Rome. One section of the gardens is dedicated to exotic species and there are the ruins of the medieval village of Ninfa, which was abandoned at the end of the 14th century. ❑

Map on page 184

Statue in the garden of Diana, in the grounds of the Palazzo Cesarini.

BELOW: Nemi, famous for its wild strawberries.

ETRUSCAN TOWNS

The Etruscans built a series of cities, founded leagues and painted frescoed tombs in northern Lazio more than 2,700 years ago. The remains of their cities make a trip through Etruria one of the most interesting archaeological excursions in Italy

Map on page 184

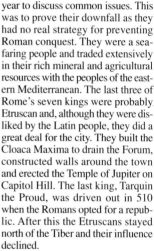

A mysterious and superstitious people whose presence in Italy can be traced to the 9th century BC, the Etruscans were known as Tirreni by the Greeks, and Tusci or Toscani by the Romans, but they called themselves Raseni. At the height of their power, in the 6th century BC, Etruscan influence spread from the Po Valley to Campania, even encompassing Ancient Rome. The Etruscans were never a united people, however, more a confederation of towns which came together once a

BELOW: one of the beautiful frescoes left behind by the Etruscans.

year to discuss common issues. This was to prove their downfall as they had no real strategy for preventing Roman conquest. They were a seafaring people and traded extensively in their rich mineral and agricultural resources with the peoples of the eastern Mediterranean. The last three of Rome's seven kings were probably Etruscan and, although they were disliked by the Latin people, they did a great deal for the city. They built the Cloaca Maxima to drain the Forum, constructed walls around the town and erected the Temple of Jupiter on Capitol Hill. The last king, Tarquin the Proud, was driven out in 510 when the Romans opted for a republic. After this the Etruscans stayed north of the Tiber and their influence declined.

There are many Etruscan settlements in Italy, including Sutri, Orvieto, Tuscania, Vulci and perhaps the most significant, Tarquinia, near Lake Bolsena. This chapter will highlight the most important ones. They can all can be reached by train from the Trastevere, Ostiense and Termini stations in Rome, or on a COTRAL bus from Lepanto metro station on Line A (ask at the tourist office for details). To see Etruscan objects, visit the museum at Villa Giulia in Rome *(see page 143)* or the Etruscan Museum in the Vatican *(see page 112)*.

Veio

The Etruscan city closest to Rome, once the largest in southern Etruria, is **Veio** ⓰. Unlike the other sites, where only tombs remain, the Archeological Area of Veio (Località Isola Farnese, Via Riserva Campetti; tel: 06-30890116; Tues–Sun 8am–2pm, until 4pm Thur and Sat; admission charge) includes parts of a swimming pool and the lower section of a temple. The striking Portonaccio sanctuary was located outside the city walls. Originally, it was decorated by a terracotta roof and culminated in a series of larger-than-life statues of various gods. A block of tufa stone and an underground gallery are the only ruins left from this construction. A statue of Apollo was found in the temple dedicated to Minerva.

Palestrina

Very little is known about the history of Praeneste, as **Palestrina** ⓱ used to be called. According to legend, it was founded by Telegonus, son of Ulysses. When Rome was in its infancy, Praeneste was already flourishing. The Romans conquered it in 338 BC, then, after civil wars in 82 BC, the Roman general Sulla, as a punitive measure, made it into a colony and settled army veterans in the region. It soon became something of a resort. Horace described it as "cool Praeneste".

Praeneste was famous, but feared, for its huge temple dedicated to the goddess **Fortuna Primigenia**, the mother of all gods. The six terraces of the mighty shrine still stand today. Adorned with statues and blazing with torches, the complex must have been an impressive sight, which could be seen from afar.

The statue of the goddess stood before the semi-circle that is now the entrance to the museum. The goddess Fortuna was worshipped in the upper part of the shrine so the Roman Barberin family built its palace neatly into the upper circle of the temple. The original palace was 11th-century, but much of the present incarnation is from the 1640s.

Palazzo Barberini now houses a museum, the **Museo Nazionale Archeologico Prenestino** (tel: 06-

BELOW: the shrine of Fortuna Primigenia, at Palestrina.

9538100; daily 9am–8pm; admission charge). Countless busts and other objects are on display, including the badly damaged remains of the statue of Fortuna. It is the top floor that contains one of the highlights of Palestrina: the **Nile Mosaic**. Dating from the 1st century BC, it probably decorated the floor of the buildings where the temple now stands. It shows, in detail, the Nile valley after the annual flood, a scene teeming with peasants, fishermen, priests, soldiers and animals.

In the lower part of the shrine, the walls of which now enclose the old town of Palestrina, lies the secretive heart of the complex. In the central **Piazza Regina Margherita** you will find the **Seminario**, which incorporates the remains of the sacred place, the *area sacra*. Most archaeologists agree that this was the entrance to the **Oracle** – one of the most important of ancient times. It was here that the citizen Numerus Sufficius is said to have unearthed the *sorti Preneste*, thin wooden sticks with oracular powers. To consult the oracle, you drew one of the wooden sticks from a box and the priests used it to predict your future.

The worship of the goddess declined with the arrival of Christianity and, with the prohibition of non-Christian worship in the 4th century, Fortuna closed her gates. In the early Middle Ages, the city was fought over by Goths, Longobards, Byzantines and papal families. The latter finally conquered the town at the beginning of the 14th century and destroyed it once again.

Apart from its goddess, Palestrina is linked with the composer Giovanni Perluigi da Palestrina, who was born here in 1525. As choirmaster of St Peter's, he was responsible for a fresh expressiveness in Catholic church music, in the spirit of the Counter-Reformation. The town also has a following among food lovers, who come in autumn to hunt the local speciality, *funghi porcini*, wild mushrooms that have been a delicacy since Roman times.

Cerveteri

Ancient remains, even older than those at Ostia, can be found near

BELOW: the Nile Mosaic in the Palazzo Barberini.

Map on page 184

Cerveteri ⓲, where an Etruscan settlement called Kysry was established in the foothills of the Tolfa range, about 45 km (28 miles) northwest of Rome and only 6 km (4 miles) from the sea. The oldest archaeological evidence dates back to the 9th century BC.

In the 7th and 6th centuries BC, Kysry became one of the most powerful cities in Etruria, with a population of around 25,000. The city boundary enclosed 150 hectares (370 acres) and was 6 km (4 miles) in circumference. Revenue came mostly from rich ore deposits in the Tolfa Hills, but also from trade with Greek cities and the Middle East.

Kysry was probably ruled by a king and, for a long time, maintained good relations with its Roman neighbours. Then, in 358 BC, it was conquered by Rome and became known as Caere. The town grew steadily poorer, but was not abandoned until the Middle Ages. The population then moved east to Ceri, renaming their abandoned town *Caere Vetus*, which developed into the modern name Cerveteri.

Nothing is left of the ancient city, but it is worth going to look at the excavation of the **Necropoli della Tomba Banditaccia** (tel: 06-9940001; summer Tues–Sun 8.30am–7pm; winter 8am–1 hour before sunset; admission charge), a necropolis on a hill where an archaeological park has been set up. Different types of tombs are laid out along a main road and side roads, like a city for the dead, all carved into the soft tufa rock.

From the simple body tombs, covered with a mound of earth, the tumulus tombs developed in the 7th century BC. On a round foundation, up to 30 metres (100 ft) in diameter, a hill was built, where rites for the dead were celebrated. Inside the tomb, one or more burial chambers were hewn out of the rock – copies of the wooden houses of the living with windows, doors and pillars.

Especially worth seeing are the 6th-century BC **Tomba dei Capitelli** and the **Tumulus II**, containing four graves belonging to one noble family, dating from the 5th century BC to the end of the 2nd century BC.

TIP

To reach Cerveteri from Rome, take the *regionale* (ie not an intercity or Eurostar) train to Pisa which stops at the town. Alternatively, a Cotral bus leaves from Lepanto station on Metro Line A.

BELOW: the 7th-century Tomba della Cornice, Cerveteri.

Cities for the Dead

One of the first things that a visitor to an Etruscan settlement will notice is that every village or city had another "city for the dead" built outside its walls – settlements that seem to show that life in the next world was just as important as life on earth – perhaps even more so, judging by the fact that dead were buried in a greater space than the living inhabited. The Etruscans had their own conception of life after death and believed not only in the everlasting soul but in the survival, in some shape or form, of the human body, so the tombs had to be suitably equipped for the person to carry on living in the next world in the way he or she had become accustomed to living on earth. Acccordingly, the dead were supplied with food and jewellery and surrounded with all the things that they had loved most when alive – even household furniture, such as beds and chairs were carved out of the rock, giving a detailed impression of Etruscan everyday life. The most stunning necropolis, the Necropoli della Tomba Banditaccia *(see above)* can be found at Cerveteri off the main Civitavecchia road.

TIP

Other important tombs in Cerveteri are the Tomba della Capanna, the Tomba dei Dolii, Tomba dei Letti e dei Sarcofagi, Tomba dei Vasi Greci, Tomba della Cornice and Tomba degli Scudi e delle Sedie.

BELOW: one of the tumulus tombs in Cerveteri.

In the 6th and 5th centuries BC, the so-called cubic graves became common. These rectangular buildings stand in regular rows of streets, reflecting the social changes that had taken place in the city. By then, prosperity had spread to the lower classes and a social levelling had taken place. Tumulus tombs were replaced by the rectangular ones; graves with many chambers gave way to graves with only one. This was partly to save space, but also a sign of a failing belief in an afterlife in which graves could be used as houses. Examples worth visiting can be found on **Via dei Monti della Tolfa** and **Via dei Monti Ceriti.**

From the 4th to the 1st century BC, the dead were buried in underground tombs called *hypogaea*. Most of these were fairly plain and contained many bodies. The richer you were, the larger your tomb. The largest is the **Tomba dei Rilievi,** belonging to the wealthy family of Matuna, which dates from the 4th century BC. It has space for 32 bodies and is decorated with coloured plaster reliefs depicting weapons,

tools, household implements, musical instruments and furnishings.

Housed in the 16th-century Castello Orsini, the **Museo Nazionale Cerite** (tel: 06-9941354; Tues–Sun 8.30am–7.30pm; admission charge) contains some of the items found in the graves, including domestic implements, vases and terracotta lamps. However, finds from Cerveteri are scattered as far afield as the British Museum, the Louvre in Paris, the Vatican's Museo Gregoriano and the Villa Giulia in Rome, which includes the famous sarcophagus of the married couple, the *Sarcofago degli Sposi.* Some of the graphic figures, fashioned by anonymous artists, are believed to have inspired great Italian masters, such as Leonardo and Michelangelo.

Tarquinia

The town of **Tarquinia** ⓲ always enjoyed a certain supremacy and prestige that the other Etruscan settlements did not have. By the 8th and 7th centuries BC Tarquinia was a rich and powerful city and became

an active commercial and industrial centre (metals, raw materials, bronze and ceramics). Its political supremacy extended over a vast area inland as far as the Cimini Mountains and Bolsena Lake. Most of the tombs found in the **Necropoli** (tel: 0766-856308; Tues–Sun 8.30am–7.30pm; until 4.30pm in winter; admission charge) 2 km (1 mile) east of the modern city were adorned with elaborate wall paintings depicting a variety of themes inspired by daily life, such as banquets, dancing and musicians, athletics or gladiatorial fights, funeral processions, and even erotic scenes.

At any given time no more than 15 of the 6,000 tombs are accessible, as they are opened in rotation in an effort to preserve the delicate paintings. The Tomba della Caccia e della Pesca (530–20 BC), which shows some lively fishing and hunting scenes, and the Tomba del Cacciatore (the Tomb of the Hunter, 530–10 BC) are among the oldest. The Tomba delle Leonesse (Tomb of the Lionesses) shows a pronounced Greek influence. One of the best-known is La Tomba dell'Orco (4th century BC), which depicts a banquet attended by the prominent Surinna family.

The atmospheric medieval town of Tarquinia, with its defensive towers, is home to the **Museo Nazionale Tarquinense** (Piazza Cavour; tel: 0766-856036; Tues–Sun 8.30am–7.30pm; admission charge), which houses one of the most important collections of Etruscan artefacts in Italy, most of which were discovered in the necropolis.

If you are travelling by car, return to Rome via **Lago di Bracciano**, famous for fishing and watersports. In **Bracciano**, the 15th-century Castello Orsini-Odescalchi is worth visiting. More idyllic, however, is the medieval village of **Anguillara** on the southern shores of the lake.

Viterbo

Viterbo is a city with roots that go back to Etruscan times. Crammed with medieval alleyways, porticoes and noble fountains it is a lovely place to visit, with historic buildings and the **Terme dei Papi** (the Baths of the Popes; tel: 0761-3501, www.terme deipapi.it; open daily), which passed to the papacy in the 11th century and became a favourite residence of the popes. The numerous sepulchral caves in the cliffs around, and the tombs that contain genuine Etruscan objects, are indisputable proof of the existence of an Etruscan town on this spot. The name of the ancient town seems, from Latin inscriptions, to have been Surrina or Sorrina. The **Museo Civico** (tel: 0761-348275; Tues–Sun 9am–7pm, until 6pm in winter; admission charge) in Piazza Crispi contains a collection of Etruscan finds such as sarcophagi with bas-reliefs, pottery urns and vases, and some bronze idols. The pottery is plain, either black or uncoloured, very different from the beautiful, ornate vases of the more luxurious cities of Vulci or Tarquinia. ❑

Map on page 184

TIP

The Necropoli and Museo Nazionale in Tarquinia can both be visited on a combined ticket.

BELOW: only the brave will step inside this curious Viterbo structure.

TRANSPORT

GETTING THERE AND GETTING AROUND

GETTING THERE

By Air

Scheduled flights land at the main airport, **Aeroporto Leonardo da Vinci** in Fiumicino (tel: 06-65951; www.adr.it), about 30 km (18 miles) southwest of Rome. The airport is served by most major national carriers, including Alitalia and British Airways. Charters come into **Ciampino airport** (tel: 06-65951; www.adr.it) about 15 km (9 miles) to the southeast of the city. Low-cost airlines easyJet and Ryanair are among many firms operating services to Ciampino *(for information on getting into the city from the airport, see page 207).*

By Train

Rome is well served by rail connections to the majority of major European cities, and the national railway, **Ferrovie dello Stato**, is efficient and relatively inexpensive. There are several categories: reservations are required for the Pendolino or Eurostar (if travelling via Paris), the fastest and most luxurious trains, and optional for the InterCity and EuroCity. You pay a supplement to use these lines, but they save time. Slower

regional trains *(diretto, espresso, regionale* or *interregionale)* stop at many stations.

You should book a seat if you plan to travel by rail to towns outside Rome. Do this at a travel agent *(agenzia di viaggio)* in the city, rather than at the station where the queues can be long. Or book by credit card online (www.trenitalia.com) or by phone (tel: 892021, no prefix; from landline phones only; 7am–9pm daily, press 2 to speak to an operator). You can pick up your tickets at machines at Termini station or on the train (ask for the "ticketless" option when booking). Both the website and phone service offer

AIRLINES

Alitalia
Tel: 06-2222 (Rome)
Tel: 0870-544 8259 (UK)
www.alitalia.com
British Airways
Tel: 199-712266 (Italy)
Tel: 0870-850 9850 (UK)
www.britishairways.com
easyJet
Tel: 848-887766 (Italy)
Tel: 0870-600 0000 (UK)
www.easyjet.com
Ryanair
Tel: 899-678910 (Italy)
Tel: 0871-246 0000 (UK)
www.ryanair.com

in-depth timetable information. If you're planning a lot of rail travel, it pays to look into various railpass offers at home and in Italy.

Train tickets are valid for two months after the date of issue and must be stamped on the day you travel at one of the station machines, or you will be fined. The only exception are Eurostar tickets which always have a booking time printed on them.

Stazione Termini is the main railway terminal, the meeting point of the two Metro lines and the main stop for many city buses. There is a tourist office opposite platform 4, and a hotel reservation booth opposite platform 20, as well as lost property, luggage deposit, cafés, restaurants and fast-food joints, a bookstore and a telephone office.

The official taxi rank is in front of the station. Do not be tempted by offers from unofficial cab drivers in the station interior.

By Coach

Most coaches arrive at the main terminus on Via Marsala next to Stazione Termini. If you are travelling on a COTRAL bus, the network which serves the Lazio region, you will arrive and depart from a Metro stop: Lepanto, Ponte Mammolo for the north or Anagnina and EUR Fermi for the south.

By Car

European (EU) driving licences are valid in Italy. Travellers from other countries normally require an international driving licence. Carry your licence, plus the vehicle registration and insurance (Green Card) documents with you when driving. If driving your own car, you may wish to take out extra insurance to cover home recovery in case of a breakdown.

Tolls are payable on motorways, including the A1. Pay in cash or with magnetic cards, available at service stations.

Motorists arriving in Rome from all directions will first hit the Gran Raccordo Anulare (GRA), the ring road. It is busy and can be alarming, but is usually the quickest way to reach one of the entry roads into the centre. During rush hour, however, there are frequently traffic jams.

The A1 Autostrada del Sole leads into the GRA from both north and south, as does the A24 from the east. If you arrive on the Via del Mare from the coast (Ostia), you can either switch on to the GRA or continue straight on into the centre.

When leaving the GRA, follow white signs for the road you want (blue ones usually lead away from the centre). The city centre sign is a white point in a black circle on a white background.

GETTING AROUND

From the Airport

From Fiumicino, there are frequent train services to the city – every 30 minutes to Trastevere Station and the Stazione Termini. Trains run from 6am to midnight with the last train from Fiumicino bound for Termini leaving at 11.37pm. It's a short taxi or bus ride to most hotels from Termini and a 15-minute tram ride or slightly longer taxi ride from Trastevere Station. At night there's a COTRAL bus that

SHUTTLE TO AIRPORT

Terravision (www.terravision.it) provides a shuttle service to and from 22 Via Marsala (beside Termini railway station and opposite the Royal Santina Hotel) to connect with Ryanair and easyJet flights. A return ticket costs €13.50 for Ciampino airport and €15 for Fiumicino airport and can be bought online or from the Arrivals Hall in Ciampino.

leaves from the international arrivals terminus every 75 minutes bound for the Termini and Tiburtina railway stations. A taxi from Fiumicino to the centre costs about €50, possibly more if it's late and you have lots of luggage.

From Ciampino, the best way to reach the centre is by taxi (about €45). Alternatively, COTRAL buses leave every half hour for Anagnina Metro station on Line A where you take the Metro to Stazione Termini. Allow at least an hour for the journey.

Orientation

It sometimes seems that all Roman roads lead to Piazza Venezia. This can produce traffic chaos, but from a visitor's point of view the square is a useful orientation point at the centre of ancient, medieval and modern Rome.

To the south of Piazza Venezia, the three roads, Via dei Fori Imperiali, Via di San Gregorio and Via delle Terme thread between the greatest monuments of Ancient Rome to the Terme di Caracalla. Northwards, Via del Corso runs through the commercial heart of modern Rome to Piazza del Popolo. To the west, Corso Vittorio Emanuele II leads through the heart of medieval Rome and across the Tiber (Tevere) to St Peter's and the Vatican. Eastwards Via Nazionale, Piazza della Repubblica and Piazza del Cinquecento lead to Stazione Termini.

An easy, and pleasant way to

get an overview of the city is to walk up the Gianicolo (Janiculum Hill) behind Trastevere.

Public Transport

Public transport is quite efficient and inexpensive, but overcrowded at peak hours. Single-use tickets costing €1 are available from bars, tobacconists and newspaper kiosks that display the ATAC (city bus company) emblem, and from vending machines in Metro stations and bus terminals. Once validated in the Metro turnstile or machine at the back of the bus, a ticket is good for bus or tram rides and/or one Metro ride for 75 minutes. Passengers caught without a ticket will be fined €51 (plus the price of the ticket) on the spot. The amount doubles if you cannot pay immediately.

Buses and trams

Bus and tram services run from 5.30am to midnight, with an all-night service on 22 bus lines, noted by the letter "N" after the number. Bus and tram stops are clearly marked and most list route numbers, the main destinations along each route and lines with night service. Board buses at either the front or rear doors and stamp your ticket immediately. Ring the bell to request the next stop and exit through the centre doors.

The 40 Express is the quickest way to get from the station to the city centre and then St Peter's. Along with the 64 (a slower version of the 40 Express with more stops), it is one of the city's most popular bus routes so watch out for pickpockets.

Five electric minibuses serve the narrow streets of the Centro Storico: the most useful are the 116 which passes through or alongside Campo de' Fiori, Piazza Farnese, Piazza Navona, the Pantheon and Piazza Barberini; the 119, which serves the area around Piazza del Popolo and Piazza di Spagna; and the 117,

BUS TOURS

ATAC's double decker open-top service (Bus No. 110) leaves every 15 minutes from Termini Station and tours the city's principal monuments. The service operates daily from 8.40am–8.25pm and the whole journey lasts about 2 hours. A special night-time version of the tour departs at 9pm in summer and 8pm in winter. Tickets can be bought at the terminus in Piazza dei Cinquecento (or on baord if you get on at one of the other 10 stops). Archeobus is a small eco-friendly minibus that serves the historic Appia Antica park. It departs every hour from Termini station between 9.45am and 4.45pm. The ticket is valid all day and the bus goes as far as the recently reopened Casa dei Quintili. Freephone for both buses: 800-281281. A combined two-day ticket for both bus tours is also available.

which goes from Piazza del Popolo to Basilica San Giovanni in Laterano. Bus 81 runs from the Colosseum to Piazza del Risorgimento near the Vatican Museum. If you are visiting the catacombs, take bus 118 from the Piramide Metro stop to the Via Appia. The No. 8 tram line links Largo Argentina in the centre to Trastevere and Monteverde in the west. From Piazza di Spagna to Stazione Termini, take Metro line A. For the Colosseum, do the same and change at Termini to line B.

For information on trams, buses or the Metro call freephone 800-431784, Mon–Sat 8am–8pm; or go to www.atac.roma.it.

COTRAL runs regional buses that connect Rome to the airports, the rest of the province and the Lazio region (freephone 800-150008 for information).

Metro

The Metro operates from 5.30am to 11.30pm and until 12.30am on Saturday night.

The city is served by two Metro lines (A and B), which intersect at Stazione Termini. There are only two lines because of the problems of circumnavigating the numerous unexcavated ruins underground. A third Metro line has been on the drawing board for years but remains very much at the conceptual stage.

Due to much-needed renovation works, Line A currently closes down at 9pm every day (and will do so until January 2008). Two shuttle services – the MA1 and MA2 – replace the metro above ground after 9pm, following roughly the same route.

Boats

Since April 2003 a public river boat service has operated along the Tiber. The service makes six stops between the Isola Tiberina (the stop is called Callata Anguillara) and the Duca D'Aosta Bridge near the Olympic Stadium.

Tickets cost €1 for a single journey of up to six stops, and can be bought on board or at any of the tourist information points (see page 231). The same company organises touristic cruises of about an hour, with commentary; romantic night-time cruises with dinner; and a boat service to the site of Ostia Antica that leaves from Marconi Bridge at 9.15am Mon–Fri. It costs €11 for a return ticket and there is a two-hour stopover. Ask at the tourist information points for more details or contact Battelli di Roma, tel: 06-6789361, www.battellidiroma.it.

Taxis

Licensed taxis are white and always have a meter. If you are approached inside railway stations or at the airport by someone muttering "Taxi, taxi" always refuse as they are likely to charge you far more than the official rate.

There are ranks outside Termini Station, outside both airports, and

in many parts of the Centro Storico, such as Largo di Torre Argentina and Piazza Venezia. Otherwise you can always hail a taxi on the street as long as it has a light on, indicating it is free; or call one of the following radio taxi services (tel: 06-3570, 06-8822 or 06-4994).

Prices for licensed taxis are fixed and start with a minimum fee of €2.35. Surcharges are made for each large piece of luggage and for journeys after 10pm and on public holidays. By law every taxi should have a card (usually in the pocket of one of the front seats) listing the various rates and charges. Outside the city centre and beyond the Grande Raccordo Anulare (the ring road) the rate per kilometre also goes up.

Driving

Generally, a car is of little use within the city. Parking is hard to find, one-way systems are complex and much of the city centre is closed during business hours, and parts of it in the evening. If you need to reach a hotel in a traffic-restricted area you must make arrangements with the reception before arriving. Local drivers have a very personal set of rules and codes which, although for the most part looks worse than it is, allows for much flashing of lights, tooting of horns and rampant acceleration at what looks like vastly inopportune moments to anyone non-Roman. During the day most cars in the city centre obey the traffic lights. However, some of Rome's traffic lights are switched to flashing amber at night: this indicates caution, although not all drivers seem to understand this.

If you are not deterred by such problems or if you wish to make extensive trips out of town, you might want to hire your own vehicle (see panel opposite). Note that all cars are required by law to keep their low-beam lights on at all times on motorways and dual carriageways.

There is a large car park under Villa Borghese (entrance at the top of Via Veneto) and one on the Gianicolo hill near the Vatican called Terminal Gianicolo (entrance from Piazza della Rovere). Several of the four- and five-star hotels in the centre have their own garage or protected parking: ask when booking. Few two- or three-star hotels are able to help with parking.

Given the lack of parking spaces, it is not surprising that a lot of cars are towed away in Rome – over 10,000 a year – so if your car is no longer where you left it, this, rather than theft, may be the reason. The Ufficio Rimozione of the traffic police (Vigili Urbani) will be able to tell you if this is the case. The fines you will have to pay to get your car back are high. Contact: Vigili Urbani, 4 Via della Consolazione. Tel: 06-67691.

A lot of cars are clamped. If this happens to you, a note on the windscreen will give you the number to call.

If you think that your car has been stolen, you can report it at the nearest police station.

Breakdown service

The Italian Automobile Association (ACI) provides an emergency breakdown service. If you need repairs, look in the Yellow Pages (Pagine Gialle) for the nearest mechanic (Autofficine), or ask the ACI. ACI breakdown and information service, freephone: 803-116. ACI information, tel: 06-491115.

Bicycles and Mopeds

Romans tend to cycle, if at all, on weekends away in Tuscany with their mountain bikes. However, on car-free Sundays (which usually take place once a month) you will see them darting along the Via dei Fori Imperiali. You can hire a bicycle by the hour, the day or the week. Riding in one of the parks is a pleasant alternative to the city streets.

Bicycle rental companies include:
Bici & Baci
5 Via del Viminale
Tel: 06-4828443 (mopeds also)
Collalti
82 Via del Pellegrino
Tel: 06-68801084

Touring Rome by moped or Vespa is not advisable for beginners or the nervous. You will need to show your licence when hiring a moped, and leave a deposit. Motorcycle rental companies include:
Happy Rent
3 Via Farini
Tel: 06-4818185
Scooters for Rent
84 Via della Purificazione
Tel: 06-4885485

On Foot

In much of the city centre the best way to get around is on foot. Most of the main sights are within easy walking distance of each other, although there are some for which you may want to use public transport.

Some parts of the centre are for pedestrians only, such as the second half of Via del Corso, roughly from the Piazza San Silvestro to Piazza del Popolo and Piazza Navona. This pedestrianised area will soon include the section that goes from Largo Argentina past the Pantheon to the Parliament. Do not rely too heavily on this, however. Moped riders in particular, but also some car drivers, often decide that they are exempt from this rule.

Cross the road with confidence, staring down nearby drivers. If you wait timidly at a pedestrian crossing for the traffic to stop, you will spend the whole day there.

Most of the centre of Rome is reasonably safe, even at night, though the areas around Stazione Termini (particularly Via Giolitti) can be deserted and, despite recent improvements, are still rather seedy.

CAR HIRE

Prices per day at all the major international firms start at approximately €60 for the smallest cars. Expect to pay a generous surcharge if you want unlimited mileage, and check exactly what is included in the insurance you are offered. All the major firms have offices at the airports and railway station and most of them have online booking services as well as sections where you can work out how much the rental will cost. Avis, Europcar and Hertz probably provide the best cover, but Italy Rent, which also has an office at the airport, has the lowest rates.

Avis
Tel: 199-100133
www.avisautonoleggio.it
Europcar
Freephone 800-014410
www.europcar.it

Hertz
Tel: 199-112211
www.hertz.it
Maggiore
Tel: 06-4880049
www.maggiore.it
Italy Rent
Freephone: 800-930032
www.italyrent.it

Several airlines also have on online car-hire booking service, for example:
EasyJet
Tel: +44-11-33883329; lines open 365 days a year for bookings
www.europcar4easyjet.com
Opodo (a company jointly owned by a number of European airlines)
Tel: +44-0871-2770090
www.opodo.com
KLM Royal Dutch Airlines
Internet bookings only:
www.klmuk.com

A CCOMMODATION

SOME THINGS TO CONSIDER BEFORE YOU BOOK THE ROOM

Choosing a Hotel

The APT office *(see Tourist Information, page 231)* publishes an annual list *(Annuario Alberghi)* showing star categories, facilities and prices of all Rome hotels. This may be obtained from the Rome EPT or through the Italian national tourist offices. Commission-free booking is available from the Hotel Reservation Service *(see page 231)*.

Hotels are rated by stars but these ratings correspond to facilities and services, not to the quality, which is often disappointing compared with what you would expect from similarly rated hotels in other major European cities. Since many hotels are located in renovated medieval or renaissance *palazzi* in the centre, the rooms and bathrooms can be a bit on the small side, and noisy.

There has been a recent explosion of designer and luxury hotels in Rome, which offer great views, memorable food, striking décor and usually a health spa; prices are high but deals can be found on their websites.

Bed & Breakfasts

The bed & breakfast sector in Rome is flourishing. Some offer the amenities of a hotel in noble *palazzi* for far more competitive prices; others are nothing more than a private room in someone's home. The APT office on Via Parigi and tourist information points have full listings of registered establishments. The Bed and Breakfast Italia Association (tel: 06-59606395, www.bbitalia.com) has over 250 options in Italy, which they vet and award with a crown system. The standard rates are posted on their website.

Hotel Areas

Rome offers countless places to stay, in every imaginable category. The following list gives a selection, concentrating on the centre. The area around Piazza Navona, the Pantheon and Campo de' Fiori offers the best introduction to the city, since you are right in its medieval heart and within easy reach of most main sights. However, there are relatively few hotels in the area, and these tend to be booked up early. This area is always lively, and that means it is also noisy.

The Aventine Hill is quieter, although a little further out. The Via Veneto area has a number of large hotels at the higher end of the scale. It is a convenient location, although the area is no longer the fashionable centre. Around Piazza di Spagna there is a more varied selection.

Many hotels can be found around Stazione Termini. This is not the most attractive area, but it is well connected with the rest of the city by public transport. A lot of the cheaper hotels are here, but there are some in the middle and luxury ranges. The area south of the station is rather insalubrious and best avoided.

Hotels slightly out of the centre may offer more facilities, such as swimming pools and parking, and they are quieter.

Prices & Booking

Prices are high and do not always reflect what is on offer. A two-star can be as good if not better than a three- or even four-star. Expect to pay anything between €80 and €250 for a three-star (depending on the season) and don't expect views for less then €200.

High season is pretty much year-round in Rome so book ahead. November to March and August are quieter and prices are lower. Bookings can be made online or by phone; sometimes a confirmation fax will be requested, as well as your credit-card details. If you want to cancel, do it a few days in advance. Prices usually include breakfast, although it is never included in the luxury and five-star category. In Bed & Breakfast accommodation, guests typically pay between €40–100 per night for a double room but prices can go as low as €25 and as high as €200.

ACCOMMODATION ◆ 211

ACCOMMODATION LISTINGS

TRANSPORT
ACCOMMODATION
ACTIVITIES
A – Z
LANGUAGE

PIAZZA DEL POPOLO, SPANISH STEPS & CORSO

Hotel Art
56 Via Margutta
Tel: 06-328711
Fax: 06-36003995
www.hotelart.it
Set in a converted seminary, this upmarket hotel is a successful blend of old and new. The reception area is contained within two futuristic pods manned by friendly and efficient staff, and the sleek lounge area (an exercise in style over comfort) is laid out in the former chapel beneath frescoed vaulted ceilings. The rooms are small but comfortable. The internal courtyard is a nice quiet corner for an evening drink. €€€€–€€€€€

Casa Howard
18/a Via Capo le Case and 149 Via Sistina
Tel: 06-69924555
Fax: 06-67946444
www.casahoward.com
Decorated with real flair, each of the 10 rooms in this stylish hotel has a different theme; those in the newer Via Sistina are slightly more luxurious. Turkish bath available at both sites. €€€

De Russie
9 Via del Babuino
Tel: 06-328881
Fax: 06-32888888
www.roccofortehotels.com
This is Rome's original designer hotel, housed in a *palazzo* by Valadier. It is chic and modern (often minimalist). The staff is knowledgeable and welcoming, and the internal courtyard overlooking a tiered garden is magical. Ask for a room with a view of Piazza del Popolo. €€€€€

D'Inghilterra
14 Via Bocca di Leone
Tel: 06-699811
Fax: 06-69922243
www.hoteldinghilterraroma.it
Old-fashioned and traditional, with unfussy service. The rooms, furnished with antiques, are cosy if on the dark side. Top-floor rooms are brighter and have terraces. Good position just off the Corso. €€€€–€€€€€

Fontanella Borghese
84 Largo Fontanella Borghese
Tel: 06-68809504
Fax: 06-6861295
www.fontanellaborghese.com
Stylish, with beautiful old tiles and hardwood floors. Well located for shopping in the Piazza di Spagna and Via dei Condotti area. The rooms overlooking the internal courtyard are quieter. €€€

Gregoriana
18 Via Gregoriana
Tel: 06-6794269
Fax: 06-6784258
Art Deco interior with a wonderful gold-and-black lift and original 1930s room numbers by the Russian fashion designer Erté. Near the Spanish Steps, it has only 20 rooms; no restaurant. €–€€

Hassler Villa Medici
6 Piazza Trinità dei Monti
Tel: 06-699340
Fax: 06-6789991

www.hotelhasslerroma.com
Situated above the Spanish Steps. Its grandeur is slightly faded but this is still one of Rome's most alluring luxury hotels. The restaurant, with roof gardens and view over the city, is particularly beautiful. €€€€€

Locarno
22 Via della Penna
Tel: 06-3610841
Fax: 06-3215249
www.hotellocarno.com
Appealing Art Deco touches (the ornate cage lift alone is memorable) though some rooms are quite basic. De luxe rooms in the new wing are lovely but cost more. Breakfast served in the garden or on the roof terrace when warm. Oodles of charm and class and the location, two minutes' from Piazza del Popolo, can't be beaten. Bicycle rental included in the price. €€–€€€

Margutta
34 Via Laurina
Tel: 06-3223674
Fax: 06-3200395
On a cobbled street near Piazza del Popolo. Rooms are small but pleasant, especially the three on the top floor which have a great view and terraces. Well priced for this chic area. €€

Nazionale
131 Piazza Montecitorio
Tel: 06-695 001
Fax: 06-678 6677
www.nazionaleroma.it
This hotel by the House

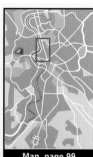

Map, page 99

of Representatives has an impressive roster of illustrious past guests, Simone de Beauvoir and Jean-Paul Sartre among them. These days, the 80 rooms more often host politicians, who appreciate its comfort, service and location. €€€€

Scalinata di Spagna
17 Piazza Trinità dei Monti
Tel: 06-6793006
Fax: 06-69940598
www.hotelscalinata.com
A small hotel in a beautiful townhouse at the top of the Spanish Steps. Some rooms open onto a large terrace, most have great views. Breakfast on rooftop terrace in summer. Book early. €€€€

PRICE CATEGORIES

For a double room in high season
€ = under €100
€€ = €100–180
€€€ = €180–260
€€€€ = €260–450
€€€€€ = €450+

TREVI & VIA VENETO

Aleph
15 Via San Basilio
Tel: 06-422 901
Fax: 06-42290000
www.boscolohotels.com
Intriguing boutique hotel. Bedrooms are inspired by 1930s design and have hi-tech touches and huge beds. Lovely spa downstairs. €€€

Ambasciatori Palace
62 Via Vittorio Veneto
Tel: 06-47493
Fax: 06-4743601
www.ambasciatoripalace.com
Central and comfortable large hotel, halfway up the leafy Via Veneto. Caters to a mainly business crowd, and can lack atmosphere but the staff are friendly and efficient. €€€€

Eden
49 Via Ludovisi
Tel: 06-478121
Fax: 06-4821584
www.hotel-eden.it
Discreet, cosy and ultra-refined with excellent, unsnooty service and a good roof garden restaurant. €€€€€

Excelsior
Via Vittorio Veneto 125
Tel: 06-47081
Fax: 06-4826205
www.starwoodhotels.com
Part of the 1950s' Dolce Vita scene, the opulent Excelsior still offers the ultimate in comfort and service. Popular with Americans. €€€€€

Fontana
96 Piazza di Trevi
Tel: 06-6786113
Fax: 06-6790024
www.hotelfontana-trevi.com
In a 13th-century monastery opposite the Fontana di Trevi. A tad pricey for quite basic rooms but it has a beautiful rooftop breakfast room. €€€

Jolly Vittorio Veneto
Corso Italia
Tel: 06-84951
Fax: 06-8841004
www.jollyhotels.it
Modern, with all amenities, including conference rooms. Air conditioned and sound proofed. High-quality service. €€€–€€€€

Modigliani
42 Via della Purificazione
Tel : 06-42815226
Fax : 06-42814791
www.hotelmodigliani.com

Maps, pages 94, 140

A lovely hotel with great views from top-floor rooms and a garden in an inner courtyard. Worthwhile last-minute deals can be had on the website. €€–€€€

PIAZZA NAVONA & PANTHEON

Abruzzi
69 Piazza della Rotonda
Tel: 06-6792021 or 06-9784131
Fax: 06-67988076
www.hotelabruzzi.it
Directly opposite the Pantheon, this hotel is not quiet in summer but all rooms have air conditioning and double glazing. They are modest but clean and quite large. The view is out of this world. €€€

Due Torri
23 Vicolo del Leonetto
Tel: 06-68806956
Fax: 06-6865442
www.hotelduetorriroma.com
A delightful hotel in a former cardinal's palace tucked away down a narrow cobbled street. Rooms are small and cosy; those on the

top floor have terraces; quiet by Rome standards. €€–€€€

Grand Hotel de le Minerve
69 Piazza della Minerva
Tel: 06-695201
Fax: 06-6794165
www.hotel-invest.com
Built within a 17th-century *palazzo* overlooking the lovely Piazza della Minerva. Vast areas of Venetian glass create spectacular public spaces. Rooms are large and there are splendid views from the roof terrace. €€€€€

Raphael
2 Largo Febo
Tel: 06-682831
Fax: 06-6878993
www.raphaelhotel.com
A distinctive ivy-covered exterior, antique furnish-

ings, art works and stunning views. Some rooms don't quite live up to expectations, but facilities and rooftop restaurant, bar and views do. €€€€

Santa Chiara
21 Via Santa Chiara
Tel: 06-6872979
Fax: 06-6873144
www.albergosantachiara.com
In a sprawling building with three wings, 100 rooms and three rooftop apartments. Feels like a luxury hotel but prices are lower. Excellent value. Ask for a room with a terrace. €€€

Sole al Pantheon
63 Piazza della Rotonda
Tel: 06-6780441
Fax: 06-69940689
www.hotelsolealpantheon.com
This 500-year-old hotel,

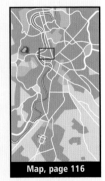

Map, page 116

a stone's throw from the Pantheon, has been renovated without spoiling the atmosphere. Front rooms have memorable views but are quite noisy. Quieter rooms overlook an internal courtyard. €€€€

CAMPO DE' FIORI & TRASTEVERE

Barrett
47 Largo Torre Argentina
Tel: 06-6868481
Fax: 06-6892971
Located between
Campo de' Fiori and the
Pantheon, with large,
comfortable rooms with
big en-suite bathrooms,
this is one of the best
value-for-money hotels
in Rome. No credit
cards accepted and no
breakfast available, but
each room is equipped
with its own coffee
maker and cafés are
not far away. €–€€

Campo de' Fiori
6 Via del Biscione
Tel: 06-68806865
Fax: 06-6874003
www.hotelcampodefiori.com
A stone's throw from
the Campo de' Fiori,
this friendly hotel has a
beautiful terrace and
small intimate rooms,
all individually deco-
rated. The cheaper
rooms have just a
washbasin; the bath-
room and toilet are
shared. The hotel
management also rents
several apartments in
the area. €€

Della Lunetta
68 Piazza del Paradiso
Tel: 06-6861080
Fax: 06-6892028
www.albergodellalunetta.it
Comfortable, clean but
very basic, Della
Lunetta is extremely
well situated between
Piazza Navona and
Campo de' Fiori. There
is no breakfast but you
can pop round to Campo
de' Fiori or Piazza Far-
nese for your morning
cappuccino. There's a
pleasant, panoramic
communal terrace that
can be used for sunning

and reading. €–€€

Pomezia
12 Via dei Chiavari
Tel: 06-6861371
Fax: 06-6861371
The rooms in this small,
accommodating hotel
just off the Corso Vitto-
rio Emanuele were reno-
vated after the
millennium, as were the
reception and breakfast
areas. They are basi-
cally furnished but com-
fortable and all have
en-suite bathrooms with
a power shower. There
is a lift and a room
equipped for people
with disabilities. For the
reasonabale price, and
considering the loca-
tion, you could not ask
for more. €–€€

Rinascimento
122 Via del Pellegrino
Tel: 06-6874813
Fax: 06-6833518
www.hotelrinascimento.com
This pleasant, family-run
hotel has well-equipped,
comfortable and charac-
teristic rooms and bath-
rooms, although they
are a bit cramped. Ask
for the room which has a
stunning, direct view of
the Chiesa Nuova –
although it naturally gets
booked early. A few of
the rooms are really tiny
with not a lot of light so
make sure you avoid
these. €€

Ripa
21 Via Luigi Gianniti
Tel: 06-58611
Fax: 06-5814550
www.ripahotel.com
Cutting-edge, clean and
functional design char-
acterise this hip hotel
near the Porta Portese
end of Trastevere. The
Ripa is well located for
Testaccio and Ostiense

(the city's hippest club-
bing areas), the Aven-
tine and Circus
Maximus, and has all
the usual extras to be
found in this price
range, including an
excellent fusion restau-
rant and its own trendy
nightclub. It's a pity
about the street it's
located in, which is a bit
of an eyesore, but
maybe the presence of
the hotel will encourage
improvements. €€€€

Santa Maria
2 Vicolo del Piede
Tel: 06-5894626
Fax: 06-5894815
www.htlsantamaria.com
Behind firmly closed
gates in this quiet and
typical Trastevere alley-
way lies a refurbished
16th-century cloister.
All the rooms are large
and comfortable with
terracotta tiling and a
view out onto a large,
sunny, porticoed central
courtyard. €€€

Smeraldo
9 Vicolo dei Chiodaroli
Tel: 06-6875929
Fax: 06-68805495
www.smeraldoroma.com
A good value hotel ben-
efitting from a central
location in a narrow
street between Largo
Argentina and Campo
de'Fiori. Its rooms are
clean and comfortable,
if on the small side, and
some of those on the
upper floors have lovely
views over the rooftops.
If these are all booked
up you can still enjoy
the views from the two
roof gardens, Avoid the
rooms overlooking
courtyard, however, as
these are on the gloomy
side. €€–€€€

Maps, pages 116, 148

Sole
76 Via del Biscione
Tel: 06-68806873
Fax: 06-6893787
www.solealbiscione.it
The main draw of this
cosy hotel is its central
location near Campo de'
Fiori. It has quiet, if basic
rooms, a pretty inner garden and a small roof ter-
race offering lovely views
of the domed church of
San Andrea della Valle.
It's very popular so book
well ahead. There's no
breakfast service, and
no credit cards are
accepted. €€

Trastevere
24a–25 Via L Manara
Tel: 06-5814713
Fax: 06-5881016
With clean simple rooms
overlooking the Piazza
San Cosimato market
square, this charming,
but down-to-earth little
hotel is a great deal for
the area. €

PRICE CATEGORIES

For a double room in
high season
€ = under €100
€€ = €100–180
€€€ = €180–260
€€€€ = €260–450
€€€€€ = €450+

TRANSPORT

ACCOMMODATION

ACTIVITIES

A – Z

LANGUAGE

PRATI & VATICAN

Atlante Star
34 Via Vitelleschi
Tel: 06-6873233
Fax: 06-6872300
www.atlantehotels.com
One of the capital's bastions of luxury. The wood-panelled rooms are decorated with antiques and the marble bathrooms all have jacuzzis.The rooftop terrace is famous for its view of St Peter's and for the haute cuisine Les Etoiles restaurant, which is booked up weeks in advance. €€€

Colors
31 Via Boezio
Tel: 06-6874030
Fax: 06-6867947
www.colorshotel.com
Bright, clean, modern and colourful hotel with individual rooms, with or without en-suite bathrooms, and dormitory accommodation. As its name implies, all the rooms are brightly painted in different colours. There is a large and fully equipped kitchen should you want

to cook, laundry facilities, a roof terrace with gazebo and no curfew for dorm accommodation. The staff are very helpful. €–€€

Columbus
33 Via della Conciliazione
Tel: 06-6865435
Fax: 06-6864874
www.hotelcolumbus.net
On the main street leading up to St Peter's, this ex-monastery has retained some of its original features, including a large, vaulted dining room, frescoes, and a garden planted with orange trees where you can sit and dine in summer. This is a large, comfortable hotel with its own parking area. Prices go down a fair bit off season. €€€€

Dei Mellini
81 Via Muzio Clementi
Tel: 06-324771
Fax: 06-32477801
www.hotelmellini.com
Close to the river in Prati, a short walk from Castel Sant' Angelo and St Peter's, and just

across the bridge from the Via del Corso and the Tridente shopping district. Rooms are spacious and elegant if a little on the old-fashioned side. There is a pleasant rooftop terrace too. Good facilities for the disabled. €€€–€€€€

Gerber
241 Via degli Scipioni
Tel: 06-3221001
Fax: 06-3217048
www.hotelgerber.it
Rooms suffer slightly from floral overload but are comfortable and quiet, and the hotel is close to the Vatican. There is a nice terrace too. Great value for money. €€

Farnese
30 Via Alessandro Farnese
Tel: 06-3212553
Fax: 06-3215129
www.hotelfarnese.com
This upmarket, four-star hotel occupies a grand, old aristocratic residence. The attention to detail and period furnishings are what make it so special. The recep-

Map, page 106

tion desk is a 17th-century altar from a deconsecrated church. The rooms are elegantly decorated with antiques, terracotta tiling, marble bathrooms and Murano lamps, with crisp linen sheets on the beds The breakfast is excellent and there is a pretty roof terrace. Lepanto Metro station is nearby and the hotel is within easy walking distance of St Peter's and the Centro Storico. €€€€

STAZIONE TERMINI, VIA NAZIONALE, COLOSSEO & FORUM

Antica Locanda
84 Via del Boschetto
Tel: 06-484894
Fax: 06-4871164
www.antica-locanda.com
As the name suggests (*locanda* means inn) this is a cosy, wood-panelled wine bar with rooms to rent upstairs. The rooms, named after famous composers and artists, are all individually furnished. Breakfast is served in the wine bar and guests can

use the roof terrace at any time of day. €€–€€€

Capo d'Africa
54 Via Capo d'Africa
Tel: 06-772801
Fax: 06-77280801
www.hotelcapodafrica.com
One of a recent slew of boutique hotels in Rome. The dramatic, palm-tree lined entrance bodes well and the design of the 64 rooms are cosy yet refreshingly contemporary – one suite has its own private

terrace. Views are delightful, and the Colosseum only a five-minute walk away. Any worries that you won't be in the thick of things will vanish once you realise how well connected you are and what a haven of comfort and peace this place is. €€€€

Fawlty Towers
39 Via Magenta
Tel: 06-4454802
Fax: 06-49382878
www.fawltytowers.org

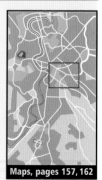

Maps, pages 157, 162

A far cry from its chaotic namesake, this efficiently-run hotel, in a pleasant street near the station, is one of the better low-budget options in the area. And there are no Basils or Manuels among the welcoming staff. There is the added bonus of a flower-filled terrace where you can relax and sunbathe. Very popular so book early. €–€€

47 Hotel
47 Via Petroselli
Tel: 06-6787816
Fax: 06-69190726
www.47hotel.com
Near Piazza Venezia, this new hotel is located on a street of sprawling but imposing government offices. The Teatro di Marcello is at one end and it leads out to the Temple of Vesta and the Bocca della Verità on the

other. It is set in an austere 1930s building which has been tastefully converted and filled with repro furnitture and original contemporary Italian art works. The views of the river are wonderful. €€€€

Forum
25 Via Tor de' Conti
Tel: 06-6792446
Fax: 06-6786479
www.hotelforumrome.com
Built around a medieval belltower off the Via dei Fori Imperiali, this luxurious, tasteful, old-fashioned hotel is ideally located for the Forum, and has a wonderful view from its roof-garden restaurant, which is one of the best in Rome. €€€–€€€€

Nerva
3 Via Tor de Conti
Tel: 06-6781835
Fax: 06-69922204

www.hotelnerva.com
At the upper end of this price scale, the décor of this hotel is nothing to get excited about but it is quiet and excellently located on the border between the Imperial Fora (the ruins can be seen from some of the top-floor windows) and the hilly bohemian Monti district, which is filled with boutiques, cafés and restaurants. €€–€€€

St Regis Grand
3 Via Vittorio Emanuele Orlando
Tel: 06-47091
Fax: 06-4747307
www.stregis.com
Situated between the station and the Via Veneto, the newly restored St Regis Grand provides a taste of 19th-century belle-époque grandeur. The

opulent establishment has retained its individuality, style and atmosphere. If you can't afford to stay here, at least try to drop in for high tea or cocktails. €€€€€

YWCA
4 Via Cesare Balbo
Tel: 06-488 0460
Fax: 06-4871028
The YWCA offers two-, three- and four-bedded rooms, for women only, and is located conveniently close to Via Nazionale and the station. There is a midnight curfew and no credit cards are accepted. There's a cosy and homely atmosphere although the interior is a bit run down. Outside, the area is somewhat deserted after dark (although it's not unsafe). €

FURTHER AFIELD

Cavalieri Hilton
101 Via Cadlolo
Tel: 06-35091
Fax: 06-35092241
www.cavalieri-hilton.it
Luxury hotel situated on top of Monte Mario, just north of the Vatican. It is quiet and spacious, and offers amenities that more central hotels lack, a swimming pool and tennis courts among them, as well as one of Rome's best restaurants (La Pergola) on the top floor, which spreads out on to the terrace in summer. €€€€€

Lord Byron
5 Via Giuseppe De Notaris
Tel: 06-3220404
Fax: 06-3220405
www.lordbyronhotel.com

Built into a former monastery, this small, first-class hotel has the atmosphere of a private club, and enjoys a serene location away from the chaos of the city centre, in the well-heeled Parioli district. Its 47 rooms are sumptuously decorated and the restaurant (Sapori del Lord Byron) is excellent. €€€€

Ostello del Foro Italico
61 Viale delle Olimpiadi
Tel: 06-3236267
Fax: 06-3242613
www.ostellionline.org
Advance reservations are strongly advised, as this 334-bed hostel is the only real hostel in Rome. It is open all year round, has a midnight

curfew and is located some way out of the centre (but is accessible by bus). €

Aventino S. Anselmo
2 Piazza Sant'Anselmo
Tel: 06-5745174
Fax: 06-5783604
www.aventinohotels.com
This appealing hotel is in fact made up of three interconnecting residential villas, nestling in a peaceful garden on the leafy and exclusive Aventine hill. Each of the villas has its own distinct atmosphere, as well as slightly different and fairly affordable rates. The public rooms have inlaid marble floors and many bedrooms are fitted with antique furniture. It's

Map, page 184

just a short walk from Testaccio and the Piramide Metro stop. €€–€€€

PRICE CATEGORIES

For a double room in high season
€ = under €100
€€ = €100–180
€€€ = €180–260
€€€€ = €260–450
€€€€€ = €450+

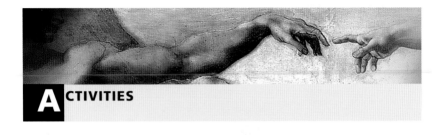

ACTIVITIES

THE ARTS, NIGHTLIFE, FESTIVALS, SHOPPING AND SPORTS

THE ARTS

Theatre

As plays are nearly always performed in Italian, an evening at the theatre is only recommended for fluent Italian speakers. A notable exception are theatrical events related to the Roma-Europa Festival *(see festivals page 220)* or some of the original-language performances put on at the ever-reliable **Teatro Argentina** (56 Largo Argentina, tel: 06-684000345, www.teatrodiroma.net). However, in some cases it is worth attending a classical drama or play in translation, if the venue itself provides the drama – particularly summer events held outdoors, whether in amphitheatres, such as the one at Ostia Antica, or at other classical sites *(see Summer Spectacle, below)*. Roman theatre embraces mainstream and contemporary theatre but the emphasis is on the tried and trusted Italian dramatists, such as Carlo Goldoni and Luigi Pirandello, musicals, or lighter, frothier stuff, often translated. However, the university theatres and smaller venues do stage experimental or fringe productions (known as "Teatro off").

One of the most interesting of these is the recently reopened **Teatro Palladium** (8 Piazza Bartolomeo Romano, tel: 06-57067761, www.teatro-palladium.it) which is attached to the University Roma 3 and puts on an interesting range of readings, films, dance and theatre events. The theatre season runs from October to early June, but there are numerous summer events linked to specific Roman festivals *(see Estate Romana, page 220)*. Rome also has a last-minute theatre box office where unsold tickets can be bought on the same day for up to 50 percent off. The counter is located at 20 Via Bari (Piazza Salerno, Policlinico Metro stop Line B); Tues–Sat 2–8pm (closed July and August).

Opera & Ballet

The opera and ballet season runs from October to June at the Teatro dell'Opera, 1 Piazza Beniamino Gigli, tel: 06-48160255 or freephone 800-016665, www.operaroma.it. The ticket office is open Tues–Sat 9am–5pm, Sun 9am–1.30pm, but tickets can also be bought on their website and picked up at the opera house on the night of the performance. Ticket prices run from reasonable to exorbitant.

The outdoor summer opera series (same numbers as above) has been held in a number of different venues in past years, including the Baths of Caracalla. The best bet for international and contemporary dance is the **Teatro Olimpico** (17 Piazza Gentile da Fabriano, tel: 06-3265991, www.teatroolimpico.it. Ticket office open daily 11am–7pm).

Classical Music

There is a great variety of venues for classical music. The season runs from October to June, but with special summer concerts there's something going on just about all year round.

The renowned, high-profile Accademia di Santa Cecilia (www.santacecilia.it), and its symphonic and chamber orchestras, hosts all its principal concerts from October to May at the new **Auditorium-Parco della Musica** (30 Viale Pietro de Coubertin, tel: 06-80241281, www.auditorium.com). Designed by Genoese architect Renzo Piano, it opened in December 2002 and features three concert halls with excellent acoustics. A 10-minute tram-ride from Piazzale Flaminio (just above Piazza del Popolo), the complex also features a large inner courtyard,

HOW TO GET TICKETS

Venues have ticket offices, phone booking lines and online booking possibilities. Failing that, the best agencies for tickets to all events, are:

Hello Ticket
Stazione Termini
34 Via Giolitti
Tel: 06-47825710
Freephone: 800-907080
www.helloticket.it (tickets can also be bought online and picked up before the performance at the venue).

Ricordi Mediastores
88 Viale G. Cesare
Tel: 06-37500375.

Orbis Servizi
37 Piazza Esquilino (behind Santa Maria Maggiore)
Tel: 06-4744776.

Messaggerie Musicali
473 Via del Corso
Tel: 06-68192349.

which is used for outdoor concerts and events.

For more information, visit www.santacecilia.it or the auditorium's website. There are many other venues for classical music including churches and outdoor venues all over Rome in summer, many of them part of the Estate Romana series of events *(see Festivals, page 220)*. Some of the most atmospheric venues are Terme di Caracalla, the Teatro di Marcello, the Fori Imperiali and the Terrazza del Pincio. Ask at a tourist information point for their monthly guide to cultural events, called *L'evento*, or check the local press for more information on classical music events.

Museums & Galleries

A €9 Museum Card, valid for 7 days, is available and covers all the sites of the Museo Nazionale Romano; a €20 ticket (Roma Archeologia Card), also valid for 7 days, covers the sites of the Museo Nazionale Romano and the Colosseum, the Palatine, the Baths of Caracalla, the Tomb of Cecilia Metella and the Villa of the Quintili. They can be bought from any participating site.

Most museums are closed on Monday though there are some exceptions. Important art exhibitions are usually open daily.

NIGHTLIFE

Roman nightlife tends to be fun rather than frenzied. Apart from a few privileged or exclusive clubs, the nightclub scene is far less adventurous than in Berlin, London or New York. In common with other capital cities, door policy determines whether you even get to cross the threshold of a club. If your look is not right you will either not get in or not fit in. As a general rule, however, in Rome it is safer to dress up rather than down, even if it makes rejection all the more humiliating.

You may be required to obtain temporary membership (a *tessera*, or membership card, should be available at the door). Entry price may include a free drink but drinks are normally quite expensive. Groups of young men together are usually not welcome and, in some clubs, a man may be turned away unless accompanied by a woman.

Trastevere is still a reliable destination for Romans in search of a good time. Slightly more alternative is Testaccio, which is clubland central, and a burgeoning gay, alternative and commercial scene is happening even further south in the industrial Ostiense quarter.

The historic quarters around Piazza Navona (around Via di Tor Millina), the Pantheon and Campo de' Fiori are timeless and contain a number of popular bars and clubs. The Via Veneto, scene of Fellini's mythical *Dolce Vita*, is still home to certain elegant nightclubs and piano bars, which tend to be patronised by middle-aged, moneyed Americans.

Most nightclubs don't get going until midnight; most close Monday night, some on Sunday too. Several of the better ones are around Via di Monte Testaccio. Recently there's been an upsurge in so-called *discobar* and *ristodisco*, which as their names suggest mean bars and restaurants where there are also DJ sets and you can dance till late.

In summer, much young nightlife moves to the beach resorts south of the city. However, the glut of summer city festivals ensures that Rome remains lively. Apart from these, the best and most typical forms of Roman nightlife tend to be centred on a leisurely meal, a musical event or chatting and drinking at one of the many outdoor bars.

Nightclubs

Akab-Cave
69 Via di Monte Testaccio
Tel: 06-5782390
Ever-popular club with two floors and a terrace garden. The music is mainly commercial dance.

Alpheus
36 Via del Commercio
Tel: 06-5747826
www.alpheus.it
Everything from "black" music and hip hop to house with live music nights that vary from rock to Latin music.

Anima
57 Via di Santa Maria dell'Anima
(Piazza Navona)
Tel: 347-8509256
A trendy, narrow bar and disco with mezzanine and sofas; serves brightly coloured cocktails to an R&B, dance and soul soundtrack.

Distillerie Clandestine
7 Via Libetta (Ostiense)
Tel: 06-57305102
www.distillerieclandestine.com
Restaurant, club and live music venue with great cocktails.

Etò
44 Via Galvani (Testaccio)
Tel: 06-5748268
Hi-tech décor, art-filled walls, big-

TRANSPORT · ACCOMMODATION · ACTIVITIES · A–Z · LANGUAGE

screen monitors and a house-music following.

Ex Magazzini
8 Via dei Magazzini Generali (Ostiense)
Tel: 06-5758040
One of the best nightclubs in town. Memorable DJ sets featuring the latest in hip hop and electronic, plus theatre performances, live music and short film festivals.

La Maison
4 Vicolo dei Granari (Piazza Navona)
Tel: 06-6833312
Very hip centrally located club with a very hip 1970s-retro feel to the décor and ambience.

La Saponeria
20 Via degli Argonauti (Ostiense)
Tel: 06-5746999
Industrial location with a retro 1970s design and music nights that range from hip hop to house. Open Thur–Sat.

Le Coppelle
52 Piazza delle Coppelle (Piazza Navona)
Tel: 06-6832410
A so-called discobar with an enviably central location and a great line in cocktails. Outdoor seating on giant sofas in summer and a very cosmopolitan vibe.

Music Venues

Alexanderplatz
9 Via Ostia (Prati).
Tel: 06-39751877
www.alexanderplatz.it
When the big names come to town, they often come to this jazz club and sushi bar, which runs the summer jazz series at the Villa Celimontana. Closed Sun.

Big Mama
18 Via San Francesco a Ripa (Trastevere).
Tel: 06-5812551
www.bigmama.it
The blues club in Rome but also hosts jazz and rock musicians. Free entry to many events.

Fonclea
82A Via Crescenzio (Prati)
Tel: 06-6896302
Jazz restaurant/pub.

Four XXXX Pub
29 Via Galvani (Testaccio)
Tel: 06-5757296.
www.fourxxxxpub.it
Unusually this is a jazz club which serves South American food.

La Palma
35 Via Giuseppe Mirri (near the Tiburtina Metro stop)
Tel: 06-4359 9029
www.lapalmaclub.it
Live bands playing new jazz and ethnic music and DJ sets.

No Stress Brasil
35 Via degli Stradivari (Trastevere)
Tel: 06-58335015
Restaurant and club. Live music every night (except Sunday), with Brazilian bands and dancers.

Palalottomattica
Piazzale dello Sport (EUR)
Tel: 199-128800
Refurbished architectural landmark in EUR; hosts major indoor concerts.

Villaggio Globale
Lungotevere Testaccio 2
Tel: 06-5757233
A large live music and cultural venue that offers alternative and world music, as well as cinema festivals, theatrical events and African food at its Roots Village.

CINEMA

Virtually all films on general release are dubbed into Italian. For English-speaking cinema, try the following (films are marked VO – *versione originale*):

Alcazar, 14 Via Cardinale Merry del Val. Tel: 06-5880099. Current film playing is shown in its original version on Monday.

Metropolitan, 7 Via del Corso. Tel: 06-32600500. Air-conditioned multi-screen cinema with one screen devoted to original-version films.

Nuovo Olimpia, 16G Via in Lucina. Tel: 06-6861068. Art-house movies often shown, as well as original-language films.

Pasquino, 10 Piazza Sant'Egidio.

Tel: 06-5815208, www.multisala-pasquino.com. Rome's only all original-language cinema, with three screens.

Warner Village Moderno, 45–46 Piazza della Repubblica. Tel: 06-47779202. Frequent original-version films on one of its screens.

CHILDREN'S ACTIVITIES

Explora-Il Museo dei Bambini, 82 Via Flaminia; Tues–Sun 9.30am–7pm; visits by prior booking only on weekends, four slots daily; entrance fee; tel: 06-3613776, www.mdbr.it. Rome's first and only children's museum. With four sections dedicated to humans, the environment, communications and society, there are plenty of signs and material in English. Kids can star in their own TV show and have fun with the interactive educational displays. There's also a nice restaurant.

Time Elevator, 20 Via SS Apostoli; daily screenings 11am–7.30pm; entrance charge; tel: 06-97746243, www.time-elevator.it. Touted as a multimedia experience that illustrates the history of Rome from the 8th century BC to the present day. Visitors sit on moving platforms, wearing headphones, for a cinematic roller-coaster ride through history with various major protagonists (such as Nero and Michelangelo) playing major parts, and a narrator to help with the chronology. Quite cheesy, but a fun introduction to the Eternal City. Memorable moments include watching Rome burn.

Museo Criminologico, 29 Via del Gonfalone; Tues–Sat 9am–1pm, Tues and Thur also 2.30–6.30pm; entrance charge; tel: 06-68300234, www.museocriminologico.it. The Rome criminological museum covers the history of the prison system in Italy, how criminal cases are solved, and how criminals were punished over the centuries, but the part (older) children will enjoy best is undoubtedly the section with torture instruments and paintings depicting various and gruesome forms of punishment.

ANNUAL EVENTS

Many festivals are linked to the Catholic church. The tourist office usually has information on what's happening.

January
6 January: culmination of Christmas fair in Piazza Navona *(see December)* celebrating **Epiphany (Befana)**, the traditional festival when good children receive presents and naughty children are given sweets shaped like coal.
17 January: **La Festa di Sant' Antonio Abate**. Blessing of animals in the church of Sant'Eusebio all'Esquilino.

March
9 March: **Festa di Santa Francesca Romana**. Cars, mopeds and taxis are driven to the church of Santa Francesca Romana to be blessed by the patron saint of motorists.
La Festa della Primavera. The arrival of spring is marked by the decoration of the Spanish Steps with a sea of azaleas.
Late March/Early April: **Giornate FAI**. The Fondo Ambientale Italiano (Environmental Fund of Italy) organises a weekend when usually closed churches, monuments and gardens can be visited.
March/April: Easter week is a

very important time of the year, from the big Mass on Palm Sunday and the distribution of palm fronds, to the mass pilgrimages for **Holy Week (Settimana Santa)** and concerts all over the city. The Pope also leads an outdoor **Mass at the Colosseum on Good Friday**, followed by a procession passing the Stations of the Cross. The week culminates on Easter morning with the Pope's Urbi et Orbi speech to the world. Call the Vatican Tourist office for more info *(see page 106)*.

April
21 April: **Il Natale di Roma**. Rome celebrates its legendary founding with fireworks, music and other events.
25 April: **La Festa della Liberazione**. Public holiday commemorating liberation of Italy by Allied forces at the end of World War II.
Late April or May: **Settimana della Cultura**. Cultural Week all over Italy when entrance is free to all state-run museums and historical sites, as well as many exhibitions, see www.beniculturali.it.

May
May Day is widely celebrated in Rome – it's the one day of the year when no buses run. A huge free concert is held in front of San Giovanni in Laterano.
Sporting Events – the Italian Open Tennis Championship is usually held in the first half of May, and the International Horse Show is at the end of the month

in the Villa Borghese.
June
29 June: **San Pietro e San Paolo**. The founders of the Catholic church are honoured with a public holiday. Special Masses are held in their basilicas.
Estate Romana starts in June *(see Festivals panel, page 220.*
July
Summer Opera Series. Opera and ballet performed in the open air at the Baths of Caracalla (also in August).
Festa de'Noantri. A street festival in Trastevere that runs for two weeks from mid-July.
Roma Alta Moda. A series of fashion shows featuring the new lines from the major design houses. The highpoint is the show on the Spanish Steps.
August
5 August: **La Festa della Madonna della Neve**. Simulated snow falls to commemorate the miraculous founding of the Basilica of Santa Maria Maggiore.
September
La Notte Bianca. A designated Saturday night when many museums, clubs, cinemas and shops stay open all night.
October
Symphonic music season begins at the auditorium, www.auditorium.com.
November
2 November: **Giornata dei Defunti**, or Day of the Dead, when the Pope celebrates Mass at the Verano cemetery.
December
8 December: **Immacolata Concezione**. The Immaculate Conception of the Virgin is celebrated around the statue of the Madonna in Piazza di Spagna.
Christmas. Major shopping streets are beautifully decorated and *presepi* (nativity scenes) set up in churches around the city.
Mercatino di Natale a Piazza Navona. Christmas arts and crafts fair with stalls selling food opens the second week of December.
31 December: **San Silvestro**: fireworks and free concerts in Piazza del Popolo and other squares.

WHAT'S ON LISTINGS

For the most comprehensive listings of what's on in Rome, pick up *Roma C'è*, a weekly booklet that comes out on Wednesday and is available from newsstands. Listings are in Italian with an abbreviated section in English. The Thursday edition of the national daily *La Repubblica* carries a supplement called *TrovaRoma* that contains full listings for the upcoming week, and the

fortnightly English magazine *Wanted in Rome* (available in all the city centre's newsstands) also has a listing section. The tourist information office and booths *(see page 231)* provide a multitude of leaflets including the monthly guide *l'evento* and a booklet that comes out every two or three months called *Tourist's Passepartout*. Online, www.trovacinema.it lists all the films currently playing.

FESTIVALS

Over the past few years the number of cultural events and festivals in Rome has almost tripled and many new buildings and museums have helped this process. The two most established festivals, which nevertheless grow every year, are the RomaEuropa Festival (www.roma europa.net or www-teatro-palladium.it) and the Estate Romana.

The **RomaEuropa Festival** is a cutting-edge event which takes place every year from mid-September to at least mid-November and covers dance (usually modern), theatre, readings, cinema and music. Every year the festival has a different theme and the performers are a highly interesting mix of well-established international performers and emerging or avant-garde troupes.

The **Estate Romana** (literally, Roman Summer) is the umbrella for the huge programme of events sponsored by the local council from June to September which sees some of the city's most attractive parks and piazzas become venues for rock, ethnic and jazz concerts, theatre performances (in Villa Ada, Villa Celimontana, at the Fori Imperiali, Piazza del Popolo, to cite but a few), outdoor

cinema (for example, in Piazza Vittorio Emanuele II and San Lorenzo), dance lessons and other cultural events such as readings, book fairs and gastronomic evenings. Every night various Roman *piazze* and venues all over town host something to suit absolutely all tastes, and some of the locations are truly spectacular. See the local press and ask at the tourist information points for details, or log on to the following website: www.romeguide.it.

Rome's **International Photography Festival** (www.fotografia festival.it) started in 2002 and has been such a success that it has expanded. It puts on a very wide range of photographic shows in the most diverse settings, from historic monuments to avant-garde backstreet galleries. Also initiated in 2002, the **International Literature Festival** of Rome (www.festivaldel-leletterature.it) hosts writers in the historic and mesmerising setting of the Basilica of Massenzio; past guests have included Günter Grass, Jonathan Coe, Alice Sebold, Paul Auster, Don Delillo, Hanif Kureishi and Salman Rushdie. Readings and debates are accompanied by jazz concerts.

SHOPPING

What to Buy

All the major designers and national chains are represented in Rome. Attractive buys include books on art and architecture, striking kitchenware, herbalists' concoctions, marbled notepaper, stylish modern lamps and old prints. Regional wines, cheeses and olive oil are also good value.

However, the city really comes into its own with leather and designer goods. Leatherware,

designer luggage, eclectic ceramics, glassware, lighting, inlaid marble tables, gold jewellery and objets d'art are excellent buys. For those with the time and excess baggage allowance to spare, browsing for textiles, antiques and hand-crafted furniture can be a pleasant occupation, as well as seeking out the growing number of artisan's boutiques offering handmade jewellery, ceramics and artworks.

As a general rule, you can't return merchandise for a refund, though you may be able to exchange items if you state your case convincingly.

Where to Buy

Shopping Centres

Several shopping centres, all outside the centre, are good places to find last season's wares (mainly clothing) with discounts up to 70 percent.

Castel Romano, south of EUR, has over 90 stores, including designer and mid-market brands such as Dolce & Gabbana, Versace, Calvin Klein, Diesel and Bruno Magli. **Fashion District** in Valmontone southeast of Rome (trains leave regularly from Termini) has over 200 shops selling mostly mid-market brands. **Galleria Alberto Sordi** on Via del Corso has just been restored to its original grandeur after years of closure and neglect. Many new shops include Rome's first Zara, a large Feltrinelli book and music store, and a megastore called Jam, dedicated to young fashion. **Margutta Arcade**, 3 Via Margutta is new, sleek and exclusive, with 21 boutiques selling upmarket jewellery, antiques and clothing.

Department Stores

Department stores are few and far between in Rome, but there are four main chains.

COIN, 7 Piazzale Appio (San Giovanni). Dependable, with some well-made and imaginative kitchen, linen and interiors items. **La Rinascente**, Piazza Fiume and 20 Largo Chigi (level with Piazza Colonna). The most elegant of the stores, with a vast range of goods, especially fashion for women and children. **Oviesse**, 62 Viale Trastevere. Basic store for household goods, clothes and cosmetics. **Upim**, 172 Via del Tritone and Piazza Santa Maria Maggiore. Economical store for household goods, cosmetics and children's clothes.

Fashion

Those into serious shopping and couture names head to the Piazza di Spagna area and explore the high-fashion temples that are **Via dei Condotti**, **Via Bocca di Leone** and **Via Borgognona**. **Prada**, **Gucci**, **Armani**, **Dolce & Gabbana**, **Trussardi**, **Valentino**, **Hogan**, **Laura Biagiotti**, **Emanuel Ungaro**, **Tod's** and **Max Mara** all succeed one another in dizzying fashion. If prices are not within your reach fear not as there are many less-expensive alternatives.

Via del Corso is a street of good budget options. Although crass in parts, it holds some true pearls for high street fashion fanatics, such as **Diesel**, **Miss Sixty**, **Benetton** and **Zara**.

Via dei Giubbonari (off Campo de' Fiori) and **Via del Governo Vecchio** (off Piazza Navona) are also great streets for exploring new and original fashions.

Via Cola di Rienzo, linking the Vatican with the Tiber (and Piazza del Popolo on the other bank) is lined with many of the mid-market and more elegant shops found in the city centre and offers a good opportunity for a change of scene.

Off to the southeast is the hilly **Monti** district where there are some interesting clothing and artisans' boutiques.

Here's a small selection of the city's countless chic boutiques:
Angelo Nepi, 28 Via Dei Giubbonari, sells colourful fitted jackets, wide linen trousers and beautiful dresses and scarves.
Arsenale, 64 Via del Governo Vecchio, is the place for local designer Patrizia Pieroni's eye-catching creations.
Carla G, 121 Via del Babuino, sells garments that are classy, well-cut and very sassy.
Ethic, 11 Piazza B. Cairoli (end of Via dei Giubbonari) is one of many branches of a casualwear company that mixes styles, genres and fabrics with a penchant for the ethnic or unusual. Great looking, well priced, but the quality is not the highest.
Furla, 22 Piazza di Spagna, and other branches around Rome, is Italy's mid-market answer to the

bag dilemma, with a widely varied, constantly changing range of leather bags and accessories. Good quality, and pleasingly modest prices.
Kristina Ti, 40 Via Mario de' Fiori, makes sexy and feminine dresses and bikinis.
Patrizia Pepe, 1 Via Frattina, is a Florentine designer who creates modern, feminine wear at user-friendly prices.
Maga Morgana, 27 and 98 Via del Governo Vecchio, specialises in Luciana Iannace's hand-knitted garments and old-fashioned dresses.

Leatherware & Shoes

Boccanera, 36 Via Luca della Robbia (Testaccio). All the big Italian (and some foreign) brands under one roof: Hogan, Tod's, Prada, Sergio Rossi and Pollini.
Bruno Magli, 6 Via Condotti. Prestigious shoemaker for over 70 years, experiencing a major rebirth.
Calzature Fausto Santini, 165 Via Santa Maria Maggiore. His main store is on Via Frattina, but this is where you get Santini's gems from past collections at half-price.
Di Cori, 53 Piazza di Spagna. All sorts of gloves.
Diomedi, 99 Piazza San Bernardo. An old-fashioned shop selling exquisite beauty cases, suitcases and briefcases.
Fendi, 419–21 Largo Goldoni. The new mega-space for Fendi's classic and cult items, created season after season.
Geox, 3 Via Frattina. Comfortable, wearable and sexy shoes – a bit like Camper shoes.
Gucci, 8 Via Borgognona. Accessories that ooze elegance, style and quality.
Fratelli Rossetti, 59 Via Condotti. Another classic Italian footwear maker, from Milan.
Nuyorica, 36–37 Piazza Pollarola. A shoe-lover's dream, with a selection by Marni, Balenciaga, Rodolphe Menudier and Sigerson Morrison. Very hip, pretty pricey.

Pollini, 22–24 Via Frattina. Classic shoes and handbags.
Tod's, 56a–57 Via Fontanella Borghese. Diego Della Valle's shoes and bags, sold here, have become cult items.

Books

Almost Corner Bookshop, 45 Via del Moro. Australian run, with well-chosen and reasonably-priced titles.
Anglo-American Book Co., 102 Via della Vite. Novels, art books, travel tomes and a section for kids, all in English; friendly staff.
Bibli, 28 Via dei Fienaroli. Large Italian-language bookshop and café; has an internet point and does nice Sunday brunches.
The English Bookshop, Via di Ripetta 248. A good range of travel, non-fiction and children's books, plus a café
Feltrinelli International, 84 Via V.E. Orlando. A large selection of English-language books.
Herder, 117 Piazza di Montecitorio. A good selection of travel books and classics.
Libreria del Viaggiatore, 78 Via del Pellegrino. Travel books in Italian and English.
Lion Bookshop, 33 Via dei Greci 33. The oldest English bookshop in Rome with a wide assortment and a coffee shop.

Gifts

Via della Conciliazione, linking the Vatican with Castel Sant'Angelo, offers a wide range of religious artefacts including Vatican coins, statues, stamps, religious books and souvenirs. Similar objects are on sale around the Vatican itself and on Via dei Cestari, between the Pantheon and Largo Argentina.
Ai Monasteri, 72 Corso Rinascimento. In an old pharmacy; it sells teas, honeys, liqueurs, ointments and potions made by monks from all over Italy.
Al Sogno, 53 Piazza Navona. Historic toy store specialising in soft toys of all shapes and sizes.
Città del Sole, 65 Via della Scrofa. A store for progressive parents and their progeny,

ARTISANS

Skilled *artigiani* (artisans) are a feature of life in Rome. Many of their workshops *(botteghe)* are open to the public and it can be a real pleasure to buy their hand-crafted, distinctive articles. The following are among the most interesting and reliable but you are bound to come across more as you wander around the historic centre *(see page 63*:

Borse Scultura, 67a Largo degli Osci, tel: 06-4469284. Exquisitely crafted leather bags and briefcases, ranging from the eccentric to the classically beautiful are made here by Claudio Sanò.

Ceramica Sarti, 21 Via Santa Dorotea, tel: 06-5882079. Domenico and Lavinia, a father-and-daughter team of skilled potters, make beautiful ceramic lamps, wall lights, bowls and baskets.

Farnese, 53–54 Via Garibaldi, tel: 06-5817566. Expensive and internationally renowned groups of artisans who create stunning ceramic tiles inspired by those found in classical Roman villas and 18th-century patrician houses. Some lovely antique items, too.

GiuncArt, 93 Via del Pellegrino, tel: 06-68806204. Specialises in anything made from grasses, rushes and bamboo. Pieces of furniture, chairs and baskets in all shapes and sizes are available, and restoration work is also done by shop owner, Umberto Giovagnoli.

La Grande Officina, 165b Via dei Sabelli, tel: 06-4450348. A

husband-and-wife team make every item here from scratch. They show off precious and semi-precious stones and pearls to maximum effect, using inventive and sometimes spectacular mountings, and fashion Balinese coins into rings. There are items to suit all budgets.

Ivano Langella, Laboratorio Artigiano, 73a Via di Ponte Sisto, tel: 333-4209100. Truly unusual jewellery made of gold, silver and bronze and incorporating pearls, horn and even plants. Ivano will make to measure in three to five days and will ship items abroad.

Officina della Carta, 26b Via di Benedetta, tel: 06-5895557. Note pads, diaries, recipe books and photo albums are crafted in this tiny workshop-boutique, where items can also be made to order.

Rachele, 6–7 Vicolo del Bollo, tel: 06-6864975. Original clothing for discerning children under the age of seven.

La Terra di AT, 13 Via degli Ausoni, tel: 06-491748. An exquisite, ethnically inspired selection of ceramics includes brightly coloured, contemporary bowls, mugs and vases as well as unusual gold- and platinum-plated jewellery.

Le Tre Ghinee, 53a Via del Pellegrino, tel: 06-6872739. This *bottega* is run by a mother and her daughters, who employ Tiffany glass and ceramics to make unusual jewellery and objets d'art, and run evening classes where they pass on their skills.

the traditional made out of bamboo and cast iron and come from all over the world.

Food and Wine

Innocenzi, 31 Via Natale del Grande. An old-fashioned treasure trove of a deli selling rice and grain out of big canvas sacks, many organic products, and ethnic foods from all over the world, as well as regional Italian delicacies.

Constantini, 16 Piazza Cavour. Over 2,000 Italian wines to choose from.

Panella, 4 Largo Leopardi. A bread and pastry shop straight out of one's dreams.

Trimani, 20 Via Goito. Good selection of wines and tempting delicacies.

Volpetti, 47 Via Marmorata. Probably the best delicatessen in Rome.

Interior Design

Architettura D'interni, 27–29 Via Bissolati. A striking store where interior design and architecture blend seamlessly.

Spazio Sette, 7 Via dei Barbieri. One of Rome's premier furniture and home furnishings stores.

Sisters, 143 Via dei Banchi Vecchi. Three women run this eccentric and opulent space selling mirrors, lights, vases and some furniture.

Tad, 155a Via del Babuino. A so-called "concept store" with all the designer lifestyle must-haves: fashion, footwear, cosmetics, magazines, furniture. There's also a florist, hairdresser and a café.

Thè Verde, 23 Via Vittoria. A lovely store selling ethnic and Oriental fabrics for the home.

MCM900, 10 Vicolo del Cedro (Trastevere). At the foot of the Gianicolo, this lovely shop is dedicated to 1900s' period pieces. Staff are informed and friendly.

Jewellery

Buccellati, 31 Via Condotti. Famous Florentine jeweller's, best known for their elaborately worked silver pieces.

crammed with educational toys, games and books.

Fabriano, 173 Via del Babuino. Quality writing paper, photo albums, wallets and travel diaries, plus a section with drawing products for children.

Musicali, 473 Via del Corso, www.messaggeriemusicali.it.

Huge music shop with a good video and DVD selection. Also sells concert tickets and international magazines. Open late.

Tè e Teiere, 85 Via del Pellegrino. Tel: 06-6868824. A tea-lover's haven with expert staff. The teas, pots and cups range from the modern and colourful to

Bulgari, 10 Via Condotti. The supreme jeweller to royalty and the stars.

Ivano Langella, 73a Via di Ponte Sisto. Not your run-of-the-mill jeweller, Langella moulds chunks of silver, gold and bronze into unusual and stunning pendants, rings and necklaces *(see Artigiani, opposite page)*.

Massimo Maria Melis, 57 Via dell'Orso. Custom-made jewellery, inspired by Roman and Etruscan artefacts.

Kitchenware

C.U.C.I.N.A., 65 Via Mario de' Fiori. Trendy, good-quality kitchenware with an appealing mix of prices.

Gusto, 9 Piazza Augusto Imperatore. Attached to the Gusto mega-restaurant *(see restaurants, page 102)* this is a delightful store with the most unusual and well-made cooking utensils and gadgets as well as a range of cookery books and magazines.

Leone Limentani, 47 Via del Portico d'Ottavia. A wide variety of discounted ceramics, crystal, china and cutlery, and Alessi products, in a dusty and rambling warehouse.

SPORT

Spectator Sports

You can find information on sporting events in two national papers devoted solely to sport: *Corriere dello Sport* and *Gazetta dello Sport* – easy enough to understand even if you speak no Italian. Many local sporting events are also listed in Rome editions of the daily papers.

Football

Sporting life in Rome, as elsewhere in Italy, revolves around football *(calcio)*. Rome's Olympic Stadium is home to both the local clubs, SS Lazio and AS Roma, who play there from September to May. For fixtures,

ticket information and official team paraphernalia, go to the Lazio Point, 34 Via Farini (near Termini) or the AS Roma Store, 360 Piazza Colonna.

Major Events

The two major sporting events that take place in Rome during the year and attract international stars and audiences, are:

Concorso Ippico Internazionale (International Horse Show) at Piazza Siena in the gardens of the Villa Borghese in May (ask at a tourist information point or log on to www.fise.it).

Also in May is the **Italian Tennis Open** (www.masters-series. com), held at the Foro Italico.

Participant Sports

Gyms

The sport Romans are most interested in is weight training at a local *palestra* (gym). The largest gym in the centre (which also has two Olympic indoor pools) is the **Roman Sport Center**, 33 Via del Galoppatoio, tel: 06-3201667 (closed Sun) on the edge of Villa Borghese (access from the car park at the top of Via Veneto).

Fitness First, 44 Via Giolitti, tel: 06-47826300, in Termini railway station is kitted out with all the latest technogym equipment.

Swimming

For a hot city, Rome is decidedly under-provided with swimming pools and most that *do* exist are privately run. The few city council pools are booked up with slot systems that are incomprehensible and inaccessible even for many Romans. Some of the luxury hotels (especially those outside the historic centre) offer access to their pools. If you choose this option be prepared to pay for it; make an afternoon of it and enjoy a pleasant cocktail by the pool.

Cavalieri Hilton Hotel, 101 Via Cadiolo (Monte Mario), tel: 06-35091 *(see Accommodation, page 215)*.

CSI Roma Nuoto, 55 Lungotevere Flaminio (Flaminio), tel: 06-3234732.

ES Hotel, 171 Via Filippo Turati, tel: 06-444841, www.eshotel.it. A truly stunning rooftop pool with a unique view of Termini's train tracks and a "different" Roman panorama below.

Hotel Parco dei Principi, 5 Via G. Frescobaldi, tel: 06-854421.

Piscina delle Rose, 20 Viale America, tel: 06-5926717. Take the Metro to EUR Palasport. A large outdoor pool with rose gardens nearby. June to September only.

Other possibilities for swimming are the beaches and the lakes. The lakes are more pleasant than the beaches closest to Rome. Swimming is possible in Lago di Bracciano, the lakes of the Castelli Romani and several other smaller lakes.

Tennis

Most tennis courts belong to private clubs and are open to members and their guests only. Check with your hotel or tourist office for clubs that allow non-members to play.

SIGHTSEEING TOURS

Walking and sightseeing tours are organised by a number of travel agencies and tour guides, both licensed and unlicensed. The quality of what's on offer varies wildly. Recommended is **Enjoy Rome**, 8/a Via Marghera, tel: 06-4451843, www.enjoyrome .com), a friendly English-speaking office near the station that organises walking tours of Rome. They range from the Vatican to the Jewish Ghetto and Trastevere. A recent addition is the food- and wine-tasting tour, and they do a night tour and one by bike. They also organise day trips to the ruins of Pompeii (south of Naples), Tivoli and Ostia Antica and can advise on cheap accommodation.

TRANSPORT

ACCOMMODATION

ACTIVITIES

A – Z

LANGUAGE

A - Z

DIRECTORY OF PRACTICAL INFORMATION

A dmission Charges

Museum admission fees vary but the major ones start at about €6 while the minor ones cost about €3. Most state or municipal museums offer free entrance to EU citizens under 18 and over 65. The entrance ticket to the Palatine can be used to visit the Colosseum. Entrance to the Roman Forum, the Pantheon, and all basilicas and churches is free, as are the Vatican Museums on the last Sunday of the month (expect long queues).

B udgeting for your Trip

Prices have rocketed in Rome in recent years, with many blaming the euro and lack of government control when it was introduced.

Things have calmed down a bit, and some prices have normalised, but hotels and restaurants were two of the worst-hit sectors and in some cases prices have doubled. Bearing this in mind, expect to pay at least €160 a night for a double room if you want to stay in the city centre somewhere decent. For a more elegant hotel the prices are well over €200 a night. In a restaurant, a three-course evening meal with wine costs about €40 a head, on average. You will pay a bit less at lunchtime, or if you find a neighbourhood *trattoria* in the suburbs or something off the beaten track, and more if you are in blatant tourist territory or in a modern minimalist restaurant with a 'creative' menu. One thing that remains very cheap is public

transport. A single tickets costs €1 and can be used for 75 minutes, and a number of passes are available. There are one-day, three-day and seven-day passes, called *Biglietto Integrato Giornaliero, Biglietto Turistico Integrato* and *Carta Integrata Settimanale*, which are good for unlimited Metro, bus and local train or regional bus travel. They need to be validated only on first use. Month-long passes, *Abbonamento Mensile*, are also available. COTRAL, the regional bus company, offers a regional daypass *(BIRG)*, which covers your round trip and in-city travel. Taxis are also cheaper than in most other capital cities, with a trip from the station to the centre (Piazza Navona) costing about €12–15 depending on the traffic.

Business Hours

Business hours vary greatly, but in general, shops open Monday–Saturday 9am–1pm and 3.30–7.30pm. Many close on Monday morning. Recently, in the touristy areas, many shops have started opening on Sunday and through lunch. Hairdressers and barbers are open all day but closed on Monday. In general, the small food shops are open 8am–1.30pm and 5.30–8pm, and closed Saturday afternoon in summer and Thursday afternoon the rest of the year. Many shops close for two weeks in August.

Churches generally open 7am–7pm with a three-hour lunch break; the four main basilicas open 7am–7pm with no lunchtime closure.

Banks open Monday–Friday 8.30am–1.30pm and 2.45–4pm; a few in the city centre also open Saturday morning.

Most currency exchange bureaux open until 7.30pm Monday–Saturday, and in very touristy areas even later.

State and city museums are closed on Monday, but there are a few exceptions: the Colosseum, the Roman Forum and the Imperial Fora, the Domus Aurea, the Vatican Museums and the Galleria Doria Pamphili are all open on Monday.

C limate

Despite some very unusual weather in the past few years (snow and hail in July, heatwaves in May), Rome can still be said to have a classic Mediterranean climate: mild-ish winters and very hot, long summers. July and August are the hottest and most humid months when it is advisable to stay indoors or in the shade in the middle of the day.

When to Visit

May, June, September and October are the best months to visit as the weather is usually sunny and warm but devoid of that heavy, airless quality. This makes moving around on foot much easier and a real pleasure. In July and August many Romans go on holiday (especially around the Feast of the Assumption on 15 August) but for the past few years the city council has put on an incredible range of outdoor, world-class concerts and other cultural events from June to September and the city is less deserted than it used to be.

What to Wear

Light summer clothes are suitable from spring to autumn. The Roman heat is sometimes alleviated by a sea breeze which can produce cool evenings even in summer, so a cardigan or jacket is useful. Wear a hat if you are sensitive to heat. Sunglasses are essential.

In summer, the likelihood of rain is slight: sometimes there is no rainfall in Rome for more than three months. If it does rain, it will probably be a downpour in a thunderstorm. There is little point in preparing for this: just run for cover. At other times of the year, some form of waterproofing is worth considering, but not worth a lot of weight in your luggage. The most likely times for rain are autumn and spring.

In winter, warmer clothes are needed, including a heavy overcoat, as it can be very cold. Indoors, you may find the heating levels are below your expectations. In response to the climate, Roman building design has always concentrated on keeping heat out, rather than creating cosy interiors.

If visiting churches, and particularly St Peter's, remember that bare arms or shorts (on men or women) and short skirts are not acceptable, and you will be refused admittance. If wearing a short-sleeved or sleeveless garment, carry a light shirt/blouse or scarf with you.

Romans, like most Italians, consider clothes important. Although they are slightly less

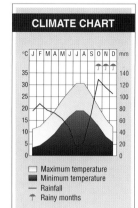

CLIMATE CHART

- ☐ Maximum temperature
- ■ Minimum temperature
- — Rainfall
- ⊤ Rainy months

obsessive than Florentines or Milanese, most will dress smartly for an evening out, a restaurant meal or a visit to the theatre. Although this is very rarely required and Rome is accustomed to casually dressed tourists, you may wish to follow local habits.

Dress codes for discos and bars vary enormously and change with the seasons and fashions. In general, however, dress is still likely to be slightly more formal than would be expected in much of Northern Europe or the USA.

Crime and Safety

The main problem tourists experience in Rome is petty crime: pickpocketing and bag snatching, together with theft from parked cars. Reduce the possibility of theft by taking elementary precautions. Leave money and valuables, including airline tickets, in the hotel safe. Carry your camera out of sight and always be discreet with your money or wallet (don't put it in your back pocket).

If you are carrying a handbag, keep it on the side away from the road, and when sitting in a café, place it firmly on your lap; one Roman speciality is the motorbike snatch. Backpacks, while convenient, make easy targets: take them off or sling them under your arm in crowds. Always keep a separate record of credit-card and cheque numbers just in case. A photocopy of your passport is also a useful precaution.

On the streets and particularly near the main tourist attractions, keep an eye on beggars, particularly the small children who crowd around you with boxes in their hands. Take extra care on crowded buses and the Metro and on bus routes frequented by tourists, such as the No. 40 Express and the No. 64.

Put a car with a foreign number plate in a garage overnight. Take your radio out, even if your insurance company will replace it, because fixing a broken windscreen means wasted time and trouble. Don't leave any items visible in the car.

If you are unlucky enough to have something stolen, report the theft to the police as soon as possible: you will need the police report for any insurance claim and to replace stolen documents. For information on the nearest police station call the central station, the Questura Centrale, 15 Via San Vitale, tel: 06-46861 or 06-46863401.

Customs

Customs restrictions on alcohol, cigarettes and some other items no longer apply to members of EU countries, although there are guide levels designed to prevent illegal trading, and the amount of goods should fall within what can reasonably be described as "for personal use". For US citizens, the duty-free allowance is 200 cigarettes, 50 cigars, 1 US quart of alcoholic beverages and duty-free gifts to the value of $100.

D isabled Travellers

Rome is a difficult city for people with disabilities. Most churches and museums and even outdoor archaeological sites have steps; streets and pavements are often uneven or cobbled, and pavements in the medieval centre are frequently too narrow for a wheelchair or have cars parked on the wheelchair access ramps. However, things are improving and the following museums have installed functioning ramps and lifts: the Vatican Museums, Galleria Doria Pamphili, Castel Sant' Angelo, St Peter's, Galleria Borghese and Galleria Nazionale d'Arte Moderna. Ask at the tourist information points for other sites with facilities for people with disabilities.

Some trains have access for the disabled, but check with the railway before travelling. Seats at the front of city buses are reserved for the disabled, and many have designated wheelchair areas in the centre. The newest trams and buses all have large central doors and access ramps; they are recognisable by the international symbol for accessibility on the front and side of the vehicle.

If travelling by car, there are free parking spaces for drivers with disabilities displaying an official placard.

Restaurants are usually helpful, but call in advance to ask about access. A number of hotels claim to offer access to travellers with disabilities: check with the individual hotel – be as precise as possible about your needs and ask detailed questions.

For more information about accessible hotels, museums and toilets, contact the association

DISABILITY SERVICE

To find out more about a special transport service for people with disabilities, which is free if you carry proof of your disability, tel: 06-46954001, www.trambus.com/trasportodisabili.htm.

COIN (tel: 06-23269231, www.coinsociale.it) who also publish leaflets on the subject.

E lectricity

Standard is 220 volts AC, 50 cycles. Sockets have either two or three round pins. For UK visitors, adaptors can be bought before you leave home, or at airports and main railway stations. Travellers from the US will need a transformer.

Embassies and Consulates

Consulates generally have answering machines on which you can leave a message in the event of a query or problem. If your passport is lost or stolen you will need to obtain a police report and have proof of your identity and suitable photos in order to get a new one: check your country's requirements before setting out.

Australia
215 Via Alessandria
Tel: 06-852721
www.italy.embassy.gov.au
Canada
27 Via G.B. De Rossi
Tel: 06-445981
www.canada.it
Ireland
3 Piazza Campitelli
Tel: 06-6979121
New Zealand
28 Via Zara
Tel: 06-4417171
South Africa
14 Via Tanaro
Tel: 06-852541
www.sudafrica.it
United Kingdom
80/a Via XX Settembre
Tel: 06-42200001
www.britain.it
United States of America
119/a Via Veneto
Tel: 06-46741
www.usembassy.it
Consulate: 121 Via Veneto
Tel: 06-46741

TRANSPORT
ACCOMMODATION
ACTIVITIES
LANGUAGE

EMERGENCY NUMBERS	
Police	113
Carabinieri	112
Fire	115
Ambulance	118

Entry Requirements

Visas and Passports

EU passport holders do not require a visa; a valid passport or ID card is sufficient. Visitors from the US, Canada, Australia or New Zealand do not require visas for stays of up to three months. Nationals of most other countries do need a visa. This must be obtained in advance from the Italian Consulate. For addresses of embassies and consulates in Rome, *see previous page*.

G ay & Lesbian Travellers

Rome has an active and vibrant gay community. The national magazine, *Babilonia*, is published monthly and is available from most newsstands. For more information on cultural events and news, contact:
Circolo di Cultura Mario Mieli, Via Efeso 2/a, tel: 06-5413985, www.mariomieli.org.
Arci-Lesbica Roma, 15 Via Stefanini, tel: 06-4180211, www.arcilesbica.it, is a group that runs a helpline and organises social get-togethers for lesbians.
Babele, 116 Via dei Banchi Vecchi, tel: 06-6876628, is a gay bookshop and a good source of information (closed Sunday and Monday morning).
Alibi, 39 Via di Monte Testaccio, tel: 06-5743448, is a predominantly gay disco. Closed Monday and Tuesday.
Coming Out, 8 Via San Giovanni in Laterano (near the Colosseum) is a mainstay of the Roman gay scene that has become so popular it is often as crowded on the pavement outside as inside.
Hangar, 69A Via in Selci (near

Via Cavour), tel: 06-48813971, is a well-established gay club. Closed Tuesday.
Luna e L'altra, 1a Via San Francesco di Sales (in Trastevere), tel: 06- 68401727. A women-only evening restaurant in the recently renovated Casa Internazionale delle Donne (International House of Women, www.casainternazionaledelle-donne.org) where food is made from seasonal produce (closed Sunday).

H ealth and Medical Care

EU residents are entitled to the same medical treatment as an Italian citizen. Visitors will need to obtain and complete an E111 form (available from post offices in the UK) before they go. This covers medical treatment and medicines, although it is still necessary to pay prescription charges and a percentage of the costs for medicines.

Note that the E111 does not give any cover for trip cancellations, nor does it provide repatriation in case of illness. For this, you will need to take out private insurance. Canadian citizens are also covered by a reciprocal arrangement between the Italian and Canadian governments.

If you are covered by a reciprocal scheme and need to visit a doctor while in Italy, take the form E111 (if an EU resident) or proof of citizenship and residence (e.g. passport) to the local health office (Unità Sanitaria Locale) which will direct you to a doctor covered by the State system and supply the necessary paperwork. Not all doctors work in the State scheme, and those who do are often busy, so be prepared to wait. A consultation with a private doctor may be quicker (and certainly requires less preparatory paperwork) but costs more, so private insurance is a good idea. Medical standards are generally high. Standards of nursing and infrastructure are sometimes less so.

If you need emergency treatment, call 113 or tel: 06-5510 (Red Cross) for an ambulance or to get information on the nearest hospital with an emergency department *(pronto soccorso)* where you will be treated free at any time of the day or night. The most central is **Ospedale Fatebenfratelli**, Isola Tiberina, tel: 06-6837299. If your child is sick go to the **Ospedale Pediatrico Bambino Gesù**, 4 Piazza Sant'Onofrio, tel: 06-68591 on the Gianicolo hill.

Medical Services

The **International Medical Center** (tel: 06-4882371) is a private referral service for English-speaking doctors who are on call for house visits 24 hours a day. The **Rome American Hospital** (69 Via Emilio Longoni, tel: 06-22551), 30–40 minutes out of the town centre by taxi, has English-speaking doctors and dentists. The **George Eastman Hospital** (287 Viale Regina Elena, tel: 06-844831) is Rome's only 24-hour dental hospital.

Chemists

Chemists *(farmacia)* can easily be identified by a green cross. Opening hours are usually Monday—Saturday 8.30am–1pm and 4–8pm. A rotating system ensures there is always a chemist within walking distance which is open at night; a list outside every chemist indicates which it will be. Purchases at night carry a surcharge.

Some chemists are also open 24 hours a day. A couple of the most central are **Farmacia della Stazione**, 51 Piazza dei Cinquecento (corner of Via Cavour), tel: 06-488 0019 and **Farmacia Piram Omeopatia**, 228 Via Nazionale, tel: 06-4880754.

I nternet

There is no shortage of Internet cafés in Rome. Try:
Easy Everything
2 Via Barberini

Tel: 06/42903388
www.easyeverything.com
Open 24 hours a day. More
than 250 computers on three
floors; offers some of the
cheapest rates in town
(especially at night). Has a
café selling light snacks and
hot and cold beverages.
The Netgate
25 Piazza Firenze
Tel: 06-6893445
Open Monday–Saturday
7am–9pm. Trained staff and
37 hi-tech computers. It also
has a café

L ost Property

For property lost on trains anywhere in Rome ask at the Termini
Station's left-luggage office *(see
below)*. For property lost in post
offices or on public transport
(except trains) go to the City
Depot, Depositeria Comunale,
1 Via Nicolò Bettoni (in the Porta
Portese area of Trastevere), tel:
06-5816040 (Monday–Friday
8.30am–1pm).

Left Luggage

The left-luggage office in Termini
station is below ground level
(level −1) at the side of platform
24 (daily 7am–midnight).
Fiumicino Airport has 24-hour
left-luggage facilities in the
international terminals.

M aps

Free city maps showing the main
sights, museum opening hours
and useful numbers are available
from the main tourist information
office and tourist information
points dotted around town *(see
page 231)*. Free and extremely
comprehensive bus maps of the
city centre are available from
ATAC (public transport company)
at 59 Via Volturno (Monday–
Friday 9am–1pm, Tuesday and
Thursday also 2.30–5pm).
Detailed transport maps of the
city and outskirts called Roma
Metro-Bus can be bought at any
newsstand.

Most newsstands sell city
maps, as do museum shops. At
the latter ask for the Mondadori
maps, available in various
languages and very durable.

Media

Newspapers and Magazines

Most important European dailies
are available on the day of publication from the Rome street
kiosks, as is the *International
Herald Tribune*.

The main Rome-based Italian
newspapers are *La Repubblica*
and *Il Messaggero*. Other Italian
newspapers such as *Il Corriere
della Sera* publish Rome editions
with local news and entertainment listings. *La Stampa* offers
serious economics coverage.

By far the most convenient
way to find out about what's on in
Rome is *Roma C'è*, a comprehensive weekly guide to everything in
the city, from museums to art
exhibitions, shopping, eating,
films, etc. It comes out on
Wednesday and can be bought
from any newsstand throughout
the week. Listings are in Italian,
but decipherable with a little
effort, and there is an abbreviated section in English.

Wanted in Rome, a fortnightly
magazine in English, is another
good source for cultural listings,
classified ads and information on
museums and sights. The website (www.wantedinrome.com) is
updated regularly and contains
local news.

Porta Portese comes out on
Tuesday and Friday, with thousands of classified ads including
a large accommodation section.
Their website (www.porta
portese.com) is updated a little
after the paper version appears.

Television

Italy has six major networks
(three owned by State broad-
caster RAI and three by the
Mediaset group owned by the
Berlusconi family) and another

two that are increasingly popular,
MTV Italia and La7. MTV is the
Italian version of the ever-popular
US music channel and La7 offers
a worthy alternative to the other
six channels, which are all connected in some way to current
premier Silvio Berlusconi.

Most hotels also offer guests
CNN, BBC World, and some French
or German channels.

Radio

The three state-owned channels,
RAI 1 (89.7 Mhz FM), RAI 2 (91.2
Mhz FM), RAI 3 (93.7 Mhz FM),
offer popular music, classical
music, chat shows and news
(RAI 3 is the most serious); see
www.rai.it for a list of programmes.

The most popular music channels are Radio Capital (95.5 Mhz
FM, www.capital.it) and Radio Dee-
jay (101 Mhz FM, www.deejay.it).

Vatican Radio One-O-Five Live
(105 Mhz FM, www.vaticanradio.org)
offers news, commentary, inter-
views and spiritual programmes
in English.

Money

The unit of currency in Italy is the
euro (€), which is divided into
100 cents. There are 5, 10, 20,
50, 100, 200 and €500 notes,
and 1, 2, 5, 10, 20 and 50 cent
coins.

Changing Money

You need your passport or identi-
fication card when changing
money, which can be a slow
operation, so allow plenty of
time. Not all banks will provide
cash against a credit card, and
some may refuse to cash

LOST CREDIT CARDS

American Express
Tel: 06-72900347
Diner's Club
Freephone: 800-864064
MasterCard
Freephone: 800-870866
Visa
Freephone: 800-819014

travellers' cheques in certain currencies. Generally speaking, the larger banks (those with a national or international network) will handle tourist transactions best.

Travellers' cheques are the safest way to carry money, but not the most economical, since banks charge a commission for cashing them, and shops and restaurants give unfavourable exchange rates if they accept them at all.

Credit Cards

Major credit cards are accepted by most hotels, shops and restaurants in Rome but are less easy to use in the countryside. Very few petrol stations accept credit cards or travellers' cheques.

Automated cash dispensers (ATMs), called Bancomat, can be found throughout central Rome, and are linked with several international banking systems, including Cirrus. The transaction fee will depend on your home bank, but rates are generally the best.

Tipping

Service is not included in a restaurant bill unless noted on the menu. It is customary to leave a modest amount as a tip, but nothing like the 10–15 percent common in other countries. Romans usually leave between €1–5, depending on how satisfied they were with the service; tourists are expected to be slightly more generous.

By law, the old cover charge, called pane e coperto (bread and table linen), has been abolished, but still appears on many menus. Keep an eye out: in many cases it has turned into a charge for bread, which you may refuse if you wish.

Postal Services

Post offices are generally open Monday–Friday 8.30am–1pm, until 2pm on Saturday (a few are open later, see below).

PUBLIC HOLIDAYS

Banks and most shops are closed on the following holidays, and banks may close early on the preceding day.
• New Year's Day (Capodanno): 1 January
• Epiphany (Befana): 6 January
• Easter Monday (Lunedi di Pasqua): variable, March–April
• Liberation Day (Anniversario della Liberazione): 25 April
• May Day (Festa del Lavoro): 1 May
• Patron Saints of Rome (SS Pietro i Paolo): 29 June
• August holiday (Ferragosto): 15 August
• All Saints' Day (Ognissanti): 1 November
• Immaculate Conception (Immacolata Concezione): 8 December
• Christmas Day (Natale): 25 December
• Boxing Day (Santo Stefano): 26 December

Stamps (francobolli) for postcards and standard-weight letters to most destinations can be bought at many tobacconists (tabacchi) and bars that sell tobacco products. Often you can buy stamps when you buy your postcards. You will only need a post office for more complicated transactions, such as sending a parcel, express letter or fax, collecting Posta Restante, or withdrawing money from a post-office account.

Italian postboxes are red, but several blue boxes specifically for foreign letters have been set up in the centre. The Italian postal system has improved considerably in recent years and now runs a pretty efficient priority post service which gets letters and cards to their destination in three days for Europe and five days to North America, Australia, Asia and Africa. (Ask for posta prioritaria when buying your stamps.) If posting valuables or important documents, send them registered (raccommandata). If sending an urgent parcel ask for posta celere, a courier-style service that is slightly slower than the private companies but far cheaper.

The Vatican runs its own postal service. When visiting St Peter's, buy Vatican-issued stamps for your postcards and post them immediately: they are only valid in the Vatican City's blue postboxes.

Faxes can be sent from and received at most hotels (but

beware of price mark-ups) and from copy shops all over the city, and are often the most efficient means of communication.

The main post office, which has just been renovated, is in Piazza San Silvestro, just off Via del Corso (Monday–Saturday 8am–7pm). The post office at Stazione Termini is also open Monday–Saturday 8am–7pm. For more information visit www.poste.it or call the post-office helpline, tel: 803160, Monday–Saturday 8am–8pm. There are many other post offices: ask at your hotel or in a local bar for the nearest – Dov'è l'ufficio postale più vicino?

R eligious Services

When the hours of services or Masses are not specified, call ahead as the times vary.

Anglican
All Saints' Anglican Church
153/b Via del Babuino
Tel: 06-36001881
Sunday Eucharist: 8.30 and 10.30am
Catholic
Santa Susanna (American)
15 Via XX Settembre
Tel: 06-42014554
Sunday Masses: 9am and 10.30am (also 6pm Saturday)
San Silvestro (British)
1 Piazza S. Silvestro
Tel: 06-6797775
Sunday Mass: 10am and 5.30pm

St Patrick's (Irish)
60 Via Boncompagni
Tel: 06-4203121
Sunday Mass: 10am
Episcopal
St Paul's within the Walls
58 Via Napoli
Tel: 06-4883339
www.stpaulsrome.it
Sunday services: 8.30am and
10.30am
Jewish
Tempio Maggiore
(Comunità Ebraica)
Lungotevere Cenci
Tel: 06-6840061
Islamic
Moschea di Roma
(Centro Islamico)
Via della Moschea (Parioli)
Tel: 06-8082167
Presbyterian
St Andrew's Church of Scotland
7 Via XX Settembre
Tel: 06-4827627
Sunday service: 11am

S tudent Travellers

The Centro Turistico Studentesco
(CTS) is a chain of travel agents
designed to meet the needs of
young and student travellers. The

main branch is at 16 Via Genova,
tel: 06-4620431, but their website (www.cts.it) lists the others.
They can provide you with student discount cards, hostel membership and bookings, cheap
flights and language courses.

T elephones

Several companies provide public pay phones, but the most
ubiquitous phones are the silver
ones run by Telecom, which
accept phone cards *(scheda tele-
fonica)* only. You can buy them in
various denominations from
tabacchi and from many newsstands. Some payphones accept
credit cards, and many bars have
coin-operated payphones. Addi-
tionally, there are a number of
far cheaper international phone-
cards available from many newsstands, and there are call
centres where you can make
your call and pay later, particularly in the area around Stazione
Termini. Currently the best for
the UK and US are Europa and
Eurocity.
   Landlines in Rome have an 06
area code which you must use

whether calling from within
Rome, from outside Rome or
from abroad. Numbers in Rome
have four to eight digits. Toll-free
numbers start with 800.
   Mobile phone numbers begin
with 3, for example 338, 340,
333, 348, and cost a lot more. If
you bring your mobile phone with
you, remember that if you are calling a local number you will need
to dial the international access
code as well as the country code
before putting in the area code
and subscriber number.
   For a number outside Italy,
first dial 00 (the international
access code), then the country
code, the area code (omitting the
initial 0, if applicable) and then
the subscriber number.
   For local directory enquiries
dial 12; for international directory
enquiries, 892412, then press 4;
for operator-assisted national
and international calls, 170.

Time Zones

Italy follows Central European
Time (GMT +1). From the last Sunday in March to the last Sunday
in September, the clocks are
advanced one hour (GMT+2). The
following times apply in summer,
when it is noon in Rome:

New York	6am
London	11am
Italy	noon
Johannesburg	noon
Sydney	8pm

Toilets

Bars are obliged by law to let you
use their toilets. This doesn't
mean that they will do so with
good grace; if you don't consume
something at the bar first they
may throw you a look, or you may
find a sign reading *guasto* (broken) attached to the door even
when this is patently not the
case; however if you ask politely
you should not have any problems. In many cases bar toilets
are locked and you will need to
ask for the key *(chiave)* at the
till; once inside you may find out

AN AUDIENCE WITH THE POPE

For many, the highlight of a visit
to Rome is attending Mass in St
Peter's or even a Wednesday
morning audience with the
Pope. Mass is celebrated daily
in St Peter's in several different
languages. Confessions are
heard in English and many other
languages in all four main
Roman basilicas: St Peter's,
San Giovanni in Laterano, San
Paolo fuori le Mura and Santa
Maria Maggiore.
   To attend an audience with
the Pope, you need to write in
advance to the Prefettura della
Casa Pontificia, 00120 Città del
Vaticano, tel: 06-69883273, or
fax them on 06-69885863.
Specify the date you would like
to attend and give a local phone
number and address (your

hotel) where tickets can be
delivered. Alternatively, go to
the *prefettura* offices in St
Peter's Square (Mon–Sat
9am–1pm) and get the tickets
in person.
   The general audiences are
held either in St Peter's Square
or in the Audience Room or, during the summer, at Castel Gandolfo, the Pope's summer
residence in the Castelli
Romani. There is no charge for
attending an audience.
   If you are in Rome for Christmas or Easter and want to
attend Midnight Mass or Holy
Week celebrations, ask the
tourist information service for
times and other information, as
you may need tickets for some
events.

TRANSPORT

that there is no soap or toilet paper. In the past few years public and modern toilets have been opened near most of the major sights and monuments. You will have to pay a small fee to use them but there is a cleaner on hand and they never run out of toilet paper.

Tourist Information

The APT offices are well stocked with information about what's going on in Rome. They also have maps which contain an updated list of opening times for museums and historical sites, plus useful information and telephone numbers. Although they cannot book accommodation for you, they do have a comprehensive list of hotels in Rome and the environs.

Alternatively, the Hotel Reservation Service, operating from a booth in Stazione Termini opposite platform 20 (daily 7am–10pm), tel: 06-6991000, www.hotelreservation.it, makes commission-free reservations.

The main Rome Tourist Office (APT) is at 5 Via Parigi, tel: 06-488991 (Monday–Saturday 9am–7pm). The APT also runs an English-speaking tourist information call centre which you can call daily 9am–7.30pm, tel: 06-82059127. Branches, known as PIT (punto informativo turistico or tourist information points), are as follows; they are all open daily from 9.30am–7.30pm:

Piazza Pia (Castel Sant'Angelo)
Piazza del Tempio della Pace (Via dei Fori Imperiali)
Piazza delle Cinque Lune (Piazza Navona)
Via Nazionale (Palazzo delle Esposizioni)
Piazza Sonnino (Trastevere)
Piazza San Giovanni in Laterano
Via dell'Olmata (Santa Maria Maggiore)
Via Marco Minghetti (Fontana di Trevi)

There is also an information point in Stazione Termini, in front of platform 4, which is open daily 8am–9pm.

The Vatican tourist office (Uffi-cio Pellegrini e Turisti) is in Braccio Carlo Magno, Piazza San Pietro (to the left of the basilica), tel: 06-69881662 (Monday–Saturday 8.30am–6.30pm).

U seful Addresses

Italian Tourist Offices Abroad
Canada: 1 Place Ville Marie, Suite 1914, Montreal, Quebec H3B 3M9, tel: 514-866 7667.
Irish Republic: 47 Merrion Square, Dublin 2, tel: 01-766 397.
UK: 1 Princes Street, London W1R 8AY, tel: 020-7408 1254.
USA: 630 5th Avenue, Suite 1565, New York, NY 10111, tel: 212-245 4822/5618.
Travel Agents in Rome
American Express, 38 Piazza di Spagna, tel: 06-67641.
CIT Italia, 65 Piazza della Repub-blica, tel: 06-4825219
Airline Contacts
Air France, 40 Via Sardegna, tel: 06-487911.
Alitalia, 11 Via Bissolati, tel: 06-2222.
British Airways, Fiumicino Airport, tel: 06-65011575; call centre: tel: 199-712 266 (no office in the city).
Air Canada, Fiumicino Airport, tel: 06-65011462.
Delta Airlines, 40 Via Sardegna, freephone: 800-477999.

W ebsites

There is a wealth of tourist information available over the web. You could try:
www.romaturismo.com (official Rome tourism site)
www.comune.roma.it (Rome city council)
www.vatican.va (Vatican)
www.treniitalia.com (train information)
www.adr.it (airport information)
www.atac.it (public transport)
www.museionline.it (museums in Italy)
www.trovacinema.it (cinema

programmes for all Italy)
www.2night.it (regularly updated and hip nightlife and entertainment guide)

W eights & Measures

The metric system is used for all weights and measures. For a quick conversion: 2.5cm is approximately 1 inch, 1 metre is about a yard, 100g is just under 4oz and 1kg is 2lb 2oz. Distance is quoted in kilometres. One kilometre equals five-eighths of a mile, so 80 km is 50 miles.

Women Travellers

Women are likely to receive considerable male attention in Rome, especially if travelling alone. Most of this is amiable and unthreatening, but to minimise unwelcome attention, dress well and mimic Italian women's behaviour: walk tall, look no one in the eye and act as though you know exactly where you are going.

Most of the centre of Rome is reasonably safe, even at night, though the areas around Stazione Termini (particularly on Via Giolitti and near Porta Maggiore) are rather seedy and unappealingly deserted at night.

ACCOMMODATION
ACTIVITIES
A – Z
LANGUAGE

LANGUAGE

UNDERSTANDING THE ITALIANS

Basic Rules

Here are a few basic rules of grammar and pronunciation: *c* before *e* or *i* is pronounced "ch" as in *ciao*. *Ch* before *i* or *e* is pronounced as "k", e.g. *la chiesa*. Likewise, *sci* or *sce* are pronounced as in "sheep" or "shed" respectively. *Gn* in Italian is rather like the sound in "onion", while *gl* is softened to resemble the sound in "bullion". Nouns are either masculine (*il*, plural *i*) or feminine (*la*, plural *le*). Plurals are most often formed by changing an o to an i and an a to an e, e.g. *il panino, i panini; la chiesa, le chiese*. Words are stressed on the penultimate syllable unless an accent indicates otherwise.
Italian has formal and informal words for "You". In the singular, *Tu* is informal while *Lei* is more polite. It is best to use the formal form unless invited to do otherwise.

Basic Phrases

Yes *Sì*
No *No*
Thank you *Grazie*
Many thanks *Mille grazie/ tante grazie/molte grazie*
You're welcome *Prego*
All right/That's fine *Va bene*
Please *Per favore/per cortesia*
Excuse me (to get attention)
Scusi (singular), *Scusate* (plural);
(to attract attention from a waiter) *Senta!* **(in a crowd)**
Permesso; **(sorry)** *Mi scusi*
Could you help me? (formal)
Potrebbe aiutarmi?
Certainly *Ma, certo*
Can I help you? (formal) *Posso aiutarla?*
Can you help me? *Può aiutarmi, per cortesia?*
I need... *Ho bisogno di...*
I'm lost *Mi sono perso/a*
I'm sorry *Mi dispiace*
I don't know *Non lo so*
I don't understand *Non capisco*
Do you speak English/French?
Parla inglese/francese?
Could you speak more slowly?
Può parlare piu lentamente, per favore?
Could you repeat that please?
Può ripetere, per piacere?
here/there *qui/là*
yesterday/today/tomorrow
ieri/oggi/domani
now/early/late *adesso/ presto/tardi*
What? *Quale/Come...?*
When/Why/Where? *Quando/ Perché/Dove?*
Where is the lavatory? *Dov'è il bagno?*

Greetings

Hello (Good day) *Buon giorno*
Good afternoon/evening
Buona sera
Good night *Buona notte*
Goodbye *Arrivederci*
Hello/Hi/Goodbye (familiar)
Ciao
Mr/Mrs/Miss *Signor/Signora/ Signorina*
Pleased to meet you (formal)
Piacere di conoscerla
I am English/American/ Irish/Scottish/Canadian/ Australian *Sono inglese/ americano(a)/ irlandese/ scozzese/canadese/ australiano(a)*
I'm here on holiday *Sono qui in vacanze*
Is it your first trip to Rome?
É il suo/la sua primo viaggio a Roma?
Do you like it here? (formal)
Si trova bene qui?
How are you (formal/informal)?
Come sta (come stai)?
Fine, thanks *Bene, grazie*
See you later *A più tardi*
See you soon *A presto*
Take care (formal/informal)
Stia bene/Sta bene
Do you like Italy/Florence/ Rome/Venice? *Le piace Italia/Firenze/Roma/Venezia?*
I like it a lot *Mi piace moltissimo*

Telephone Calls

the area code *il prefisso telefonico*
I'd like to make a reverse-charge (collect) call *Vorrei fare una telefonata a carico del destinatario*

May I use your telephone?
Posso usare il telefono?
Hello (on the telephone) *Pronto*
My name's *Mi chiamo/Sono*
Could I speak to…? *Posso parlare con…?*
Sorry, he/she isn't in *Mi dispiace, è fuori*
Can he call you back? *Può richiamarLa?*
I'll try later *Riproverò piu tardi*
Can I leave a message?
Posso lasciare un messagio?
Please tell him I called
Gli dica, per favore, che ho telefonato
Hold on *Un attimo, per favore*
a local call *una telefonata urbana*
Can you speak up please? *Può parlare più forte, per favore?*

In the Hotel

Do you have any vacant rooms?
Avete delle camere libere?
I have a reservation *Ho fatto una prenotazione*
I'd like… *Vorrei*
a single/double room *una camera singola/doppia*
a room with twin beds *una camera a due letti*
a room with a bath/shower
una camera con bagno/doccia
for one night *per una notte*
for two nights *per due notti*
How much is it? *Quanto costa?*
On the first floor *Al primo piano*
Is breakfast included? *E compresa la prima colazione?*
Is everything included? *E tutto compreso?*
half/full board *mezza pensione/ pensione completa*
It's expensive *E caro*
Do you have a room with a balcony/view of the sea? *C'è una camera con balcone/con una vista del mare?*
a room overlooking the park/the street/the back *una camera con vista sul parco/che da sulla strada/sul retro*
Is it a quiet room? *E una stanza tranquilla?*
The room is too hot/cold/ noisy/small *La camera è troppo calda/fredda/rumorosa/piccola*

We have one with a double bed
Ne abbiamo una doppia/matri-moniale
Could you show me another room please? *Potrebbe mostrarmi un altra camera, per favore?*
Can I see the room? *Posso vedere la camera?*
What time does the hotel close?
A che ora chiude l'albergo?
I'll take it *La prendo*
big/small *grande/piccola*
What time is breakfast? *A che ora è la prima colazione?*
Please give me a call at… *Mi può chiamare alle…*
Come in! *Avanti!*
Can I have the bill, please?
Posso avere il conto, per favore?
Can you call me a taxi, please?
Può chiamarmi un taxi, per favore?
dining room *la sala da pranzo*
key *la chiave*
lift *l'ascensore*
towel *un asciugamano*
toilet paper *la carta igienica*

At a Bar

I'd like… *Vorrei…*
coffee:
(small, strong and black) *un caffè espresso;* **(with hot, frothy milk)** *un cappuccino;* **(weak, served in tall glass)** *un caffè lungo;* **(with alcohol, probably brandy)** *un caffè corretto*
tea *un tè*
lemon tea *un tè al limone*
herbal tea *una tisana*
hot chocolate *una cioccolata calda*
(bottled) orange/lemon juice *un succo d'arancia/di limone*
orange squash *aranciata*
freshly squeezed orange/lemon juice *una spremuta di arancia/di limone*
mineral water (fizzy/still) *acqua minerale gassata/naturale*
with/without ice *con/senza ghiaccio*
red/white wine *vino rosso/ bianco*
(draught) beer *una birra (alla spina)*

a bitter (Vermouth, etc) *un amaro*
milk *latte*
(half) a litre *un (mezzo) litro*
bottle *una bottiglia*
ice-cream *un gelato*
cone *un cono*
pastry/brioche *una pasta*
sandwich *un tramezzino*
roll *un panino*
Anything else? *Desidera qualcos'altro?*
Cheers *Salute*

In a Restaurant

I'd like to book a table *Vorrei prenotare una tavola*
I have a reservation *Ho fatto una prenotazione*
lunch/supper *pranzo/cena*
we do not want a full meal *Non desideriamo un pasto completo*
Could we have another table?
Potremmo spostarci?
I'm a vegetarian *Sono vegetari-ono/a*
Is there a vegetarian dish? *C'è un piatto vegetariano?*
May we have the menu? *Ci dia la carta?*
wine list *la lista dei vini*
What would you recommend?
Che cosa ci consiglia?
What would you like as a main course/dessert? *Che cosa prende di secondo/di dolce?*
What would you like to drink?
Che cosa desidera da bere?
a carafe of red/white wine *una caraffa di vino rosso/bianco*
fixed-price menu *il menù a prezzo fisso*
dish of the day *il piatto del giorno*
home-made *fatto in casa*
VAT (sales tax) *IVA*
cover charge *il coperto/ pane e coperto*
that's enough/no more/thanks *Basta così*
the bill, please *il conto per favore*
Is service included? *Il servizio è incluso?*
Where is the lavatory? *Dov'è il bagno?*
Keep the change *Va bene così*
I've enjoyed the meal *Mi è piaciuto molto*

Menu Decoder

Antipasti – Starters

antipasto misto **mixed hors d'oeuvres: cold cuts, cheeses, roast vegetables (ask for details)**
buffet freddo **cold buffet**
caponata **aubergine, olives, tomatoes**
insalata caprese **tomato and mozzarella salad**
insalata di mare **seafood salad**
insalata mista/verde **mixed/green salad**
melanzane alla parmigiana **fried or baked aubergine with parmesan and tomato**
mortadella/salame **similar to salami**
pancetta **bacon**
proscuitto **ham**
peperonata **grilled peppers drenched in olive oil**

Primi – First Courses

gli asparagi **asparagus (in season)**
brodetto **fish soup**
brodo **broth**
crespolini **savoury pancakes**
gnocchi **potato and dough dumplings**
la minestra **soup**
il minestrone **thick vegetable soup**
pasta e fagioli **pasta and bean soup**
il prosciutto (cotto/crudo) **(cooked/cured) ham**
i supplì **rice croquettes**
i tartufi **truffles (fresh in season, otherwise bottled or vacuum-packed)**
la zuppa **soup**

Secondi – Main Courses

La Carne **Meat**
allo spiedo **on the spit**
arrosto **roast meat**
ai ferri **grilled without oil**
al forno **baked**
al girarrosto **spit-roasted**
alla griglia **grilled**
involtini **skewered veal, ham, etc**
stagionato **hung, well-aged**
ben cotto **well-done (steak)**

media cottura **medium**
al sangue **rare**
l'agnello **lamb**
la bresaola **dried salted beef**
la bistecca **steak**
il capriolo/cervo **venison**
il carpaccio **wafer-thin beef**
il cinghiale **wild boar**
il controfiletto **sirloin steak**
le cotolette **cutlets**
il fagiano **pheasant**
il fegato **liver**
il filetto **fillet**
la lepre **hare**
il maiale **pork**
il manzo **beef**
l'ossobuco **shin of veal**
la porchetta **roast suckling pig**
il pollo **chicken**
le polpette **meatballs**
il polpettone **meat loaf**
la salsiccia **sausage**
il saltimbocca (alla Romana) **veal escalopes with ham**
le scaloppine **escalopes**
lo stufato **braised, stewed**
il sugo **sauce**
la trippa **tripe**
il vitello **veal**

Frutti di Mare **Seafood**
affumicato **smoked**
alle brace **charcoal grilled**
al ferro **grilled without oil**
fritto **fried**
alla griglia **grilled**
ripieno **stuffed**
al vapore **steamed**
acciughe **anchovies**
l'anguilla **eel**
l'aragosta **lobster**
il baccalà **dried salted cod**
i bianchetti **whitebait**
il branzino **sea bass**
i calamari **squid**
i calamaretti **baby squid**
la carpa **carp**
le cozze **mussels**
i crostacei **shellfish**
il fritto misto **mixed fried fish**
i gamberi **prawns**
i gamberetti **shrimps**
il granchio **crab**
il merluzzo **cod**
le ostriche **oysters**
il pesce **fish**
il pescespada **swordfish**
il polipo **octopus**

il risotto di mare **seafood risotto**
le sarde **sardines**
le seppie **cuttlefish**
la sogliola **sole**
surgelati **frozen**
il tonno **tuna**
la triglia **red mullet**
la trota **trout**
le vongole **clams**

I Legumi/La Verdura – Vegetables

a scelta **of your choice**
gli asparagi **asparagus**
la bietola **(similar to spinach)**
il carciofo **artichoke**
i carciofini **artichoke hearts**
le carote **carrots**
il cavolo **cabbage**
la cicoria **chicory**
la cipolla **onion**
i contorni **side dishes**
i fagioli **beans**
i fagiolini **French beans**
fave **broad beans**
il finocchio **fennel**
i funghi **mushrooms**
l'indivia **endive/chicory**
l'insalata mista **mixed salad**
l'insalata verde **green salad**
la melanzana **aubergine/eggplant**
le patate **potatoes**
le patatine fritte **chips/fries**
i peperoni **peppers**
i piselli **peas**
i pomodori **tomatoes**
le primizie **spring vegetables**
il radicchio **red, bitter lettuce**
i ravanelli **radishes**
ripieno **stuffed**
rughetta **rocket**
spinaci **spinach**
la verdura **green vegetables**
la zucca **pumpkin/squash**
zucchini **courgettes**

La Frutta – Fruit

le albicocche **apricots**
le arance **oranges**
le banane **bananas**
le ciliege **cherries**
il cocomero **watermelon**
i fichi **figs**
le fragole **strawberries**
frutti di bosco **fruits of the forest**
i lamponi **raspberries**
la mela **apple**
la pera **pear**

TRANSPORT

la pesca **peach**
le uve **grapes**

I Dolci – Desserts

al carrello **desserts from the trolley**
la cassata **Sicilian ice cream with candied peel**
il dolce **dessert/sweet**
le fritelle **fritters**
un gelato (di lampone/limone) **(raspberry/lemon) ice cream**
una granita **water ice**
una macedonia di frutta **fruit salad**
un semifreddo **semi-frozen dessert (many types)**
il tartufo (nero) **(chocolate) ice-cream dessert**
il tiramisù **cold, creamy rum and coffee dessert**
la torta **cake/tart**
zabaglione **sweet dessert made with eggs and Marsala**
zuccotto **ice-cream liqueur**
la zuppa inglese **trifle**

Basic Foods

aceto **vinegar**
aglio **garlic**
burro **butter**
formaggio **cheese**
frittata **omelette**
grissini **bread sticks**
marmellata **jam**
olio **oil**
pane **bread**
pane integrale **wholemeal bread**
parmigiano **parmesan cheese**
pepe **pepper**
riso **rice**
sale **salt**
senape **mustard**
uova **eggs**
zucchero **sugar**

Sightseeing

abbazia (badia) **abbey**
basilica **church**
biblioteca **library**
castello **castle**
centro storico **old town/historic centre**
chiesa **church**
duomo/cattedrale **cathedral**
fiume **river**
giardino **garden**
lago **lake**

mercato **market**
monastero **monastery**
monumenti **monuments**
museo **museum**
parco **park**
pinacoteca **art gallery**
ponte **bridge**
ruderi **ruins**
scavi **excavations/archaeological site**
spiaggia **beach**
torre **tower**
ufficio turistico **tourist office**
il custode **custodian**
il sacristano **sacristan**
Aperto/a **Open**
Chiuso/a **Closed**
Chiuso per la festa/per ferie/per restauro **Closed for the festival/holidays/restoration**

At the Shops

What time do you open/close?
A che ora apre/chiude?
Pull/Push (sign on doors)
Tirare/Spingere
Entrance/Exit *Entrata/Uscita*
Can I help you? (formal) *Posso aiutarla?*
What would you like? *Che cosa desidera?*
I'm just looking *Sto soltanto guardando*
How much is this? *Quanto viene?*
Do you take credit cards? *Accettate le carte di credito?*
I'd like... *Vorrei...*
This one/that one *questo/quello*
Have you got...? *Avete...?*
We haven't got (any) *Non (ne) abbiamo*
Can I try it on? *Posso provare?*
the size (for clothes) *la taglia*
What size do you take? *Qual'è la sua taglia?*
the size (for shoes) *il numero*
Is there/do you have...? *C'è (un/una)...?*
Yes, of course *Si, certo*
No, we haven't (there isn't) *No, non c'è*
That's too expensive *È troppo caro*
Please write it down for me *Me lo scriva, per favore*
cheap *economico/a buon prezzo*

Do you have anything cheaper? *Ha niente che costa di meno?*
It's too small/big *È troppo piccolo/grande*
brown/blue/black *marrone/blu/nero*
green/red/white/yellow *verde/rosso/bianco/giallo*
pink/grey/gold/silver *rosa/grigio/oro/argento*
No thank you, I don't like it *Grazie, ma non è di mio gusto*
I'll take it/I'll leave it *Lo prendo/lo lascio*
This is faulty. May I have a replacement/refund? *C'è un difetto. Me lo potrebbe cambiare/rimborsare?*
Anything else? *Altro?*
The cash desk is over there *Si accomodi alla cassa*
Give me some of those *Mi dia alcuni di quelli lì*
(half) a kilo *un (mezzo) kilo*
100 grams *un etto*
200 grams *due etti*
more/less *piu/meno*
with/without *con/senza*
a little *un pochino*

Types of Shops

antique dealer *l'antiquario*
bakery/cake shop *la panetteria/pasticceria*
bank *la banca*
bookshop *la libreria*
boutique/clothes shop *il negozio di moda*
butcher's *la macelleria*
chemist's *la farmacia*
delicatessen *la salumeria*
dry cleaner's *la tintoria*
fishmonger's *la pescheria*
florist *il fioraio*
food shop *l'alimentari*
greengrocer's *l'ortolano/il fruttivendolo*
grocer's *l'alimentari*
hairdresser's *il parucchiere*
ice-cream parlour *la gelateria*
jeweller's *il gioielliere*
leather shop *la pelletteria*
market *il mercato*
newsstand *l'edicola*
post office *l'ufficio postale*
shoe shop *il negozio di scarpe*
stationer's *la cartoleria*
tobacconist *il tabaccaio*
travel agency *l'agenzia di viaggi*

ACCOMMODATION
ACTIVITIES
A – Z
LANGUAGE

Travelling

aeroplane *l'aereo*
airport *l'areoporto*
arrivi/departures
arrivi/partenze
boarding card *un biglietto di bordo*
boat *la barca*
bus *l'autobus/il pullman*
bus station *l'autostazione*
coach *il pullman*
couchette *la cucetta*
connection *la coincidenza*
ferry *il traghetto*
ferry terminal *la stazione marittima*
first/second class *la prima/ seconda classe*
flight *il volo*
left-luggage office *il deposito bagagli*
platform *il binario*
port *il porto*
porter *il facchino*
railway station *ferrovia (la stazione ferroviaria)*
return ticket *un biglietto andata e ritorno*
single ticket *un biglietto solo andata*
sleeping car *la carrozza letti/ il vagone letto*
smokers/non-smokers *fumatori/non-fumatori*
station *la stazione*
stop *la fermata*
ticket office *la biglietteria*
train *il treno*
WC *gabinetto*

At the Station

(trains, buses and ferries)
Can you help me please? *Mi può aiutare, per favore?*
Where can I buy tickets? *Dove posso fare i biglietti?*
at the ticket office/at the counter *alla biglietteria/allo sportello*
What time does the train leave/arrive? *A che ora parte/arriva il treno?*
Can I book a seat? *Posso prenotare un posto?*
Are there any seats available? *Ci sono ancora posti liberi?*
Is this seat free/taken? *E libero/occupato questo posto?*

I'm afraid this is my seat *E il mio posto, mi dispiace*
You'll have to pay a supplement *Deve pagare un supplemento*
Do I have to change? *Devo cambiare?*
Where does it stop? *Dove si ferma?*
You need to change in Rome *Bisogna cambiare a Roma*
Which platform does the train leave from? *Da quale binario parte il treno?*
The train leaves from platform one *Il treno parte dal binario uno*
When is the next train/bus/ferry for Naples? *Quando parte il prossimo treno/ pullman/ traghetto per Napoli?*
How long does the crossing take? *Quanto dura la traversata?*
What time does the bus leave for Siena? *Quando parte l'autobus per Siena?*
How long will it take to get there? *Quanto tempo ci vuole per arrivare?*
Next stop, please *La prossima fermata per favore*
Is this the right stop? *È la fermata giusta?*
The train is late *Il treno è in ritardo*
Can you tell me where to get off? *Mi può dire dove devo scendere?*

Directions

right/left *a destra/a sinistra*
first left/second right *la prima a sinistra/la seconda a destra*
Turn to the right/left *Gira a destra/sinistra*
Go straight on *Va sempre diritto*
Go straight on until the traffic lights *Va sempre diritto fino al semaforo*
Is it far away/nearby? *È lontano/vicino?*
It's 5 minutes' walk *Cinque minuti a piedi*
It's 10 minutes by car *Dieci minuti con la macchina*
opposite/next to *di fronte/ accanto a*
up/down *su/giù*
traffic lights *il semaforo*
junction *l'incrocio, il bivio*
building *il palazzo (could be a*

palace or a block of flats)
Where is...? *Dov'è...?*
Where are...? *Dove sono...?*
Where is the nearest bank/petrol station/bus stop/hotel/garage? *Dov'è la banca/il benzinaio/la fermata di autobus/l'albergo/ l'officina più vicino?*
How do I get there? *Come si può andare?* (or: *Come faccio per arrivare a...?*)
How long does it take to get to...? *Quanto tempo ci vuole per andare a...?*
Can you show me where I am on the map? *Può indicarmi sulla cartina dove mi trovo*
You're on the wrong road *Lei è sulla strada sbagliata*

Health

Is there a chemist's nearby? *C'è una farmacia qui vicino?*
Which chemist is open at night? *Quale farmacia fa il turno di notte?*
I feel ill *Sto male/Mi sento male*
Where does it hurt? *Dove Le fa male?*
It hurts here *Ho dolore qui*
I suffer from... *Soffro di...*
I have a headache *Ho mal di testa*
I have a sore throat *Ho mal di gola*
I have a stomach ache *Ho mal di pancia*
Have you got something for air sickness? *Ha/Avete qualcosa contro il mal d'aria?*
Have you got something for sea sickness? *Ha/Avete qualcosa contro il mal di mare?*
It's nothing serious *Non è niente di male*
Do I need a prescription? *Ci vuole la ricetta?*
antiseptic cream *la crema antisettica*
insect repellent *l'insettifugo*
sticking plaster *il cerotto*
sunburn *scottato del sole*
sunscreen *la crema antisolare*
tissues *i fazzoletti di carta*
toothpaste *il dentifricio*
upset-stomach pills *le pillole anti-coliche*

FURTHER READING

TRANSPORT

Food and Wine

Italian Wines, by Maureen Ashley (Sainsbury's/Websters International).
Italian Wines, by Phillip Dallas (Faber & Faber).
Italian Food, by Elizabeth David (Penguin Cookery Library).

History & Society

The Early History of Rome, by Livy (Penguin).
Daily Life in Ancient Rome, by Jerome Carcopino (Peregrine).
The Roman Emperors, by Michael Grant (Weidenfeld and Nicolson).
The Caesars, by Allan Massie (Secker & Warburg).
The Decline and Fall of the Roman Empire, by Edward Gibbon (Dent and Penguin).
The Last Years of the Roman Empire (Croom Helm).
A History of Rome, by Michael Grant (Faber).
Rome: Biography of a City, by Christopher Hibbert (Penguin).
The Italians, by Luigi Barzini (Hamish Hamilton).

Art & Literature

The Aeneid, by Virgil (Penguin).
Meditations, by Marcus Aurelius (Penguin).
Lives of the Artists, by Giorgio Vasari (Penguin).
The Life of Benvenuto Cellini, by Benvenuto Cellini, translator John Addington Symonds (Macmillan).
Rome, by Emile Zola (Paris and New York).
Portrait of a Lady, by Henry James.
The Woman of Rome and *Roman Tales*, by Alberto Moravia (Oxford University Press).

A Violent Life, by Pier Paolo Pasolini (Carcanet).
Fellini on Fellini, by Federico Fellini (New York).

Famous Travellers

Pictures from Italy, by Charles Dickens (Granville).
Italian Journey, by Johann Wolfgang von Goethe, translated by W.H. Auden & Elizabeth Mayer (Pantheon Books and Penguin).
Italian Hours, by Henry James (Century).
The Fountains of Rome and *A Traveller in Rome*, by Henry V. Morton (Methuen).

FEEDBACK

We do our best to ensure the information in our books is as accurate and up-to-date as possible. The books are updated on a regular basis, using local contacts who painstakingly add, amend and correct as required. However, some mistakes and omissions are inevitable and we are ultimately reliant on our readers to put us in the picture.
We would welcome your feedback on any details related to your experiences using the book "on the road". We will acknowledge all contributions, and we'll offer an Insight Guide for the best letters received.

Please write to us at:
Insight Guides
PO Box 7910
London SE1 1WE
United Kingdom
Or send e-mail to:
insight@apaguide.co.uk

Byron in Italy, by Peter Quenell (Viking Press, New York).
The Grand Tour, by Christopher Hibbert (G.P. Putnam, New York).

Travel Companions

Rome: A Literary Companion, by John Varriano (John Murray).
The Rome Address Book (Berlitz Cityscope).

Other Insight Guides

Insight Guide: Italy covers the whole country, with features on food and drink, culture and the arts. Other titles cover Northern Italy, Southern Italy, Rome, Venice, Florence, Umbria, Tuscany, Sicily and Sardinia.
Insight Pocket Guides, including a pull-out map, feature tailor-made itineraries and are ideal for short breaks. Guides in the Italian series include: Venice, Rome, Milan, Florence, Sicily, Sardinia and Tuscany.
Insight Compact Guides are inexpensive, mini-encyclopaedias with a star-rated system of all the sites worth seeing Titles include Florence, Milan, Rome, Tuscany, Venice, the Italian Riviera and the Italian Lakes. Rome features in three new Insight Guide series:
Shopping in Rome, **Eating in Rome** and **Museums in Rome** are handy-sized, illustrated guides, all packed with useful information.
Insight Fleximaps combine clear, detailed cartography with essential travel information. The laminated finish makes the maps durable and weatherproof. Italian maps include *Florence, the Italian Lakes, Milan, Rome, Sicily, Tuscany* and *Venice*.

ACCOMMODATION ACTIVITIES A – Z LANGUAGE

ART & PHOTO CREDITS

akg-images London 21
American Numismatic Society 197T
Ping Amranand 4C, 18, 20, 22, 23, 85
Archiv Gumpel 26
Archivo Iconograifico, S.A/Corbis 179
The Art Archive/Galleria Borghese Rome/Dagli Orti 143T
Gaetano Barone 45
Jonathan Blair/Corbis 189
Bridgeman Art Library/Vatican Museums & Galleries, Vatican City, Rome 32/33
Cephas 8B, 57
Giuliano Colliva/The Image Bank 107T
Jerry Dennis 7B
GiovannaDunmall 53
The Garden Picture Library/Alamy 205
Patrizia Giancotti 12/13, 167, 182/183, 194, 196, 197, 199T, 199, 201, 202, 203, 204
Albano Guatti 14/15, 200
Ronald Grant Archive 41
Frances Gransden back cover bottom, 3B, 74T, 75T, 86T, 89T, 95T, 129T, 133T, 140, 143, 167T, 169T, 223T, 186L, 187, 190, 192T, 193T, 193
Robert Harding Picture Library/Alamy 55
John Heseltine 73, 105
Jim Holmes 19, 42, 44, 68, 175
Italian Cultural Institute 30

Philippa Lewis/Corbis 179T
Marka/Kay Reese & As 201T
Mary Evans Picture Library 24
Anna Mockford/Nick Bonetti 1, 6TR, 7TR, 8TL, 9CL, 9BR, 10/11, 16, 29, 36, 50, 51, 64/65, 66/67, 75, 77, 78, 79, 82T, 83, 84, 86/87, 88, 96, 97, 98, 100, 103, 109, 109T, 117, 117T, 118, 119T, 119, 120, 121T, 122, 126, 127, 128, 129, 130L/R, 131L/R, 133L, 134, 135, 138, 139, 141, 142, 147, 149T, 150T, 152, 153T, 153, 154T, 154, 156, 157, 158T, 158, 163, 164T, 164, 172, 173, 174, 177
The Museum of Modern Art/Film Stills Archive 40
Gerd Pfeifer 198,
Pictures Colour Library 104
Andrea Pistolesi 34, 35, 39, 56, 72, 92, 98, 100, 114
Mark Read 5T
Rosenfeld Images/The Anthony Blake Picture Library 54
Alessandra Santarelli 4T, 5B, 6CL, 6BL, 9T, 37, 49, 58, 59, 60L/R, 61L/R, 62, 63, 76, 98T, 101, 115, 123, 125, 132, 146, 149, 155, 160, 176, 178, 180L/R
Vidal Sierakowski/Rex Features 31
STR/AFP/Getty Images 28
View Pictures/Alamy 48
Bill Wassman back cover left & right, 2/3, 38, 52, 74, 80, 81, 82, 93, 110, 121, 133R, 135T, 161, 166, 169, 186R, 188, 191, 192
Kurt-Michael Westermann/Corbis 195

PICTURE SPREADS

Pages 46/47: all Scala except centre top David Ball/Corbis and bottom centre right Massimo Listri/Corbis
Pages 90/91 top row left to right: akg-images London/Erich Lessing, akag-images London; centre row: akg-images London, Scala, Image State/Alamy; bottom row: Scala, akg-images London/Erich Lessing
Pages 112/113 all Scala except centre right Frances Gransden
Pages 144/145: top row left to right: Anna Mockford/Nick Bonetti, Alessandra Santarelli, centre row Anna Mockford/Nick Bonetti, Alessandra Santarelli; bottom row Alessandra Santarelli, Anna Mockford/Nick Bonetti
Pages 170/171: top row left to right Corbis, Scala, Corbis; bottom row: The Art Archive/Dagli Orti, A. Tessore/Aisa, Corbis

Map Production: Dave Priestley and Stephen Ramsay.
© 2005 Apa Publications GmbH & Co. Verlag KG Singapore Branch, Singapore

ROME STREET ATLAS

The key map shows the area of Rome covered by the atlas
section. An index of street names and places of interest
shown on the maps can be found on the following pages.
For each entry there is a page number and grid reference.

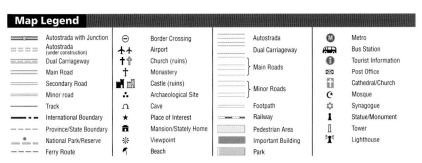

Map Legend

Autostrada with Junction	⊖	Border Crossing		Autostrada	Ⓜ	Metro
Autostrada (under construction)	✈	Airport		Dual Carriageway	🚌	Bus Station
Dual Carriageway	✝ ✝	Church (ruins)		Main Roads	ⓘ	Tourist Information
Main Road	✝	Monastery			✉	Post Office
Secondary Road	🏰 🏛	Castle (ruins)		Minor Roads	✝	Cathedral/Church
Minor road	∴	Archaeological Site			☪	Mosque
Track	∩	Cave		Footpath	✡	Synagogue
International Boundary	★	Place of Interest		Railway	✦	Statue/Monument
Province/State Boundary	🏠	Mansion/Stately Home		Pedestrian Area	▯	Tower
National Park/Reserve	❄	Viewpoint		Important Building	⌘	Lighthouse
Ferry Route	⸙	Beach		Park		

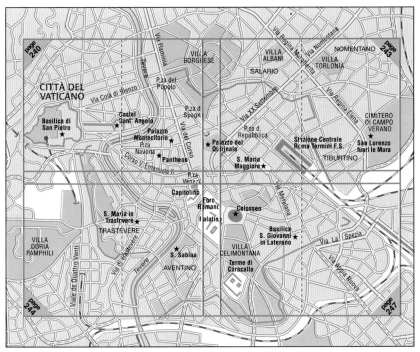

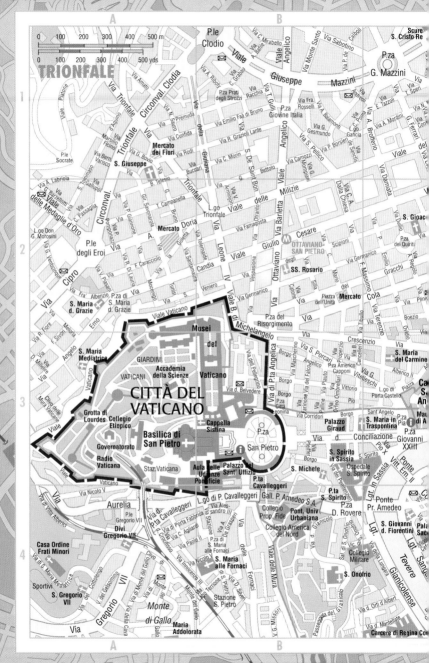

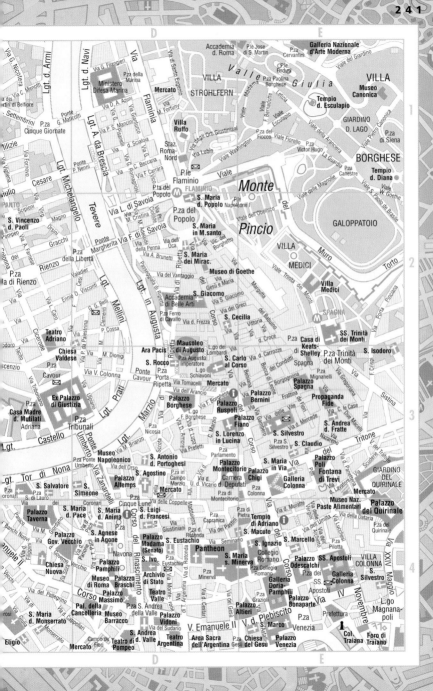

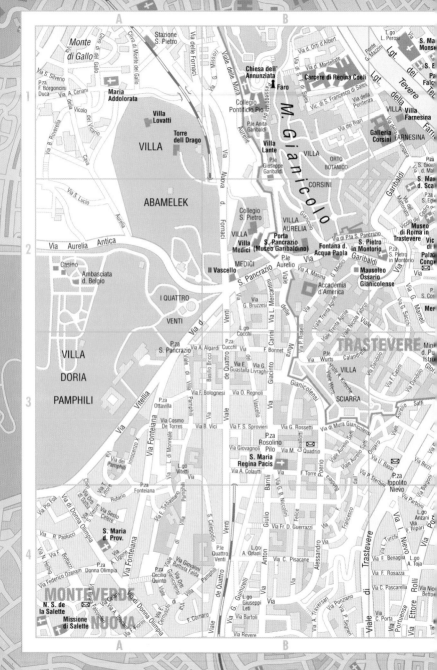

A

Monte
di Gallo

Via S. Silverio
P.za
F. Borgoncini
Duca

Stazione
S. Pietro

Chiesa dell'
Annunziata

B

Via d. Orti d'Albert

Ponte
G. Mazzini

L.go
L. Perosi

S. Ma
Mons

Via de Monte del Gallo
Chivo di dei Gallo

Via A. Ceriani

Maria
Addolorata

Villa
Lovatti

Torre
dell' Drago

Faro

Collegio
Pontificio Pio

P.le Anita
Garibaldi

Via di Mantellate

Carcere di Regina Coeli

Vic. di S. Francesco di Sales

Via della
Penitenza

S. E.
Pa
Falc

Via di Monte del Gallo
Chivo di del Gallo

Via della
Vicolo
del Vicario

VILLA

Villa
Lante

VILLA
AURELIA

M. Gianicolo

VILLA

ORTO
BOTANICO

VILLA
Villa
Farnesina

FARNESINA

Galleria
Corsini

S. Giov
d. Mal

S. Ma
d. Scal

P.za
S. Egi

ABAMELEK

Via Aurelia Antica

Casino

Ambasciata
d. Belgio

VILLA

DORIA

PAMPHILI

I QUATTRO

VENTI

Collegio
S. Pietro

VILLA
Villa
Medici

Il Vascello

MEDICI

Porta
S. Pancrazio
(Museo Garibaldino)

CORSINI

Fontana d.
Acqua Paola

P.le
Aurelio

Via A. Masina

S. Pancrazio

Via

Vicolo del
Museo
di Roma in
Trastevere

S. Pietro
in Montorio

Vic
di

Palaz
Cong

P.le
Giuseppe
Garibaldi

Garibaldi

Via di P.ta S. Pancrazio

S. Pietro
in Montorio

Via

Accademia
d'America

Mausoleo
Ossario
Gianicolense

Via

P.
S. Cos

Mer

Via
G. Bruzzesi

Via d.

Venti

Via L. Mercantini

Viale

delle

Via

Viale Trenta Aprile

Via Trenta Aprile

Viale Nicola Fabrizi

TRASTEVERE

Min
d. Pu
Istru

Via

L.go
Cocchi

P.za
S. Pancrazio

Via A. Algardi
Basilio Bricci

Cucchi

Carini

F. Bonnet

P.le
Wurts

VILLA

Via A. Krische

Calandrelli

Viale

SCIARRA

Glor

Via F. Casini

Dandolo

Via d. Quattro

Viale

Via E.
Guastalla Livraghi

Via E.
Giacinto

Via P. Roselli

Gianicolensi

Dandolo

Via Giovanni

Saffi

Via F. Bolognesi

Via O. Regnoli

Vitellia

Via
Pamphili

P.za
Ottavilla

Via Cosmo
De Torres

Via B. Vici

Via F. S. Sprovieri

P.za
G. Rossetti

Via di Mura Gianicolensi

Via Aurelio Saffi

Cavallotti

Quadrio

P.za
Rosolino
Pilo

Via G.

Via M.

Aurelio

Via Aurelio Saffi

Viale
Aurelio Saffi

Via U. Bassi

Ongaro

P.za
Ippolito
Nievo

Via Bezzi

Via Innocenzo X
Via dei
Pamphili

Via Pio Foà

Chivo di Donna Olimpia
Via T.
Littore

S. Maria
Regina Pacis

Via A. Colautti

Barrilli

F. Torre

Poerio

Via P. Sterbini

Via R. Paolucci

Via Sesto
Celere

S. Maria
d. Prov.

Via A. Ugone

P.za
Cecilio
Quinto

Via Federico Ozanam

N. S. de
la Salette

Missione
di Salette

MONTEVERDE
NUOVA

Via N. Helbig
Via F. Bonaj

Via E. Sebastiani

P.za
Fonteiana

Via Donna Olimpia

Via di Monreale

S. Calepodio

P.za
Giacomelli

Via G. Giacometti

F. Cornaro

Via G.
Giuseppe
Leti

Via G. Bartoli

Via Revere

P.le
Quattro
Venti

L.go
A. Orlandi

Giulio

Via Giovanni
Battista Falda

Venti

Via Fr. D. Guerrazzi

Anton

Via C. Pisacane

Alessandro

Felice

Francesco

Via
Ponziano

Via di Trastevere

Viale

Via P. Segneri

Via A. Traversari

Via C. Porta

Via
Ponziano

Via G. Turchi

Via I. Nievo

Via I. Toja

Via F. Rosazza

Via C. Pascarella

Rolli

Via Ettore

Via Parboni

L.go
Anzani

Via
Ripari

Via Nice
Better

Porta

Via Portuense

A

B

TUSCOLANO

STREET INDEX

GENERAL INDEX

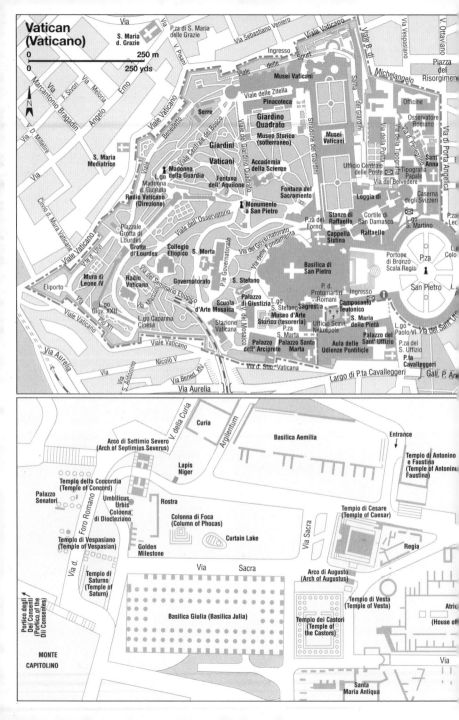

Vatican (Vaticano)

0 — 250 m
0 — 250 yds

Via
Via
P.za di S. Maria delle Grazie
S. Maria d. Grazie
Via Sebastiano Veniero
Viale Vaticano
Viale Vaticano
Viale B.º di
Michelangelo
V. Vespasiani
V. Ottaviano
Via di Porta Angelica
Piazza del Risorgimen
Ingresso
Sport
Salita dei giardini
Via della Posta
Via della Tipografia
Via del Pellegrino
Via del Belvedere
Officine
Osservatore Romano
Sant' Anna
Musei Vaticani
Viale delle
Viale delle Zitella
Pinacoteca
Giardino Quadrato
Museo Storico (sotterraneo)
Musei Vaticani
Ufficio Centrale delle Poste
Tipografia Papale
Caserna degli Svizzeri
Serre
Marcantonio Bragadin
Via F. Sivori
Via Melaria
Angelo
Via D. Millelire
Via
Erno
V. Pisani
Viale Vaticano
Viale Benedetto
Viale Centrale del Bosco
Giardini Vaticani
Accademia della Scienze
Loggia di
Cortile di San Damaso
Stanze di Raffaello
Cappella Sistina
Raffaello
L.go S. Martino
P.za Le
Giardini Quadrato
Madonna della Guardia
L.go Madonna d. Guardia
Radio Vaticano (Direzione)
S. Maria Mediatrice
Fontana dell' Aquilone
Fontana del Sacramento
Monumento a San Pietro
Viale dell'Osservatorio
P.za del Forno
P.za del Governatorato
Portone di Bronzo Scala Regis
Piazzale Grotta di Lourdes
Grotta di Lourdes
Collegio Etiopico
S. Marta
S. Stefano
Basilica di San Pietro
San Pietro
P.za
Colo
Clivio d. Mura Vaticana
Via d. Tiri
Via del Seminario Etiopico
Governatorato
P.le Governatorato
Via del Governatorato
Via delle Fondamenta
P. d. Protomartiri Romani
Ingresso
Mura di Leone IV
Radio Vaticana
Eliporto
L.go Giov. XXII
L.go Capanna Cinese
Viale Vaticano
Via Aurelia
Via S. Antonino
Nicolò V
Via Bened. XV
Via d. Staz. Vaticana
Via Aurelia
Scuola d'Arte Mosaica
Stazione Vaticana
Palazzo di Giustizia
Museo d'Arte Storico (tesoreria)
P.za S. Marta
S. Stefano
Sagrestia
Ufficio Scavi, Nekropole
Camposanto Teutonico
S. Maria della Pietà
L.go Paolo VI
Via de Sant'
Palazzo dell' Arciprete
Palazzo Santa Marta
Aula delle Udienze Pontificie
Palazzo del Sant' Uffizio
P.za del S. Uffizio
P.ta Cavalleggeri
Gall. P. Ar
Largo di P.ta Cavalleggeri
MONTE CAPITOLINO

Foro Romano

V. della Curia
Curia
Argilentum
Basilica Aemilia
Entrance
Arco di Settimio Severo (Arch of Septimius Severus)
Lapis Niger
Tempio di Antonino e Faustina (Temple of Antoninus Faustina)
Tempio della Concordia (Temple of Concord)
Palazzo Senatori
Umbilicus Urbis
Colonna di Diocleziano
Rostra
Colonna di Foca (Column of Phocas)
Curtain Lake
Via Sacra
Tempio di Cesare (Temple of Caesar)
Tempio di Vespasiano (Temple of Vespasian)
Golden Milestone
Via Sacra
Arco di Augusto (Arch of Augustus)
Regia
Tempio di Vesta (Temple of Vesta)
Atrio (House of
Tempio di Saturno (Temple of Saturn)
Porticato degli Dei Consenti (Portico of the Dii Consentes)
Basilica Giulia (Basilica Julia)
Tempio dei Castori (Temple of the Castors)
Via
Santa Maria Antiqua